STUDY OF JAPANESE SWORDS

Chronological Study of Japanese Swords and Japanese History

By Yurie Endo Halchak

Loosema Hakverdian
Technology Consultant

Copyright © 2021 by Yurie Endo Halchak

All rights reserved. No part of this publication may be reproduced, distributed, or transmitted in any form or by any means, including photocopying, recording, or other electronic or mechanical methods, without the prior written permission of the publisher, except in the case of brief quotations embodied in critical reviews and certain other noncommercial uses permitted by copyright law. For permission requests, write to the publisher, addressed "Attention: Permissions Coordinator," at the address below.

Alpha Book Publisher
www.alphapublisher.com
ISBN: 978-1954297258

Ordering Information:
Quantity sales. Special discounts are available on quantity purchases by corporations, associations, and others. For details, contact the publisher at the address above.
Orders by U.S. trade bookstores and wholesalers. Visit www.alphapublisher.com/contact-us to learn more.

Printed in the United States of America

Author

Yurie Endo Halchak was raised in Minato-ku, Tokyo, Japan; the family later moved to Kamakura. She graduated from Meiji University, received a bachelor's degree in literature and a curatorship license. The internship for the curator license was done at *Nihon Bijutsu Token Hozon Kyokai* (日本美術刀剣保存協会: The Japanese Sword Museum, often called NBTHK) in Tokyo. She also earned a bachelor's degree in Economics at the California State University of Northridge.

Her study of Japanese swords began through the influence of her father, a metal-related manufacturing company owner, who collected Japanese swords and other art objects. She studied Japanese swords in a study group run by a friend of his as well as at home with her father on his collection. Currently, she lives in Los Angeles.

Table of contents

Part 2 is a detailed part of the corresponding chapter.

TABLE OF CONTENTS	P. 1
Preface	P. 4
1 | Timeline	P. 6
2 | Joko-to (上古刀)	P. 9
3 | Names of Parts (名称)	P. 15
4 | Heian Period History 794 – 1192 (平安時代)	P. 17
5 | Heian Period Swords (平安時代太刀)	P. 21
6 | Kamakura Period History 1192 – 1333 (鎌倉時代歴史)	P. 26
7 | Overview of the Kamakura Period Swords (鎌倉時代刀概要)	P. 29
8 | Middle Kamakura Period: Yamashiro Den (鎌倉中期山城伝)	P. 32
9 | Middle Kamakura Period: Bizen Den (鎌倉中期備前伝)	P. 36
10| Jokyu-no-ran 1221 (承久の乱)	P. 40
11| Ikubi Kissaki (猪首切先)	P. 43
12| Middle Kamakura Period: Tanto (Dagger 鎌倉中短刀)	P. 48
13| Late Kamakura Period: Genko (鎌倉末元寇)	P. 52
14| Late Kamakura Period Swords (鎌倉末太刀)	P. 56
15| The Revival of Yamato Den (大和伝復活)	P. 61
16| Late Kamakura period Tanto: Early Soshu Den Tanto (鎌倉末短刀)	P. 66
17| Nanboku-cho Period History 1333-1392 (南北朝歴史)	P. 71
18| Nanboku-cho Period Sword (南北朝太刀)	P. 75
19| Nanboku-Cho Tanto (南北朝短刀)	P. 80

20	Muromachi Period History （室町時代歴史）	P. 85
21	Muromachi Period Sword （室町時代刀）	P. 88
22	Sengoku Period History （戦国時代歴史）	P. 93
23	Sengoku Period Sword （戦国時代刀）	P. 96
24	Sengoku Period Tanto （戦国時代短刀）	P. 101
25	Edo Period History 1603 – 1867 （江戸時代歴史）	P. 105
26	Over view of Shin-to: Ko-to & Shin-to Difference （新刀概要）	P. 109
27	Shin-to Sword -- Main Seven Regions (Part A: 主要７刀匠地)	P. 113
28	Shin-to Sword -- Main Seven Regions (part B: 主要７刀匠地)	P. 117
29	Bakumatsu Period History 1781 - 1867 （幕末歴史）	P. 121
30	Bakumatsu Period: Shin Shin-to 1781 - 1867 （新々刀）	P. 124
31	Sword Making Process	P. 127
32	Japanese swords after WWII	P. 133
33	Information on Today's Swordsmiths	P. 135
34	Part 2 of -- 1 Timeline	P. 138
35	Part 2 of -- 2 Joko-To (上古刀)	P. 141
36	Part 2 of -- 3 Names of the Parts	P. 144
37	Part 2 of -- 4 Heian Period History 794 - 1192 (平安時代)	P. 145
38	Part 2 of -- 5 Heian Period Sword 794 - 1192 (平安時代太刀)	P. 148
39	Part 2 of -- 6 Kamakura Period History 1192 - 1333 (鎌倉時代歴史)	P. 153
40	Part 2 of -- 7 Overview of Kamakura Period Sword	P. 157
41	Part 2 of -- 8 Middle Kamakura Period: Yamashiro Den(鎌倉中期山城伝)	P. 161
42	Part 2 of -- 9 Middle Kamakura Period: Bizen Den (鎌倉中期備前伝)	P. 166
43	Part 2 of -- 10 Jyokyu-no-Ran & Gotaba-joko 1221 （承久の乱）	P. 169

44	Part 2 of -- 11 Ikubi Kissaki（猪首切先）	P. 173
45	Part 2 of -- 11 Ikubi Kissaki（猪首切先） continued from Chapter 44	P. 178
46	Part 2 of -- 12 Middle Kamakura Period Tanto（鎌倉中期短刀）	P. 182
47	Part 2 of -- 13 Late Kamakura Period: Genko（鎌倉末元寇）	P. 185
48	Part 2 of -- 14 Late Kamakura Period Sword: Early Soshu Den（鎌倉末刀）	P. 189
49	Part 2 of -- 15 The Revival of Yamato Den（大和伝復活）	P. 193
50	Part 2 of -- 16 Late Kamakura Period Tanto: Early Soshu-Den（鎌倉末短刀）	P. 198
51	Part 2 of -- 17 Nanboku-cho Period History 1333 – 1392（南北朝歴史）	P. 203
52	Part 2 of -- 18 Nanboku-cho Period Swords（南北朝太刀）	P. 207
53	Part 2 of -- 19 Nanboku-cho Tanto（南北朝短刀）	P. 212
54	Part 2 of -- 20 Muromachi Period History 1392 - 1467（室町時代歴史）	P. 216
55	Part 2 of -- 21 Muromachi Period Sword（室町時代刀）	P. 221
56	Part 2 of -- 22 Sengoku Period History（戦国時代歴史）	P. 225
57	Part 2 of -- 23 Sengoku Period Sword（戦国時代刀）	P. 230
58	Part 2 of -- 24 Sengoku Period Tanto（戦国時代短刀）	P. 235
59	Part 2 of -- 25 Edo Period History 1603 - 1867（江戸時代歴史）	P. 238
60	Part 2 of -- 26 Overview of Shin-to（新刀概要）	P. 242
61	Part 2 of -- 27 Shin-to Main 7 Regions (part A: 主要 7 刀匠地)	P. 244
62	Part 2 of -- 28 Shin-to Main 7 Regions (part B: 主要 7 刀匠地)	P. 250
63	Part 2 of -- 29 Bakumatsu Period History 1781 - 1867（幕末歴史）	P. 254
64	Part 2 of -- 30 Shin Shin-to: Bakumatsu sword（新々刀）	P. 259
65	The Sword Observation Process	P. 261
BIBLIOGRAPHY		P. 266

Preface and Biography

Preface

This book is a series of entry-level lectures on Japanese sword and its history for those who are interested in studying Japanese art swords.

The Japanese sword was basically designed as a weapon, but Japanese swordsmiths imbued qualities of grace and beauty into the blades as well as functional superiority. The intricate patterns of surface and texture formed by their highly developed forging and tempering techniques were used only in Japan. In the past, the Japanese looked at the swords as a spiritual symbol of *Samurai,* temples, and shrines. Nowadays, the Japanese regard swords as a cultural art object made of steel.

Varieties of the appearance of swords are closely related to historical events. Textures, contours, and tempering designs are characteristics of a particular school (*Den* 伝) of swordsmiths. This is a series of lectures that discuss each period's history then talk about the swordsmiths' schools that were active in a particular province at the time. Because of that, each section starts with the history of the time. It is necessary to discuss the history to see the flow of the events that affected the swords' shape and style.

Since the subject matter covers many centuries, I will concentrate more on "*Ko-to*" (古刀), which appeared from the *Heian* period (平安時代 794 - 1185) until the end of the *Sengoku* period (戦国時代 16th cent). These lectures will be discussed with my illustrations and photos of swords from my father's collection* and the Sano Museum Catalogue**. Also, I referenced the book, "*Nihon-to no Okite to Tokucho* (日本刀の掟と特徴: The Rules and Characteristics of Japanese Sword)" by Mr. *Honami Koson*. This is the book my sword teacher, *Mori Sensei,* used as the textbook in his class. Other referenced books are, "*Token no Mikata* (刀剣のみかた: The Way to Look at Swords)" by Mr. *Yuichi Hiroi* whom I have known since my intern days in the Japanese Sword Museum, "*Nihonto Taikan* (日本刀大鑑)," "*Nihonto Koza* (日本刀講座)," and several more. The detailed information on those Referenced books is in the bibliography.

Biography

I was born and raised in *Minato-ku*, *Tokyo*, Japan. Then we moved to *Kamakura* in my late teens. Currently, I live in Los Angeles. I graduated from Meiji University and received a bachelor's degree in literature and a curatorship license. The required internship for the curator license was done at *Nihon Bijutsu Token Hozon Kyokai* (日本美術刀剣保存協会: The Japanese Sword Museum, often called NBTHK) in *Tokyo*. Also, I graduated from the California State University of Northridge and received a bachelor's degree in Economics.

My father owned a manufacturing company that dealt with metal. As his hobby, he had collected Japanese swords and other types of Japanese art objects. He was one of the administrators of *Nihon Bijutu Token Hozon Kyokai*. He had been long deceased.

One of my father's friends, *Mori Sensei* who was also the main administrator of the organization, used to have a Japanese sword study group in his house near my house. I joined the study group. *Mori sensei*'s class was a very rare and valuable kind because he was able to bring in top-quality swords as study materials because of his position in the museum. The kind of swords we studied with were top-quality museum swords, like *Juyo Bunkazai* (Important Cultural Properties), *Juyo-Bijutsuhin* (Important Art Object). I don't know how he managed to do it, but he even brought one National Treasure sword. Keep in mind things were a little different over 50 years ago. Those were the kind of swords people could only see through the glass display cases.

Also, I studied the swords with my father since he kept many swords in our house. Some photos of his swords are in pages of many chapters in this book.

*My father took the photos of his swords; those were his swords when the photos were taken.

**Some photos are from Sano Museum Catalogue. The permission to use them was granted by the Sano Museum.

1 | TimeLine

Let's look at the diagram below. At the beginning of each chapter, a timeline like the one below will be shown. It will be a good reference to see which time period the subject matter is being discussed.

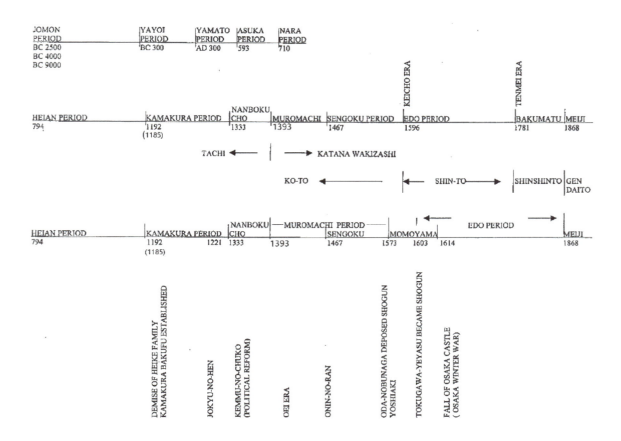

From the *Jomon* period to the *Nara* period, the short top line is the time we call the *Joko-to* period in terms of the history of Japanese swords. The term "Japanese sword" we use today refers to the swords made after the *Heian* period (平安 794-1185). Usually, *Joko-to* is in the category of archaeological study. In the next chapter, we will discuss *Joko-to*. The bottom timeline and short descriptions below are the timeline we see in Japan's general history books. The middle timeline is more specific for the sword study. My discussion will follow the middle timeline. The timeline diagram will appear at the beginning of each chapter for easy reference. The swords I discuss in this book are grouped together based on the shape, style, and trend of the time.

The difference between Tachi (太刀), Katana (刀), Wakizashi (脇差), Tanto (短刀)

Swords made before *the Muromachi* period (before 1392) are called *Tachi* (太刀). Swords made after the *Muromachi* (室町) period are called *Katana* (刀) and *Wakizashi* (脇差). *Katana* and *Wakizashi* were worn together. *Tanto* is a short dagger. *Tanto*s were made throughout time. The difference between *Tachi* and *Katana* is how they were worn. *Tachi* was suspended from one's waist belt, the blade side facing down. *Katana* and *Wakizashi* (called *Daisho* 大小 means large and small) were thrust between the belt and body two together, the blade side up. Usually, *Tachi* is longer than *Katana*. *Wakizashi* is shorter than *Katana*. *Tanto* is the shortest. When you face the swordsmith's inscribed name, if the blade comes on the right, that is *Tachi*. When you face the swordsmith's inscribed name, if the blade comes on the left, that is *Katana* and *Wakizashi*.

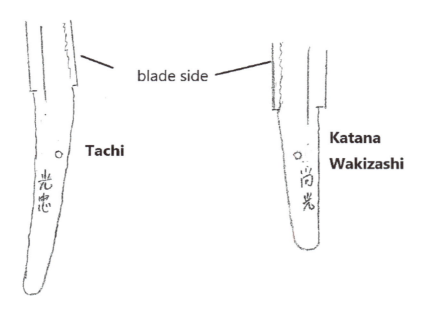

Ko-to (古刀) Shin-to (新刀) Shin Shin-to (新々刀) Gendai-to (現代刀)

Ko-to is the swords made between the *Heian* period (794-1192) and the beginning of the *Keicho* Era (1596-1614). *Shin-to* is the sword made between the *Keicho* Era (1596-1614) and the *Tenmei* Era (1781-1789). *Shin Shin-to* is the swords made during

Bakumatu time (幕末期 1781-1868). *Gendai-to* is from the *Meiji* Restoration (明治 1868) through today. Even though the names of the eras or time changed overnight due to the political or dynastical changes through history, the changes in the sword style were always gradual.

In general history, the *Bakumatsu* time is simply the last part of the *Edo* period. However, for the sword classification, the *Bakumatsu* time is from around the *Tenmei* era (天明 1781) through the beginning of the *Meiji* 1868.

2 | Joko-to (上古刀)

Joko-to means swords made before the *Heian* period. *Joko-to* is not part of the sword study. The sword study starts from the *Heian* Period. *Joko-to* is in the category of the archaeological field.

Jomon (縄文) period   9000 B.C.

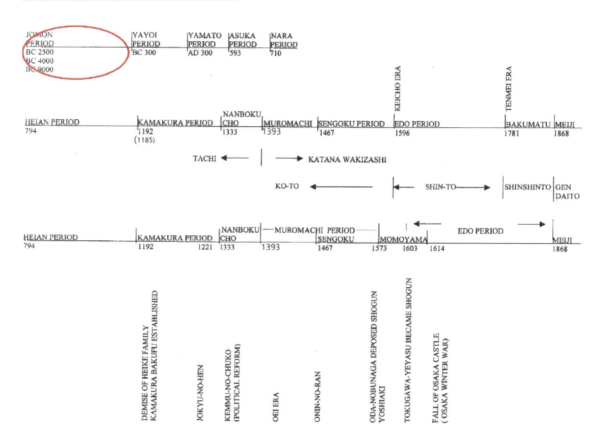

The *Jomon* period goes back to 9000 B.C. This is the time of Paleolithic and Neolithic times. The characteristic of the time was the rope design (*Jomon* 縄文) on their earthenware.

We found a stone sword made during this time. This is one-piece, approximately 27 to 31 inches (70 to 80 cm) long. This is not a Neolithic type scraper. This stone sword was made for ceremonial purposes.

Yayoi (弥生) period   300B.C to 300A.D (approximately)

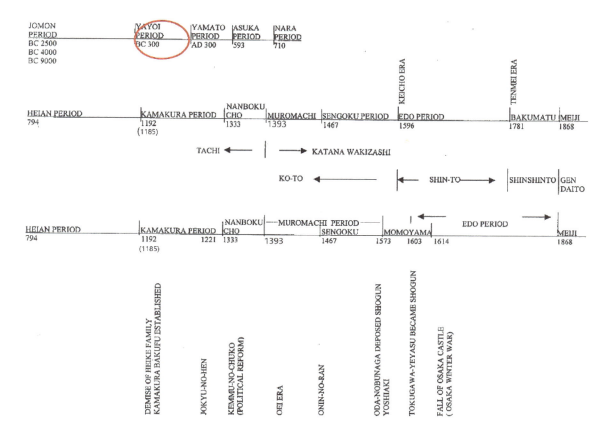

Around 300 B.C., the *Yayoi* culture replaced the *Jomon* culture. *Yayoi* culture characteristics show on their earthenwares. They were a rounder, smoother, softer design, and the techniques were much improved since the *Jomon* time. They were named *Yayoi* culture because the objects of this time were unearthed in the *Yayoi-cho* area (name of the place) near *Tokyo* University in *Tokyo*. They also discovered bronze artifacts such as a bronze sword *(Doken* 銅剣*)*, bronze pike (*Do-hoko* 銅矛), bronze mirrors *(Do-kyo* 銅鏡*)*, bronze musical *instruments (Do-taku* 銅鐸*)*. Those were imported from China and Korea, but the Japanese started to make their bronze items in the late *Yayoi* period. Although iron artifacts were hardly discovered, it is said that we have evidence that the iron objects already existed then.

Himiko （卑弥呼）

It is said that according to the Chinese history book, "*Gishi Wajinden*" (魏志倭人伝), around 300 A.D., there was a country called *Yamataikoku* (邪馬台国) that controlled about 30 small domains in Japan. The head of the country was a female figure called *Himiko* (卑弥呼), a shamanism maiden. She sent a messenger to the Chinese dynasty in 239 A.D., and she was given the title as the head of Japan (親魏倭王), a bronze mirror, and a longsword (5 feet long). Today, we still don't know the exact location of the *Yamataikoku*. This Chinese history book *"Gishi Wajinden"* (魏志倭人伝) explains how to get to *Yamataikoku*, but if we follow the book's directions precisely, we end up in the middle of the ocean, south of *Kyushu* (九州). We still have a big debate over the precise location of *Yamataikoku*.

Yamato (大和) period   300 A.D. --- 593 A.D

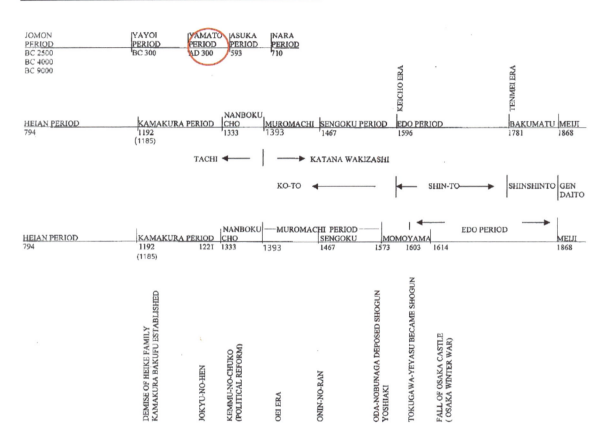

At the end of the *Yayoi* period, Japan was divided into small domains. These domains were reigned by local clans called *Go-zoku*(豪族). Around 400 A.D. most powerful *Go-zoku* united the country and named it *Yamato-chotei* (大和朝廷). This is the first Japanese imperial court, the origin of the current Japanese Imperial family. They were very powerful to be able to build the enormous tombs called *Kofun* (古墳) for themselves. In one of the famous *kofun*, *Ogonzuka Kofun* (黄金塚古墳) in *Osaka,* we found swords among other things. The hilt of the sword was made in Japan, while the blades were made in China. On the surface of the hilt, they depicted the design of a house. The other objects we found from the *Kofun* were objects like armors, mirrors, iron tools, and jewelry.

Outside of the *kofun,* it was a common practice to place *Haniwa* (clay figurine). Those *Haniwa* were smiling people, animals, houses, soldiers wearing swords, and sometimes simple tubes shaped *Haniwa* (埴輪). We think they placed *Haniwa* as a retaining wall purpose or a dividing line for the sacred area. Judging from the writings on the back of mirrors and swords, people used *Kanji* (Japanese characters) around the 5 to 6th century.

Asuka (飛鳥) period   593 ---710

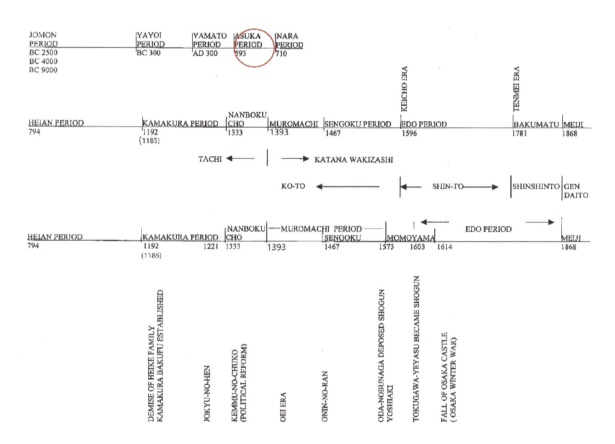

At the end of the *Yamato* period, after a long power struggle, *Shotoku Taishi* (聖徳太子) became a regent in 593 (beginning of the *Asuka* period). *Shotoku Taishi* established the political system and set up the first Japanese constitution (憲法 17 条). He protected and encouraged Buddhism and built the *Horyuji* temple (法隆寺) in *Nara*. The face of *Shotoku Taishi* had been on 10,000-yen bills for a long time. During the *Asuka* time, we see *Kanto Tachi* (環頭太刀). The shape of the hilt had a ring shape. *Kan* (環) means ring and *To* (頭) means head. Also, on the ring shape hilt, we see some inscriptions, such as the Emperor's name, location, and numbers. The number indicates the number of year the particular Emperor was enthroned. Those were all straight shape swords.

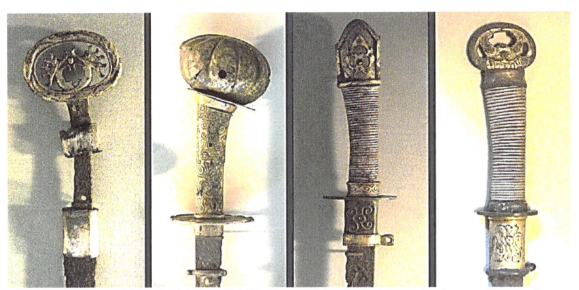

Hilts of Japanese straight sword. Circa 600 AD. From Wikipedia Commons, the free media repository

Nara (奈良) period   710 ---794

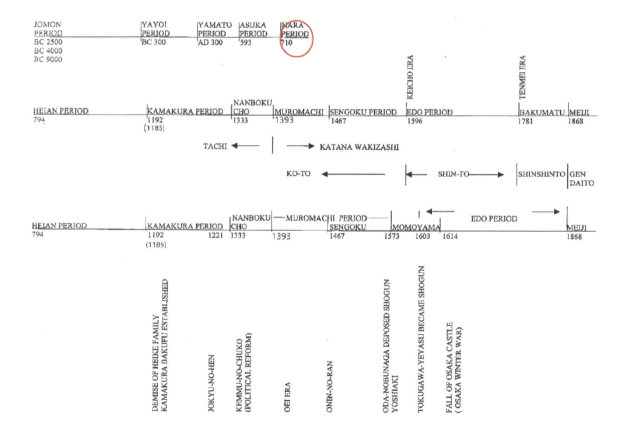

In 710, the capital city was moved to *Nara*, called *Heijo-kyo* (平城京). The shape of *Joko-to* was straight, usually 25 inches (60 –70 cm) long. They were suspended from the waist belt. Some swords came from China, and others were made in Japan. Many swords were found from *Kofun* and *Shoso-in* (正倉院) during the *Nara* period. *Shoso-in* is a storage building where belongings of *Shomu Emperor* (聖武天皇) were stored. Among other items, 55 swords were found from there. Those swords were called *Warabite-tachi*. *Warabi* (Bracken) is the name of an edible wild plant that grows in Japan. These swords were called *Warabite-tachi* because the hilt's shape resembles *Warabi,* whose stem curls up at the top.

The photo is from Creative common free media from Word online pictures

3 | Names of parts

Here are the names of the parts of a sword. The length of a sword means the length between the tip of the blade and the top of the *Nakago* (the hilt) as shown in the last illustration. The curvature of a sword is an important factor for connoisseurs to appraise the sword because it often indicates the time and region the particular sword was forged.

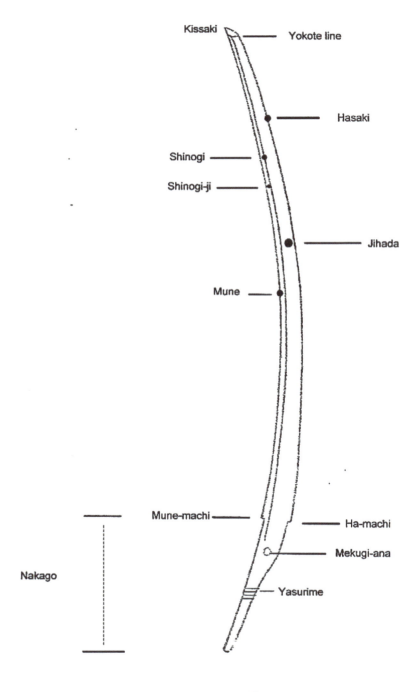

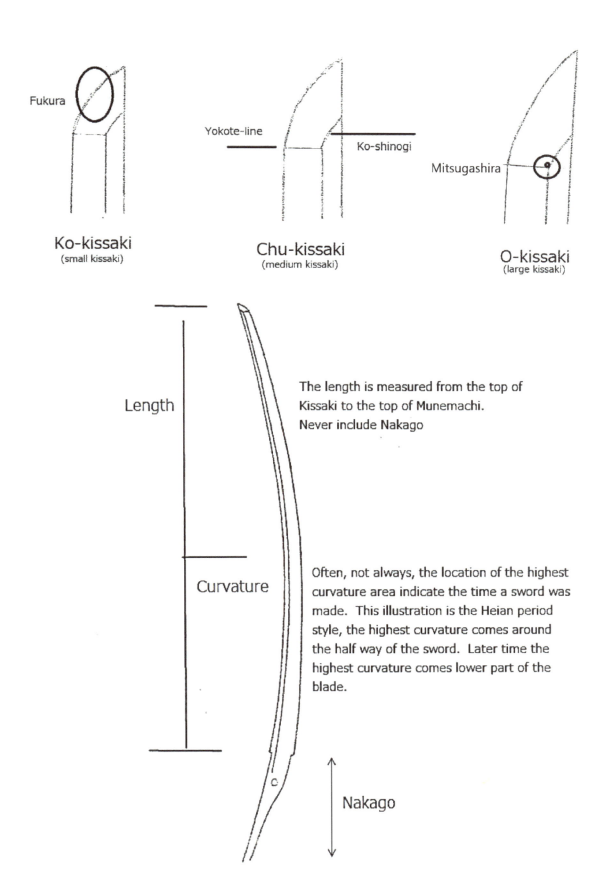

4 | Heian period History   794–1192 (平安時代歴史)

Heian Period (平安時代) is from the time the Emperor *Kanmu* (桓武天皇) moved the capital city to *Heian-Kyo* (平安京) in 794, that is *Kyoto* (京都) today.

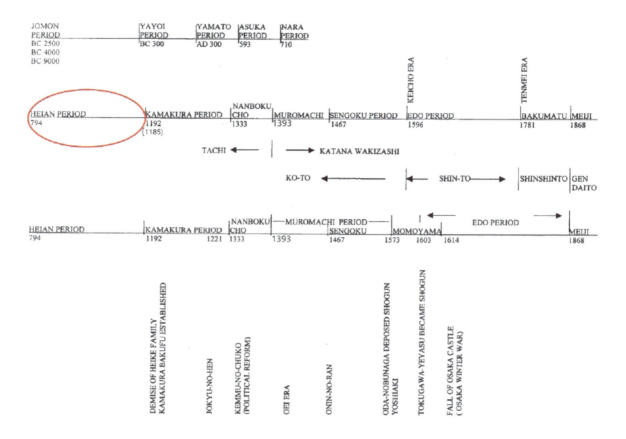

The circle above indicates the time we discuss in this section

During the *Heian* period, the emperors ruled Japan. However, in the early part of this time, the *Fujiwara* family, a very wealthy aristocrat family, had real political power. The *Fujiwara* family managed their daughters to marry the emperors. They obtained power through those marriages. The family was called "*Sekkan-ke*" (摂関家), which means the guardian's family or the Emperor's representative.

In those days, aristocrats led an elegant, refined lifestyle and cultivated a graceful culture. Many essays and novels were written by female authors during the time. The most famous one is "*Tales of Genji* (源氏物語)" written by *Murasaki Shikibu* (紫式部). The Imperial court held ceremonies quite often followed by elaborate and extravagant banquets. The imperial social life played an important role for aristocrats to get ahead in their political careers. Women also actively participated in the ceremonies. Many high-ranking officials had several huge houses. Sometimes those houses were inherited by their daughters, and the daughters lived in the house.

The way of courting was very different then. To begin a romantic relationship, a man would write a poem called "*Waka*" to a lady he set his eyes on and would have his servant bring the poem to her, hoping she would write him back a corresponding poem. Once he was accepted by the lady, first he was allowed to visit her for a short time from some distance away. As the relationship deepened, he visited her more often and stayed longer. Once they were married, and if she was his first legal wife, she lived with him in his house. However, if she was not the first legal wife, she remained in her home, and he would visit her for a few days or longer at a time. The wife's family raised their children. In those days and up until the next *Kamakura* period, the women's lineage was considered important. By the middle of the *Heian* period, the Emperors regained their political power since their mothers were not from the *Fujiwara* family.

Scene from "*TALES OF GENJI.*"   Bought in Kyoto

Origin of Samurai

Although the *Heian* Imperial court and aristocrats had a graceful and elegant life, they did not have a strong political power to control the country. There were many thieves, constant fires, and fights everywhere. The Imperial court, aristocrats, and temples began hiring armed guards or security forces to protect themselves in order to maintain public peace. Those hired hands were the origin of *Bushi* (武士) or *Samurai* (侍). *Samurai* spread their presence and grew larger in power as they formed groups and quelled uprisings. Eventually, two powerful *Samurai* clans emerged: One was *Heishi* (平氏) or often called *Heike* (平家), the other, *Genji* (源氏). Little by little, they gained power in the Imperial court. After many power struggles between them, *Heishi* started to control the Imperial court by having their daughters married to the emperors. Later in the *Heian* period, the political power was shifted to the *Heishi*. They became tyrannical and arrogant. This behavior created many enemies. The *Genji* clan, together with the *Fujiwara* family, started a war against the *Heishi*. The *Genji* pushed the *Heishi* to the final battleground called *Dan-no-ura* (壇ノ浦) in 1185 and destroyed them. This battle was the famous *Genpei-Gassen* (源平合戦). The collapse of the *Heishi* was the end of the *Heian* period.

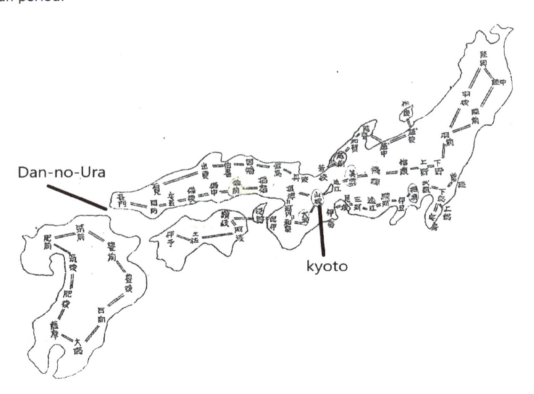

The *Heian* period was the time when curved swords appeared for the first time. Until then, swords had straight blades. Historical studies on Japanese swords start from this point. The elegant, graceful lifestyle and culture the dominant *Fujiwra* family created then were certainly reflected upon the swords' style. A group of swordsmiths in the *Kyoto* region created a particular sword style called *Yamashiro Den* (*Yamashiro* School). The shape of their blades shows a graceful line. The most well-known sword among *Yamashiro-Den is Sanjo-Munechika* (三条宗近), which is a national treasure today. The style of *Yamashiro* Den represents *Heian* period swords.

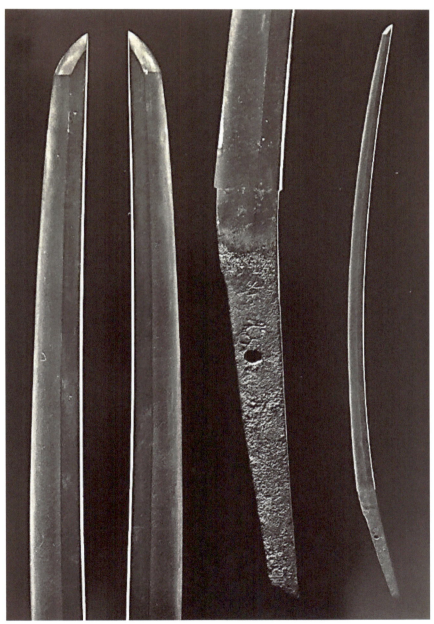

Sanjo Munechiak (三条宗近) From Showa Dai Mei-to Zufu (昭和大名刀図譜) by NBTHK
Owned by Tokyo National Museum

5 | Heian Period Sword (平安時代太刀)

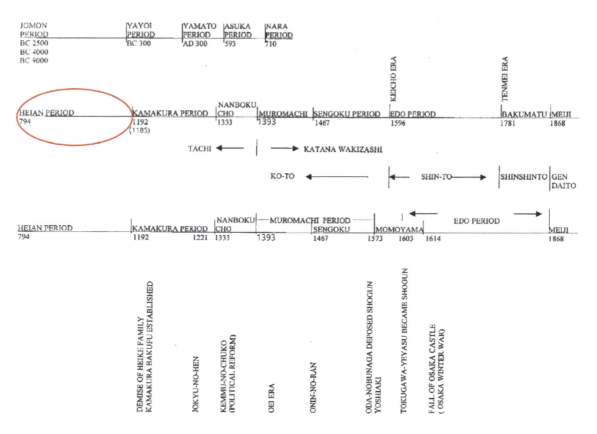

The circle above indicates the time we discuss in this section

The *Heian* period is the time when the shape of the swords changed to the present curved shape. Until then, swords were straight. It is a commonly accepted idea that the study of Japanese swords begins from the *Heian* period. Swords before the *Heian* period are in the category of archaeology. The main reason for that is the sword-making technique saw a significant improvement after the *Heian* period.

The elegant, graceful lifestyle of the *Heian* culture then reflected upon the swords' style. A group of swordsmiths in *the Kyoto* region created a particular sword style called *Yamashiro Den* (*Yamashiro* School). The shape of their swords shows a graceful line. The most famous sword of this time is *Sanjo-Munechika* (三条宗近 last page), a national treasure today. The style of *Yamashiro Den* represents *Heian* period swords.

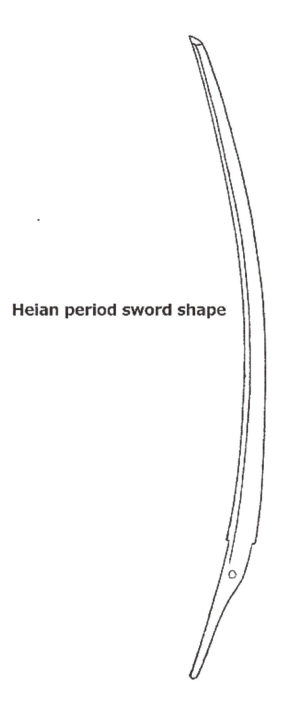

Heian period sword shape

General Heian period sword style

The shape ---------------The length of a sword is approximately 30 inches ± a few inches. It has an elegant and graceful shape with a narrow blade and a small *kissaki* (小切先). The curvature is deep. This style is called *Kyo-zori* (京反り) or *Torii-zori* (鳥居ぞり). With the *Kyo-zori* style, the deepest part of the curvature comes around the halfway of the blade. The lower part of the sword flares out, making an A-line shape like the lower part of the Eiffel Tower. This flaring shape is called *funbari* (踏ん張り).

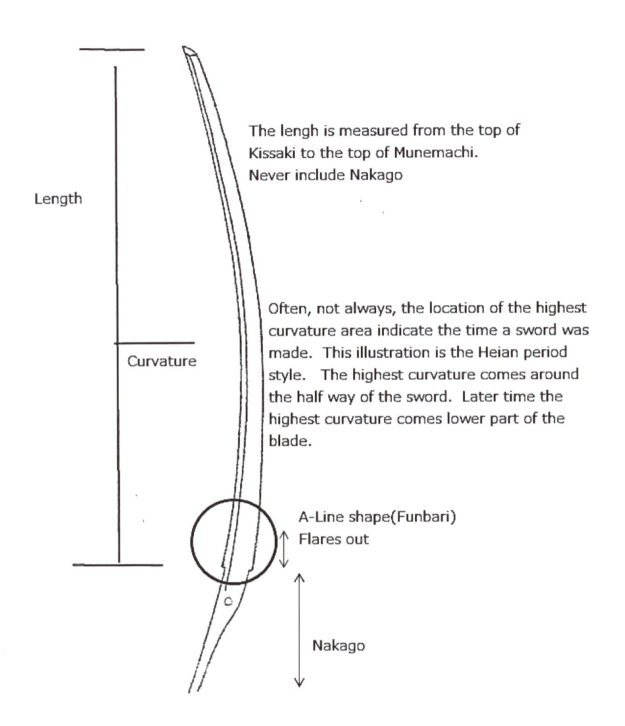

Length

The lengh is measured from the top of Kissaki to the top of Munemachi. Never include Nakago

Curvature

Often, not always, the location of the highest curvature area indicate the time a sword was made. This illustration is the Heian period style. The highest curvature comes around the half way of the sword. Later time the highest curvature comes lower part of the blade.

A-Line shape(Funbari) Flares out

Nakago

Hamon(刃文)---------- *Hamon* is the line that was created when the sword was tempered. The *Hamon* on the *Heian* period swords is narrow and usually *Suguha* (直刃). *Suguha* means a straight line. The *Hamon* is also *Nie*-base. *Nie*(沸) is a tiny particle in the *Hamon*. As shown below, if you look closely, you will see fine sand-like particles in the *Hamon* line.

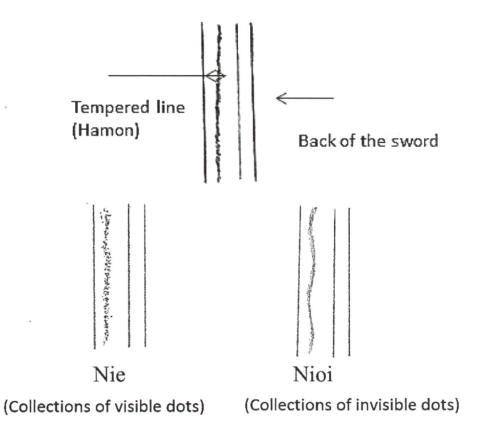

Ji-hada (地肌) --------Fine wood-grained pattern. The location of *Ji-hada* (or *Ji-tetsu*) is between *Hamon* and *Shinogi* (see Chapter 3 | Names of Parts)

Nakago (中心)-------- *Nakago* is the hilt area. Sword makers inscribed his name there. The *Nakago* during the *Heian* period is often *Kijimomo* (雉腿) shape. *Kijimomo* means the shape of a pheasant thigh.

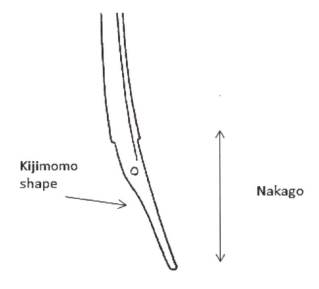

Hi and engrave ---------- *Hi* (樋) means an engraved straight line. *Hi,* and other engraved designs are rare during the *Heian* period. These became more common later time.

Kissaki (切先） ---------- The *Heian* sword's *kissaki* is *Ko-gissaki,* meaning small *kissaki*. The *Hamon* line on the *Kissaki* is called *Boshi*. In this period, the type of *Boshi* design is called *Komaru,* meaning small, round, and wrapping the tip.

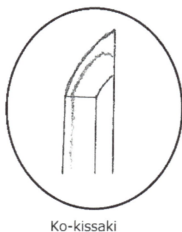
Ko-kissaki
(small kissaki)

Chu-Kissaki
(medium Kissaki)

O-Kissaki
(large Kissaki)

Swordsmiths in the Heian period

Yamashiro school ------------------------ Sanjo Munechika(三条宗近) Sanjo Yoshiie(三条吉家)
　　　　　　　　　　　　　　　　　　　　　Gojo Kananaga (五条兼長) Gojo Kuninaga (五条国永)
Yamato school ---Senju-in (千手院)
Ko-Bizen school ------------------Bizen Tomonari(備前友成) Bizen Masatsune-(備前正恒)
　　　　　　　　　　　　　　　　-　　　　　Bizen Kanehira (備前包平)
Hoki (伯耆) ---Yasutsuna (安綱) Sanemori (真守)
Buzen (豊前) --------- --Cho-en (長円) Sinsoku (神息)
Satsuma (薩摩) --Naminohira (波平)

6 | Kamakura Period History 1192 – 1333 (鎌倉時代歴史)

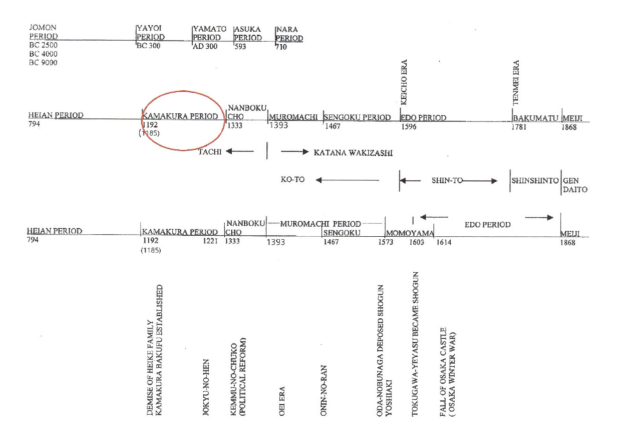

The circle above indicates the time we discuss in this section

The *Kamakura* period (鎌倉) was the golden age of sword making. Many valuable swords we have now were made during the *Kamakura* period. The war between the *Genji* clan and the *Heishi* clan demanded more swords and more swordsmiths in the late *Heian* period.

Through and after the *Genpei-Gassen* (源平合戦: The final battle between the *Genji* and the *Heishi*), sword-making techniques improved significantly. Also, Emperor *Gotoba* at that time encouraged sword-making and treated swordsmiths respectfully. As a result, swordsmiths in the *Kamakura* era created a large number of valuable swords. Since the swords' styles vary considerably during this time, we usually categorize them into three chronological groups: swords in the early, in the middle, and the late *Kamakura* period.

The name of the *Kamakura* period came from the name of a place, *Kamakura*, where the head of the *Genji* clan, *Minamoto-no-Yoritomo* (源頼朝), established a new government, *Kamakura Bakufu* (鎌倉幕府).

Kamakura Bakufu (鎌倉幕府)

At the end of the *Heian* period, the *Genji* and the *Heishi* (also called the *Heike*) were the two major powerful *Samurai* groups. After their first fight, the *Heishi* killed the *Genji*'s top and banished his young son, *Minamoto-no-Yoritomo* (源頼朝), to *Izu* Island. For *Kyoto* people back then, *Izu* Island was such a remote place with their limited transportation means.

The *Heishi* became the top of the society. They were so powerful that it was once said, "If you are not a part of the *Heishi*, you are not a human." Such arrogant people, however, naturally created many enemies.

In the meantime, *Yoritomo* grew into a fine young man on the Island. He met *Hojo Masako* (北条政子), a daughter of a small local official, *Hojo Tokimasa* of *Izu Island*, and married her. Eventually, *Yoritomo* raised an army with the help of his wife's family and his *Genji* relatives. They attacked the *Heishi*, chased them away from *Kyoto*, and won the war. This ended the *Heian* period. It was 1185.
As a result, *Yoritomo* became the *Shogun* in 1192, and the political and military power shifted from *Kyoto* to *Kamakura*.

The imperial court and aristocrats remained in *Kyoto*. While *Kamakura Bakufu* (Government) had the military, police, and political power, the imperial court had the administrative authority. Although they were like two big rivals, they controlled the country in different fields and kept the balance between them.

From Wikimedia Commons, the free media repository Taira -no-Kiyomori painted 14th century by Fujiwara Tamenobu, owned by Imperial Household Agency

From Wikimedia Commons, the free media repository. Minamoto-no-Yoritomo by Fujiwara Takanobu, owned by Jingo-ji.

7 | Overview of the Kamakura Period Swords (鎌倉時代刀概要)

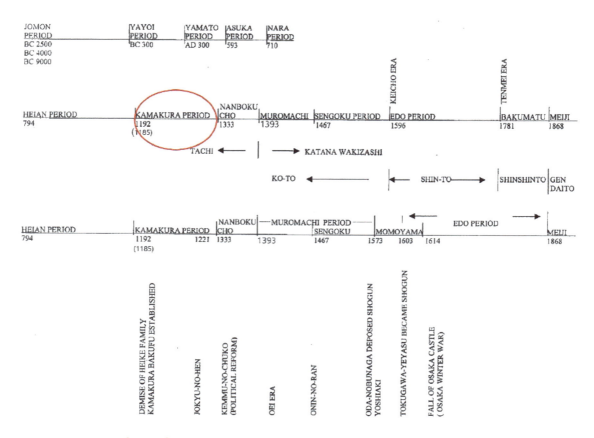

The circle above indicates the time we discuss in this section

Introduction Of The Five Main Sword School (Den)

There are five major sword schools (*Den*): *Yamashiro Den* (山城), *Bizen Den* (備前), *Soshu Den* (相州), *Yamato Den* (大和), and *Mino Den* (美濃). During the *Heian* period, *Yamashiro Den* was the main and most active school. A school called *Ko-bizen* (meaning old *Bizen*) during the *Heian* period is a part of *Bizen Den*. However, we take the *Ko-bizen* separately since their style is slightly different from the later *Bizen Den* but somewhat close to the *Yamashiro Den* as we see it later.

During the *Heian* period, the swordsmiths of *Yamashiro Den* lived around *Kyoto*, the capital of Japan then. In the early *Kamakura* period, *Yamashiro Den* maintained the similar sword style they created in the *Heian* period. *Bizen Den* appeared in the middle *Kamakura* period. *Soshu Den* appeared in the late *Kamakura* period in *Kamakura* area. *Mino Den* appeared in the *Muromachi* period, which comes much later.

The Early Kamakura Period (鎌倉)

We divide the *Kamakura* period into three stages: the early, the middle, and the late *Kamakura* period. The sword style in the early *Kamakura* period was almost the same as the one in the previous *Heian* period. *Yamashiro Den* was continuously the most active school through the early *Kamakura* period.

The Middle Kamakura Period

In the middle *Kamakura* period, we have three different styles of the sword to discuss: the *Yamashiro Den* style, the *Bizen Den* style, and the *Ikubi-kissaki* (猪首切先) style, which was new at that time. We can say that among the *Ikubi-kissaki* swords, seldom sees the mediocre sword.

The previous section described the *Kamakura Bakufu* (鎌倉幕府: government) had political and military power, yet the Emperor was still on the throne in *Kyoto*. Emperor *Gotoba* raised an army and attacked the *Kamakura* government to regain political control. This war (1221) is called *Jyokyu-no-Ran* (承久の乱). The war changed the look of swords to a sturdier shape. This style is what we call the *Ikubi-kissaki*.

The Late Kamakura Period (after the Mongolian Invasion)

During the late *Kamakura* Period, *Soshu Den* emerged in addition to *Yamashiro Den* and *Bizen Den*. After the two *Mongolian* Invasions called *Genko* (元寇) in 1274 and 1281, longer and broader swords with longer *Kissaki* began to appear. The *Soshu Den* swordsmiths forged this type of sword

Engravings on Sword

Engravings on a sword in the *Ko-to* era (*Heian* to *Keicho* era) have three purposes. One is to reduce the weight of the sword. *Hi, Bohi, Gomabashi* (wide, narrow, short, or long grooves) are examples. The second is for religious purposes, for which swordsmiths often carved Buddhistic figures. The third is for decoration. In the *Shin-to* era (from *Keicho* time and after), it became mainly for decoration purposes.

The figures below are examples of the engravings.

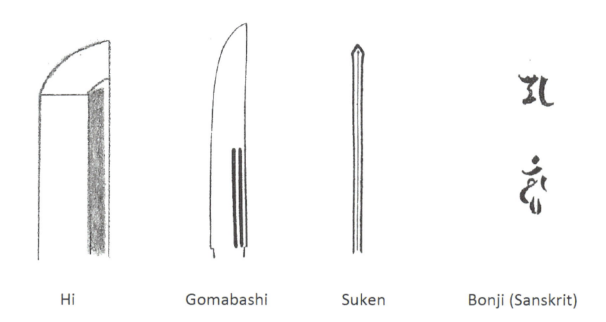

Hi   Gomabashi   Suken   Bonji (Sanskrit)

8 | Middle Kamakura Period: Yamashiro Den (鎌倉中期山城伝)

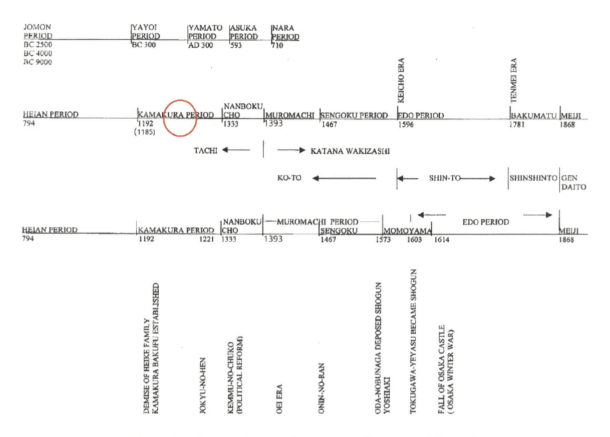

The circle above indicates the time we discuss in this section

The characteristics of Yamashiro Den swords

Sugata (shape)-----In general, the blade is narrow, especially near the *Yokote* line. The bottom of the blade has *fundari* (A-line shape). *Kasane* is thick. The curvature type is usually *Kyo-zori* (the deepest curvature comes at about the middle). It has a small *Kissaki* with *Fukura*. *Shinogi* is <u>thick</u> with *Gyo-no-mune* or *Shin-no-mune*. Please see the three illustrations below for *Sugata*.

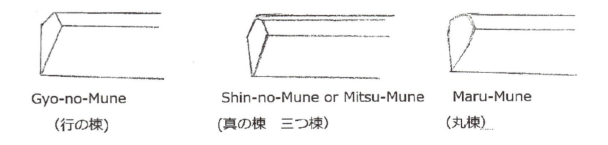

Gyo-no-Mune　　　Shin-no-Mune or Mitsu-Mune　　　Maru-Mune
(行の棟)　　　　　(真の棟　三つ棟)　　　　　　　　(丸棟)

32
Alpha Book Publisher

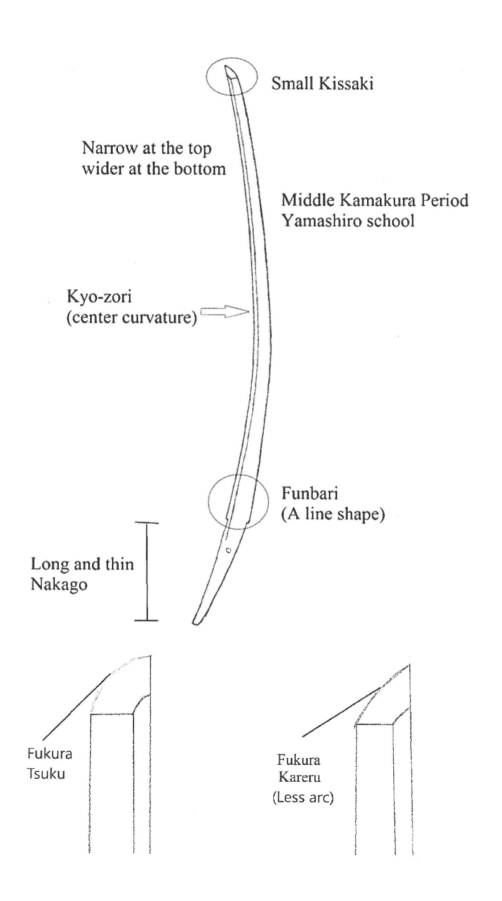

Horimono (Engraving)--------The tip of a *Hi* (樋, groove) follows the exact shape of the *Ko-shinogi* line. Sometimes you may see *Bonj* (Sanscrit) and *Suke*n (see the illustration).

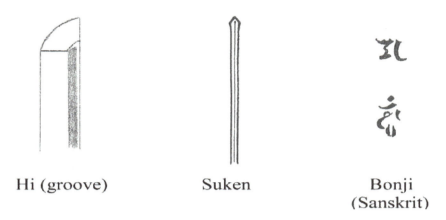

Hi (groove)   Suken   Bonji (Sanskrit)

Nakago (hilt: 中心) -----------------------Long and thin with curvature

Hamon (tempered line: 刃文) -----------------Mostly *Suguha* (straight line), *Niju-Ba* (double *Hamon*), or *Suguha* with an irregular wavy line. Sometimes a thin gold lightning-like line called *Inazuma* faintly appears. The tempered line is mostly *Nie*. Below is *Suguha*.

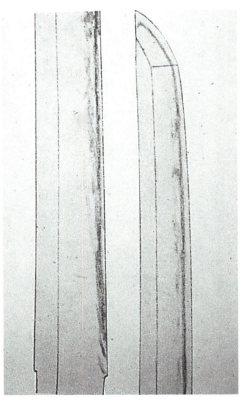

Bungo-no-Kuni-Yukihira (豊後国行平)*   Sano Museum Catalog Permission granted

* *Bungo-no-Kuni-Yukihira* was a *Yamashiro Den* swordsmith from the *Bungo* area.

Boshi (鋩子) ---------------------- *Komaru-boshi* (small round) *Omaru-boshi* (large round)

Ji-hada (地肌)-----Well forged fine surface. Small burl pattern. *Jinie* (地沸) on the surface.

Names of the swordsmiths during the middle Kamakura period

Ayano-kouji group	Ayanokouji sadatoshi (綾小路定利)
Awataguchi group	Awataguchi kunituna (粟田口国綱)
Rai group	Rai kuniyuki (来国行) Rai Nijikunitoshi (来国俊)

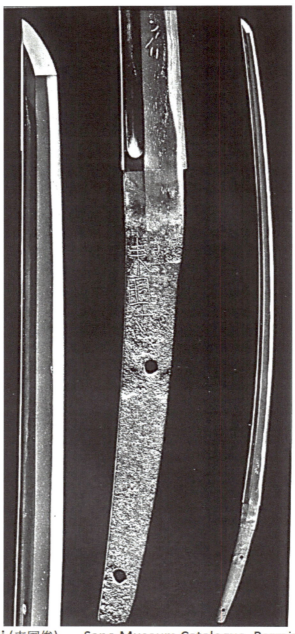

Rai Kunitoshi (来国俊)   Sano Museum Catalogue, Permission granted

9 | Middle Kamakura period: Bizen Den (鎌倉中期備前伝)

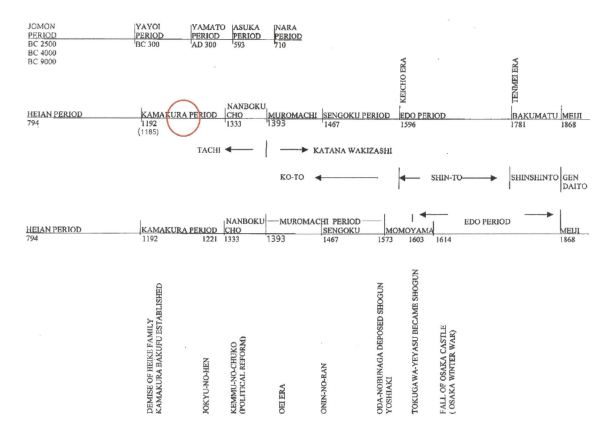

The circle above indicates the time we discuss in this section

There are many swordsmiths in the *Bizen* (備前) school during the early *Kamakura* period. However, their sword style is usually somewhat similar to that of the *Yamashiro* school. Therefore, they are called *Ko-bizen* (古備前), which means old *Bizen*.

The true *Bizen* school style emerged in the Middle *Kamakura* period. *Bizen* province had many advantages to produce great swords. The area produced high-quality iron and a large amount of firewood for fuel. Also, its location was conveniently situated to come from different places. Naturally, many swordsmiths came to the place and produced swords in quantities. Due to the competition among those swordsmiths, *Bizen* swords' quality is generally higher than that of other schools. Thus, it is not easy to appraise *Bizen* swords since they had many subtle variations among the many swordsmiths.

The following three features are the most distinctive characteristics of *Bizen* school.

1. *Nioi*-base tempered line. *Nioi*-base tempered line is finer dots than *Nie*-base. Dots are so small that they look almost like a line. Technically, the tempering processes of

these two are the same. See the illustration below.
2. *Ji-hada* (surface of the body) looks soft.
3. Reflection (*Utsuri*) appears on the surface.

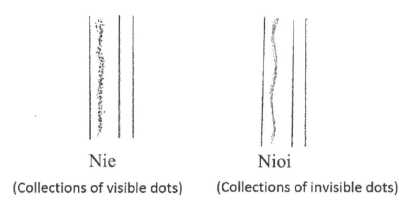

Sugata (shape) ---The length is about 33 inches ± a few inches. The blade is slightly wide and looks stout. The curvature of the blade is *Koshizori* (腰反), which means the deepest curvature comes at a lower part. The body has an average thickness. Small *Kissaki*.

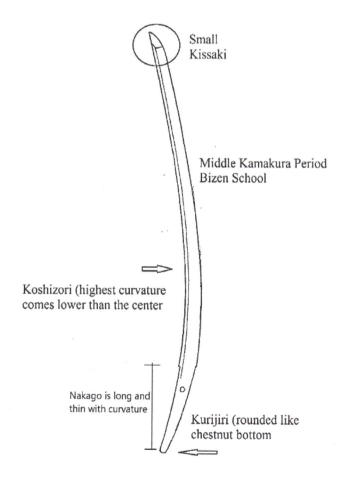

Horimono (engraving) -----------Engravings are rare. The shape of the tip of *Hi* is all the way up to *Ko-shinogi* and fills up the entire area.

Nakago -------- Long and thin with curvature. The end of *Nakago* is rounded and looks like a shape of the bottom of a chestnut (*Kuri*). This shape is called *Kurijiri*. See the illustration of the sword above.

Hamon (tempered area pattern) ------ *Nioi* base. The tempered area is wide, and the width is even. Also, the size of *Midare* (irregular wavy tempered pattern) is uniform.

Boshi ---------- The same tempered pattern continues to go up to the *Boshi* area, and it often shows *Choj- midare* (clove-shape wavy pattern) or *Yakizume*.

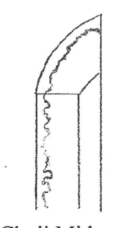   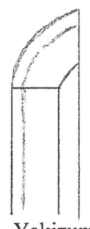

Choji Midare   Yakizume
(Clove pattern continues into Boshi)   (Hamon ends without return)

Ji-hada ------------- Fine and well forged. Steel looks soft. On the steel surface, the small wood grain pattern and the large wood grain pattern are mixed together. *Chikei* (condensation of *Nie*) and *Utsuri* (cloud-like reflection) appear.

Bizen Den Sword Smiths during the Middle Kamakura Period

Fukuoka Ichimonji (福岡一文字) group ----------------- Norimune (則宗)　Sukemune (助宗)

Yoshioka Ichimonji (吉岡一文字) group -----------------Sukeyoshi (助吉)　Sukemitsu (助光)

Shochu Ichimonji (正中一文字) group ----------------------Yoshiuji (吉氏)　Yoshimori (吉守)

Osafune (長船) group -----------------Mitsutada (光忠) Nagamitu (長光) Kagemitsu (景光)

Hatakeda(畠田) group ------------- -----------------------------Moriie (守家) Sanemori (真守)

Ugai (鵜飼) group ---Unsho (雲生)　Unji (雲次)

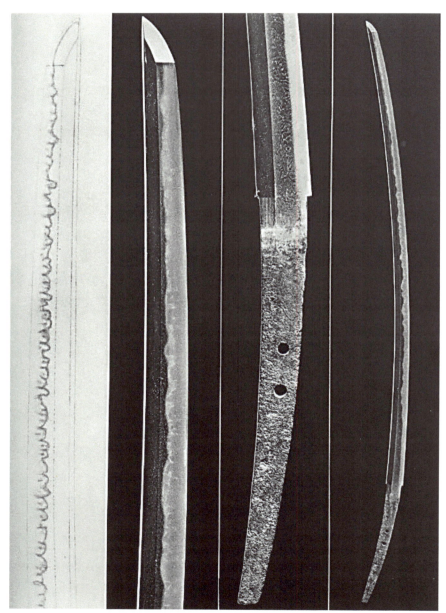

Fukuoka Ichimonji (一文字) from "Nippon-to Art Swords of Japan"
The Walter A. Compton Collection

10 | Jokyu-no-Ran 1221 （承久の乱）

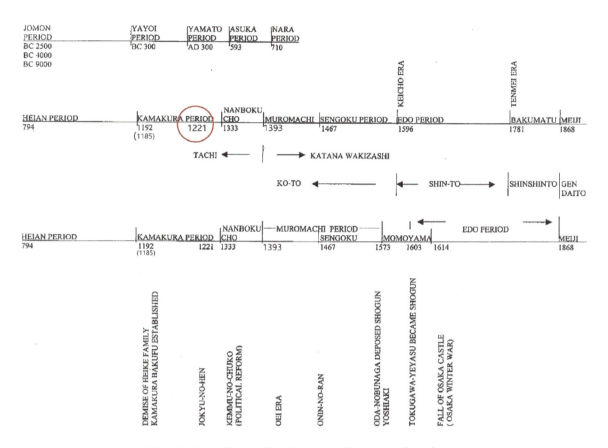

The circle indicates the time we discuss in this chapter.

Jokyu-no-Ran (承久の乱)

After *Minamoto-no-Yoritomo* (源頼朝) died, his son, *Yoriie* (頼家) succeeded the *Shogun* position. His mother, *Hojo Masako* (北条政子) *Yoritomo*'s wife, thought her son was too incompetent. She was afraid that others could take over the *Kamakura Bakufu* (*Kamakura* government). To prevent this from happening, she established a council system consisting of 13 members including herself, her father, *Hojo Tokimasa* (北条時政) and her brother, *Hojo Yoshitoki* (北条義時).

In time, *Shogun Yoriie*'s in-law became powerful. During the *Heian* and the *Kamakura* period, the wife's family was considered very important.

To suppress her son's in-laws, *Masako* and her father, *Tokimasa,* plotted an assassination of *Yoriie* and killed him.

After *Yoriie*'s death, Masako's younger son, *Sanetomo* (実朝), became the next *Shogun*. Now, his grandfather, *Hojo Tokimasa's* second wife, wanted her son-in-law to be the next *Shogun*. To please his young wife, *Hojo Tokimasa* attempted to kill *Sanetomo*, but failed. Finding this plot, *Hojo Masako* imprisoned her father, *Tokimasa*. Although *Sanetomo* was *Masako's* son, she was again very disappointed in his incompetence. In the end, *Shogun Sanetomo* was killed by his nephew *Kugyo,* the son of the previous *Shogun, Yoriiee*.

After all these incidents, *Masako's* brother, *Hojo Yoshitoki,* took control of the *Kamakura Bakufu* and brought a figurehead from the *Fujiwara* family, a powerful aristocrat family in *Kyoto*. After all the turmoil, the *Hojo* family eventually took full control of the *Kamakura Bakufu* (government).

Meanwhile, in *Kyoto*, Emperor *Gotoba* had been planning an attack on the *Kamakura Bakufu*. He had built up military power. When *Sanetomo* was killed, Emperor *Gotoba* saw the chance to attack *Kamakura*. He ordered local feudal lords to attack the *Kamakura Bakufu,* but very few followed the order. Instead, the *Hojo* family captured the Emperor and exiled him to *Oki island*. It was in 1221 and called *Jokyo-no-Ran* or *Jokyu-no Hen*.

Emperor *Gotoba* was the one who really encouraged sword making and treated swordsmiths respectfully. After the *Jokyu-no-Ran*, the Imperial family's power decreased, and the *Kamakura Bakufu* became a powerful and stable regime. From the time of *Minamoto-no-Yoritomo*'s death to the end of the *Jokyu-no-Ran*, the *Kamakura Bakufu* was still an unstable government. It was *Hojo Masako* who led the *Kamakura Bakufu* to a stable regime. She was called "*Ama Shogun*" or a "Nun *Shogun*." She was a sharp and talented but tough, critical, and often mean politician.

Kamakura people (I am one of them) like *Hojo Masako* very much. *Minamoto no Yoritomo* and *Hojo Masako* were both buried in *Kamakura* City. *Minamoto no Yoritomo* at *Shirahata* Shrine (白幡神社), and *Hojo Masako* at *Jufukuji Temple* (寿福寺).

Kamakura is about one hour from *Tokyo* by train on the *Yokosuka* line. Both *Jufuku-Ji* temple and *Shirahata* shrine are within walking distance from *Kamakura* station.

Jufuku-ji (寿福寺) Temple from Wikimedia Commons, the free media repository

The tomb of *Minamoto-no-Yoritomo's*. From Wikimedia Commons, the free media repository

11 | Ikubi kissaki (猪首切先)

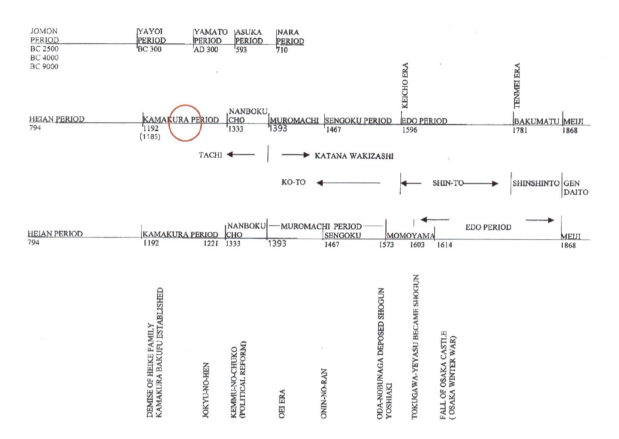

The circle indicates the time we discuss in this chapter.

Through the experience of the war of *Jokyu-no-Ran* (Chapter 10), the sword's trend changed to a wider, sturdier, and grander style. The swords made around this time are called *Ikubi-kissaki*. *Ikubi* means a wild boar's neck. *Ikubi-kissaki* style swords have a stout look *kissaki* that looks like the boar's neck.

The middle *Kamakura* period was the golden age of Japanese sword making. Many top swordsmiths created great swords during this time. Experts agree that there is no mediocre sword among *Ikubi-kissaki* swords

Ikubi Kissaki Sword

SUGATA (shape) ------------------ Originally 3 feet or longer. They were often shortened in later years. Wide width. Thick *Kasane* (thick body) with *Hamaguri-ha,* which means the sword's cross-section is shaped like a clam. The difference in the width between the near *Yokote* line and *Machi* is minimal. *Shinogi* is high, and its width is narrow. The cross-section of an *Ikubi-kissaki* sword is shown below.

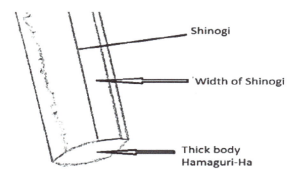

KISSAKI ------------- *Ikubi-kissaki*. *Ikubi* means the neck of a wild boar. It is thick, short, and stout-looking. *Kissaki* is short and wide at the *Yokote* line. The illustration below shows an exaggerated image of an *Ikubi-kissaki*.

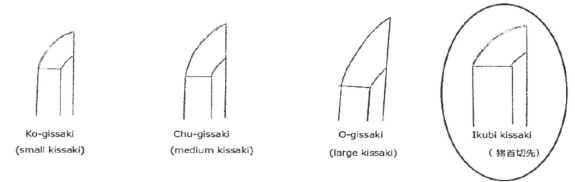

Hamon (刃文) ------ *Kawazuko-choji* (tadpole-head shape pattern). *O-choji* (large clove-shape pattern), *Ko-choji* (small clove-shape pattern), a mix of *O-choji* and *Ko-choji*, or *Suguha-choji*. *Suguha-choji* has a straight line mixed with *Choji* pattern (clove-shape).

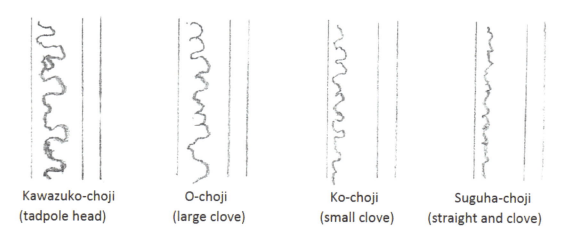

Boshi (鋩子) --------- *Yakizume*: the *hamon* ends almost at the tip of *kissaki,* no turn back. *Sansaku Boshi*: The *hamon* narrows at the *yokote* line, created by *Nagamitsu* (長光), *Kagemitsu* (景光), and *Sanenaga* (真長). See the below for *Yakizume* and *Sansaku Boshi*.

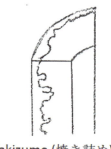
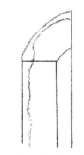

Yakizume (焼き詰め)　　　Sansaku Boshi （三作鋩子）

Ikubi Kissaki Sword Smiths

Fukuoka Ichimonji Group (備前福岡一文字) -----------Fukuoka Ichimonji Norimune (則宗)
Kamakura Ichimonji Group(鎌倉一文字) --------------Kamakura Ichimonji Sukezane (助真)
Soshu Bizen Kunimune Group(相州備前国宗)------------------Soshu Bizen Kunimune (国宗)
Bizen Osafune Group(備前長船)--------------------------Bizen Osafune Mitsutada(長船光 忠)
　　　　　　　　　　　　　　　　　　　　　　　　　　　　　Nagamitsu(長光)
Ugai Group--- Ugai Unji (鵜飼雲次)

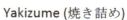

Bizen Osafune Nagamitu (備前長船長光)　Sano Museum Catalogue (permission granted)

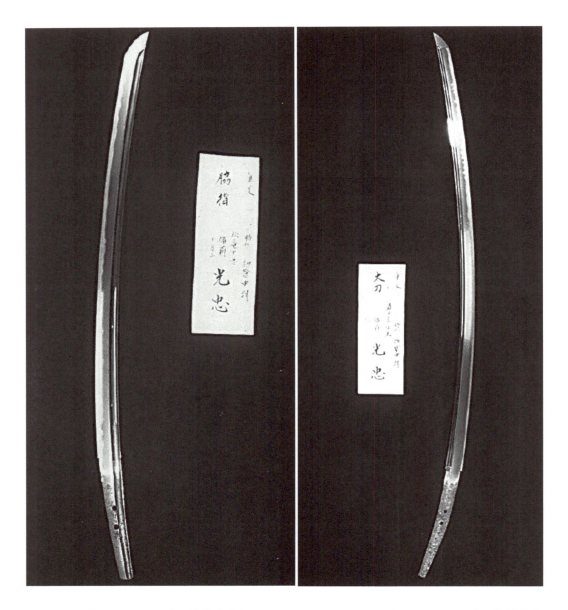

Bizen Osafune Mitsutada (長船光忠)　　　　　Bizen Osafune Mitsutada (長船光忠)
Once my family sword. My father did the calligraphy and took these pictures for himself.

12 | Middle Kamakura period: Tanto (Dagger 鎌倉中期短刀)

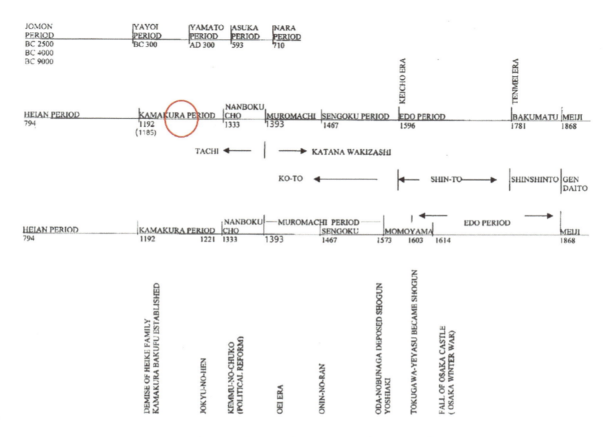

The circle above indicates the time we discuss in this section

It is very rare to see a *Tanto* (短刀 dagger) made during the *Heian* period. During the middle *Kamakura* period, a large number of high-quality *Tanto* were made. They were called *Takenoko-zori* shaped *Tanto*. *Takenoko* means bamboo shoot. The back of the *Tanto* curves inward slightly.

Middle Kamakura Period
Yamashiro School Tanto

Takenoko-zori
(bamboo shoot shape)

Sugata (shape)----------*Hirazukuri*. It means there is no *Shinogi, Yokote* line. See the illustration above. The standard *Tanto* size is about 10 inches. The width is not too wide, not too narrow, very well-balanced in size. The body is slightly thick. High *Gyo-no-mune* (行の棟) and *Shin-no-mune* (真の棟)

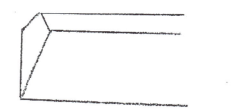

Gyo-no-Mune
(行の棟)

Shin-no-Mune or Mitsu-Mune
(真の棟　三つ棟)

Hamon (刃文) --------------------- The tempered area is narrow. *Nie* base. *Suguha-midare* (straight line pattern with irregular wavy pattern) or *Suguha-choji* (straight line pattern with small *Choji*). The tempered edge line may show a frayed look.

Boshi (tempered line at Kissaki area) ---------------------------*Yakizume, Kaen, Nie-kuzure.*

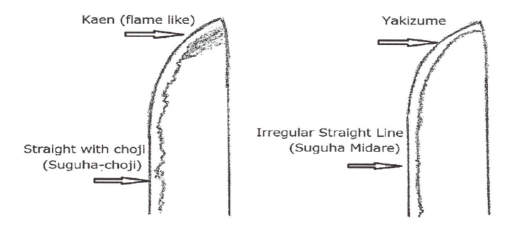

Engravings (彫刻) ---------- Often, different kinds of engravings are done at the lower part of the body.   These may be a groove or two grooves, Sanskrit, Suken (spear), dragon, etc. For Sanskrit and spear, look at the illustration inside Chapter 8.

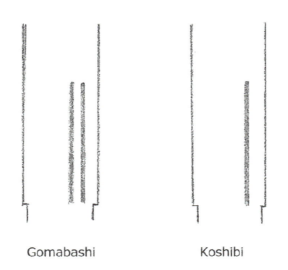

Swordsmiths who created Tanto in the Middle Kamakura Period
Awataguchi group(粟田口)-----------------------------------Awataguchi Yoshimitu (粟田口吉光)
Rai group (来) --Rai Kunitoshi(来国俊)
Soshu Group (相州) -------------------------------------- Shintougo Kunimitu (新藤五国光)
Bizen group (備前) -- Bien Kagemitu (備前景光)
Bungo no Kuni Group (豊後の国) --------------------- Bungo-no-kuni Yukihira (豊後の国行平)

50
Alpha Book Publisher

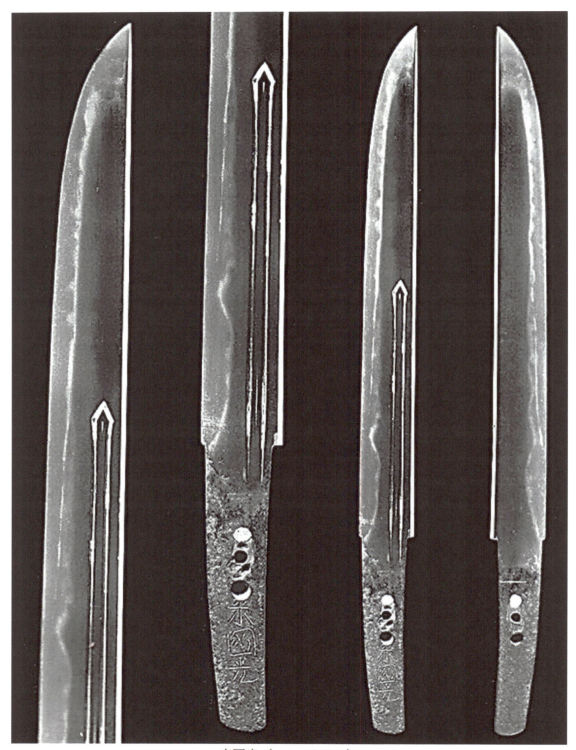

来国光 (Rai Kunimitsu)

13 | The Late Kamakura Period: Genko (鎌倉末元寇)

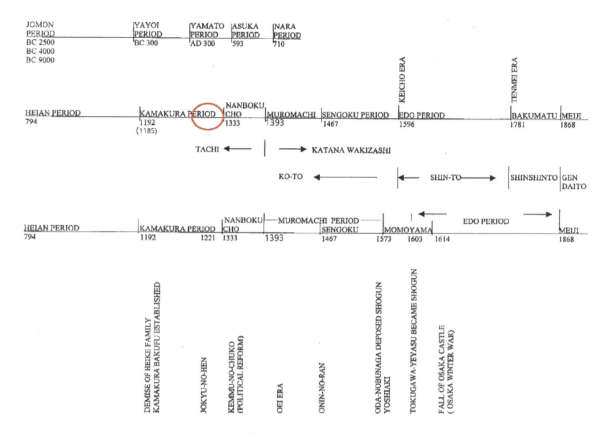

The circle above indicates the time we discuss in this section

Genko 元寇 (1274 and 1281)

The grandson of Genghis Kahn, Kublai Kahn, attempted to invade Japan twice in 1274 and 1281. Both times, a strong typhoon hit Japan. Mongols sent a large number of soldiers with all kinds of supplies on a huge number of ships to Japan. Those ships had to stay side by side and front and back very close to each other in the limited area offshore of *Kyushu*. When the strong wind came, ships were swayed, hit each other, and capsized. Many people fell into the ocean, drowned, and lost supplies in the water. Even though Mongol soldiers landed and fought with the Japanese army, they did not have much choice but to leave Japan because of the typhoon and ships wrecking. As a result of this strong wind, Japan was saved and looked as if Japan won. This is the time the famous Japanese word, "*Kamikaze*" (divine wind) was created.

Actually, Mongols had many more superior weapons than the Japanese. They had guns, while the Japanese did not. Their group fighting method was much superior and more effective than the Japanese one-to-one fighting method.

After the Mongolian invasion, the need for changing the style of the *Ikubi Kissaki* sword became obvious. When swords were used in a war, the area most frequently damaged was the *Kissaki* area. Japanese soldiers used mostly *Ikubi-kissaki* swords in this war. An *Ikubi-kissaki Tachi* has a short *Kissaki*. When a damaged area of the *Kissaki* was whetted out, the top part of the *Yakiba* (tempered area) disappears, and the *Hi* (a groove) goes up too high into the *Boshi* area (top triangle-like area). Short *Ikubi-kissaki* becomes even shorter, and the *Hi* goes up too high into the *Boshi* area. Aesthetically, it is not appealing. Functionally, it does not work well. To compensate for the flaw, a new style began to appear in the latter part of the *Kamakura* period.

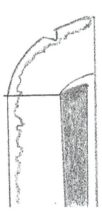 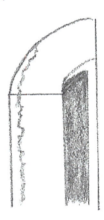

During the latter part of the *Kamakura* period, the swordsmiths began to create a new swords style to compensate for this fault. Also, the pride and confidence had grown among people after driving the Mongols away, which reflected on the swords' appearance. Generally speaking, the *Hamon* and the shape of the body became stronger and showier.

Kamakura area became a very prosperous place under the power of the *Hojo* family. A large number of swordsmiths moved to *Kamakura* from *Bizen, Kyoto,* and other places during this time, and they created a new style. This is the beginning of the *Soshu Den* (*Soshu* is the *Kanagawa* area now). Many famous top swordsmiths appeared during this time.

One of the famous swordsmiths is *Goro-Nyudo Masamune* (五郎入道正宗). You can easily visit *Masamune's* tomb in *Kamakura*. It is in *Honkaku-Ji* temple that is about 5 to 6 minutes' walk from the *Kamakura* train station.

While I was attending the sword study group of *Mori Sensei* (teacher), one of the students I studied with was the 24th generation of the direct descendants of *Masamune*. Although he does not bear the name of *Masamune*, he has been making wonderful swords in *Kamakura*. He also makes superb kitchen knives. The name of his shop is "*Masamune Kogei* (正宗工芸)," and it is located a short walk from Kamakura station. To find his place, ask at the information center in the train station.

With Mr.Tsunahiro Yamamura,
the 24th generation of Masamune, in May 2019

Honkaku-Ji Temple Masamune's tomb is here.

14| Late Kamakura Period Swords (鎌倉末太刀)

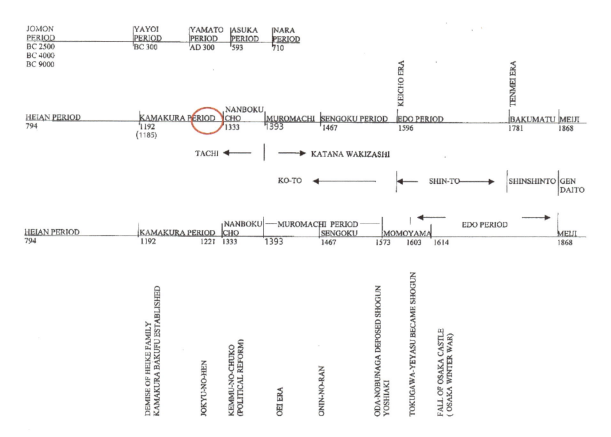

The circle above indicates the time we discuss in this section

The beginning of the *Soshu* style

A new sword style called *Soshu Den* emerged after the Mongolian invasion in the latter part of the *Kamakura* period. Kamakura region became prosperous under the rule of the *Hojo* family (北条). Many swordsmiths moved to Kamakura. Those people were *Kunituna* group (国綱) from *Yamashiro* area and *Fukuoka Ichimonji Sukezane* (福岡一文字助真) and *Kunimune* (国宗) from *Bizen* area. They are the origin of *Soshu Den* (相州伝). A star swordsmith, *Goro-Nyudo-Masamune* (五郎入道正宗), appeared during this time.

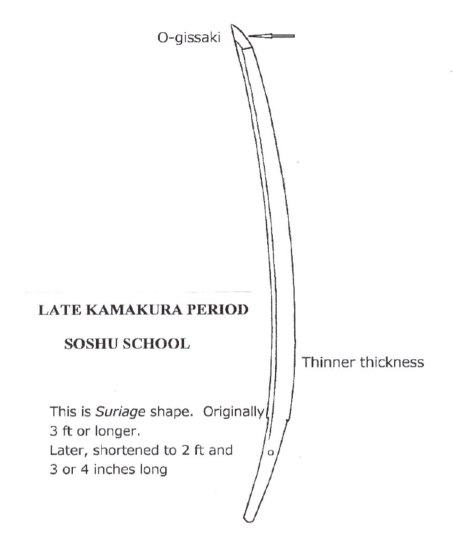

LATE KAMAKURA PERIOD

SOSHU SCHOOL

This is *Suriage* shape. Originally 3 ft or longer.
Later, shortened to 2 ft and 3 or 4 inches long

Sugata (Shape 姿) ------- *O-kissaki* (large-kissak: 大切先) and *Chu-kissaki* (medium *kissaki*: 中切先). The tip of *Hi* ends lower (see below illustration). *Hamaguri- ha* was no longer in style. The body became thinner. The original length was approximately 3 feet or longer, but the majority of them were shortened to 2 feet and 3 or 4 inches at a later time. The shortened sword is called *O-suriage* (大磨上).

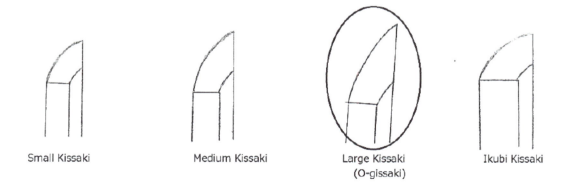

Small Kissaki   Medium Kissaki   Large Kissaki (O-gissaki)   Ikubi Kissaki

The *Hi* ends lower than *Yokote* Line

Hamon (刃文) ---------------- Narrow *Hamon* or wide *Hamon*.
Narrow Hamon --------------A mix of *Suguha* (straight) and *Ko-choji* (small clove-like pattern), and *Ko-gumome* (small half-circle like pattern). Small *Nie* base. (shown below)

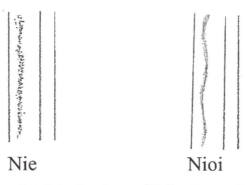

Nie   Nioi

(Collections of visible dots)   (Collections of invisible dots)

Wide Hamon----------*Notare midare* (wavy), *O-gunome*. *Nie* base. *Ashi-iri* (short line toward the blade, the right drawing below). *Inazuma* (lightning-like line) or *Kinsuji* (bright line) may appear on a tempered line. However, *Inazuma* and *Kinsuji* require trained eyes to be detected. It is hard for beginners to see the *Inazuma* or *Kinsuji*.

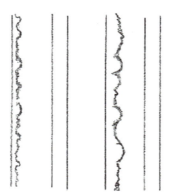

Ashi-iri

Boshi-------------The main body and *Boshi* has the same type of *Hamon*. At the tip of the *Kissaki,* turn back a little or *Yakizume*. You may also see *O-maru* (large round), *Ko-maru* (small round), *Kaen* (flame like), or *Nie-kuzure*. *Yakizume* and *Kaen*, see Chapter 12.

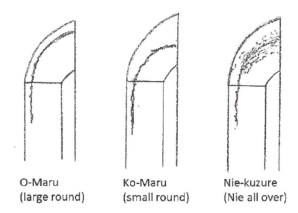

O-Maru (large round)   Ko-Maru (small round)   Nie-kuzure (Nie all over)

Ji-hada (between shinogi and tempered line) -------Strong *Ji-nie* (地沸) that is the sand-like small dots appears on *Ji* (between tempered line and *Mune*). *Yubashiri* (a cluster of *Ji-nie*), *Kinsuji* (bright, radiant line formed by *Nie*), *Inazuma* (a lightning-like irregular line), or *Chikei* (similar to *Kinsuji*) appears on *Ji-hada*.

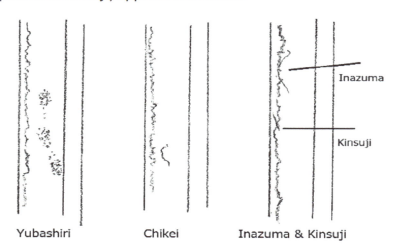

Yubashiri   Chikei   Inazuma & Kinsuji

Soshu School Swordsmiths in the late Kamakura Period

From *Bizen* (備前)--------Fukuoka Ichimonji Sukezane (福岡一文字助実), Kunimune (国宗)
From *Yamashiro* (山城)------------------------------ Toroku- Sakon- Kunituna (藤六左近国綱)

The above three swordsmiths were the origin of the *Soshu Den* (school) in *Kamakura*. Later, *Tosaburo-Yukimitu* and his son, the famous *Goro Nyudo Masamune,* appeared.

More *Soshu Den* swordsmiths other than above

From Yamashiro (山城) --------- Rai Kunitsugu (来国次), Hasebe Kunishige (長谷部国重)
From Etchu (越中) province ---------------------Go-no-Yoshihiro (郷義弘) Norishige (則重)
From Mino (美濃) province --Kaneuji (兼氏) Kinjyu (金重)
From Chikuzen (筑前) province ---Samoji (左文字)

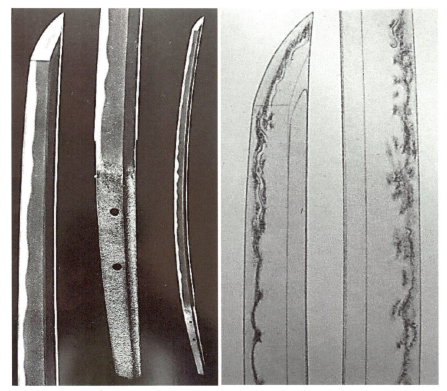

Goro Nyudo Masamune(正宗) His *hamon* is like ocean waves. (Sano Museum Permission granted)

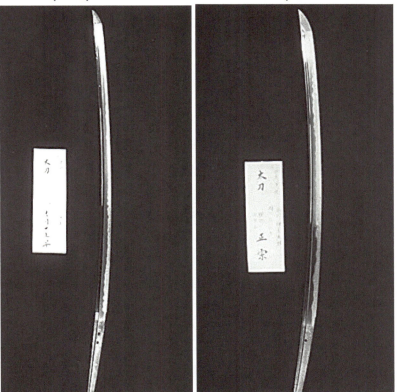

Yoshioka Ichimonji (吉岡一文字)　　　Masamune (五郎入道正宗) Once my family sword

15 | The Revival of Yamato Den   (大和伝復活)

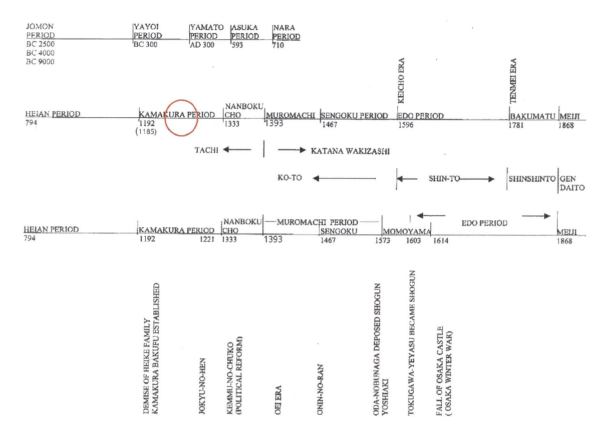

The circle above indicates the time we discuss in this section

It is said that the first sword-making started from *Yamato* province (present *Nara* prefecture) during the *Nara* period (710 to 794). In the early sword-making days, their forging techniques were primitive. At that time, many swordsmiths lived in *Yamato*, yet as time passed the sword-making declined in this area.

At the end of the *Kamakura* period, several powerful Buddhist temples in the *Yamato* area had power struggles against each other. Temples had a strong political and military power to control a large territory called *Shoen* (荘園) with their large number of warrior monks called *Sohei* (僧兵). The most powerful group was called *Nanto Sohei* (南都僧兵)*. The groups of *Sohei* demanded more swords to arm themselves. The high demand for swords from *Sohei* revitalized the *Yamato Den* (school) and increased the number of swordsmiths in the *Yamato* area. As a result, *Yamato Den* became active again. The *Yamato Den* style is somewhat similar to that of *Yamashiro Den*.

*Nanto Sohei (南都僧兵)----------------Since around the 11th century, Buddhist temples had become powerful under the protection from the *Joko* (retired emperors). Those temples had a large number of *Sohei* (low-level monks who also acted as soldiers). When power struggles started among the temples, *Sohei* fought as their soldiers on the battlefields. *Nanto Sohei* were such soldiers at *Kofuku-Ji Temple* (興福寺). Several large temples such as *Todai-Ji* (東大寺) Temple controlled the *Yamato* area.

Sugata (姿: Shape) ----------------- Not much difference in style at the early part of *Yamato Den* and *Yamashiro Den*. *Shinogi* is high. *Mune* is thin. Some types of *Yamato Den* have shallow *sori* (curvature).

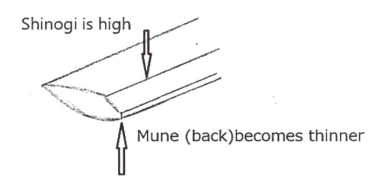

Hamon (刃文：Tempered line) ------------------Narrow tempered line. Mainly *Nie* (沸). *Chu-suguha-hotsure* (中直刃ほつれ: a medium straight line with a frayed pattern), *Ko-choji-midare* (小丁子: a mixture of small clove-like pattern and irregular wavy lines), *Ko-midare* (小乱: small irregular wavy lines), *Ko-gunome-komidare* (小五の目小乱: small continuous half-circles mixed with wavy lines).

The main characteristic of the *Yamato Den* style sword is *Masame* (straight grain). Their tempered line often shows *Nijyu-ha* (double straight lines), *Hakikake* (tracing of a broom mark), *Uchinoke* (a crescent-shape line), or combinations of them. See the illustration below.

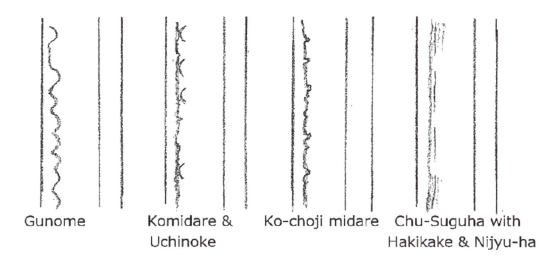

Gunome   Komidare &   Ko-choji midare   Chu-Suguha with
                 Uchinoke   Hakikake & Nijyu-ha

Boshi (鋩子: Tempered line at *Kissaki* area) ---------- On the *Boshi* area, a straight grain *Hamon* pattern appears. *Yakizume or Kaen*. (Refer Chapter *12 Middle Kamakura period: Tanto*). *O-maru, Ko-maru, Nie-kuzure*. (Refer Chapter 14 Late Kamakura Period Sword. See the illustration below.

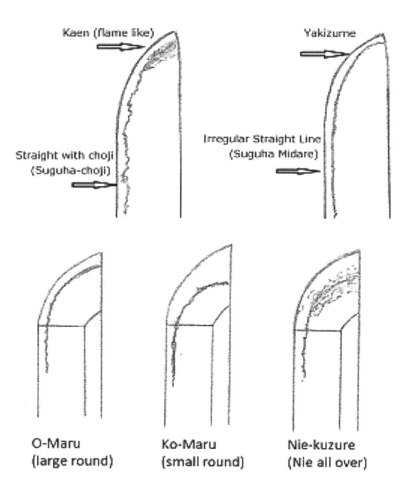

Ji-hada (地肌：Area between *Shinogi* and tempered line)------------Mostly *Masame-hada* (straight grain pattern 柾目肌). Fine *Ji-nie, Chikei,* or *Yubashiri*. (Refer to Chapter 14 Late Kamakura Period Sword (鎌倉末太刀). See below.

<u>**Nakago (Hilt)**</u>---------------------Often shows *Higaki Yasuri* (檜垣), the finishing file pattern, as shown below.

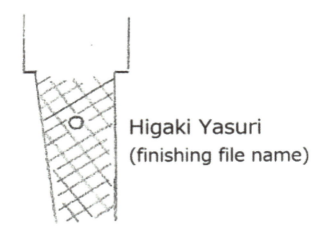

Names of the groups inside *Yamato Den*

Taima(当麻) Group---Taima Kuniyuki(当麻国行)
　　　　　　　　　　　　　　　　　　　　　　　　　　　　　　　　Taima Tomokiyo(当麻友清)
Shikkake (尻懸) Group-- Shikkake Norinaga (尻懸則長)
Tegai (手掻) group -- Tegai Kanenaga (手掻包永)
　　　　　　　　　　　　　　　　　　　　　　　　　　　　　　　　Tegai Kanekiyo(手掻包清)
Hoshou (保昌) group-- Hosho Sadamune (保昌貞宗)
　　　　　　　　　　　　　　　　　　　　　　　　　　　　　　　　Hosho Sadayoshi (保昌貞吉)

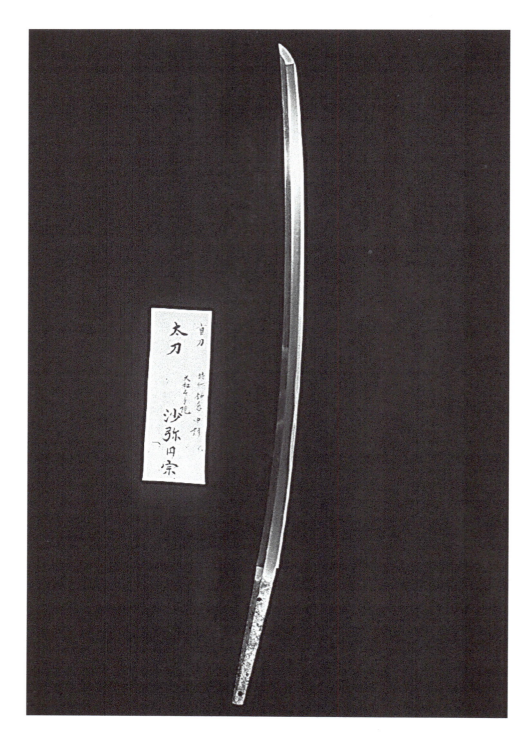

Yamato Senjuin Saya Enso (大和千手院沙弥円相宗) once my family sword

16 | Late Kamakura Period: Soshu Den Tanto (相州伝短刀)

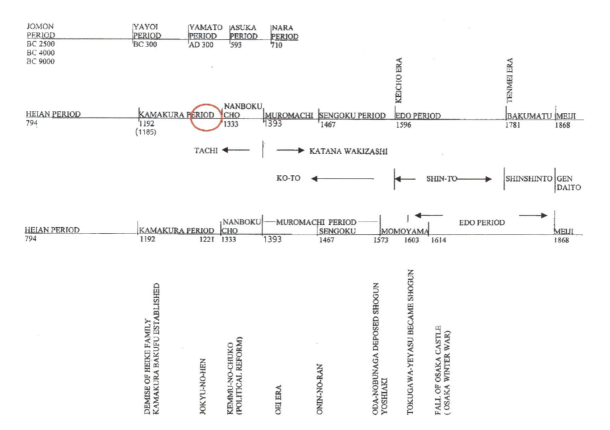

The circle above indicates the time we discuss in this section

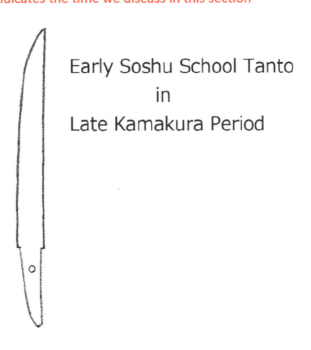

Early Soshu School Tanto
in
Late Kamakura Period

Sugata (姿: Style)---Three types of Tanto appeared (as below)

1. *Takenoko-zori* -------------- Approximately 10 inches long. However, during the middle *Kamakura* period, they were slightly longer than 10 inches. *Hirazukuri* shape. The width is a little wider than that in the mid-*Kamakura* period. Refer Chapter 12 Middle Kamakura Period Tanto (鎌倉中期短刀）.

2. *Chukan-zori*--------*Mune* side is straight, *Hirazukuri*, wide *Mihaba* (width). Slightly thick body. *Fukura Kareru* (see illustration below).

3. *Saki-zori* -----Bend outward at the top, *Hirazukuri, Fukura Kareru*.

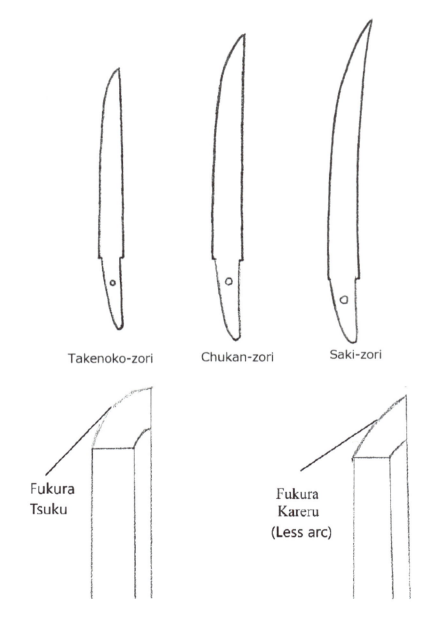

Takenoko-zori   Chukan-zori   Saki-zori

Fukura Tsuku

Fukura Kareru (Less arc)

Hi (樋: Grooves) and Horimono (彫り物: Engravings)-------------Often *Hi* (groove) shows on the *Mune* side. Sometimes *Ken* (dagger) and *Bonji* (Sanskrit) are curved inside the wide *Hi*. Refer to Chapter 12 Middle Kamakura Period: Tanto for *Hi*,

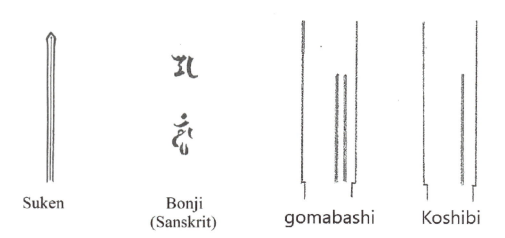

Suken　　　Bonji (Sanskrit)　　　gomabashi　　　Koshibi

Hamon (刃文: tempered line) ------------- *Hamon* is almost the same as the one on the Late *Kamakura* period swords. Refer to Chapter 14, Late Kamakura Period Sword. Some *Tanto* may have wide *Hamon* and others narrow. Often narrow *Hamon* appears at the lower part, then wider *Hamon* at the top. The work of *Hamon* around the *Fukura* area is the widest and most showy.

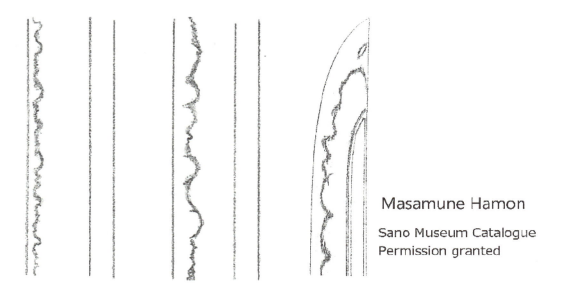

Masamune Hamon
Sano Museum Catalogue
Permission granted

Ji-hada (地肌: the area between Hamon and Shinogi) -------*Ji-hada* is excellent with a lot of *Ji-nie* (*Nie* work on *Ji-hada*). *Yubashiri* and *Chikei* (created by a cluster of Nie) shows.

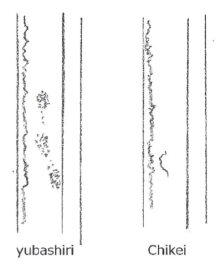

yubashiri Chikei

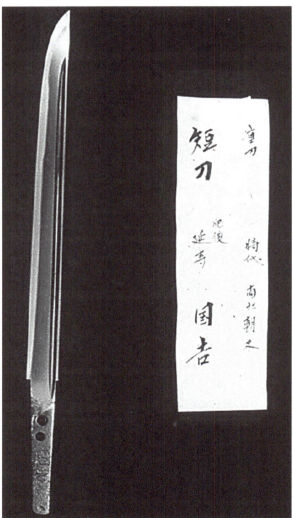

Enju Kuniyoshi Once my family sword

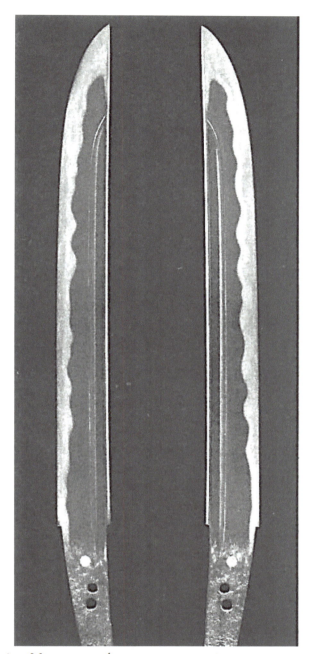

Komatsu Masamune (Sano Museum Catalog, permission granted)
*This *Tanto* shape is rare for Masamune.

Swordsmiths created the Soshu Den style in the late Kamakura Period

Soshu Den (school) -------------------Yukimitsu (行光), Masamune (正宗), Sadamune (貞宗)
Yamashiro Den (school)------------------------Rai Kunitsugu (来国次), Rai Kunimitsu (来国光)
Yamato Den (shool) --Taema Kuniyuki (当麻国行)
Chikuzen province---Chikuzen Samoji (筑前左文字)

17 | Nanboku-cho Period History 1333-1392 (南北朝歷史)
Northern and Southern Dynasty

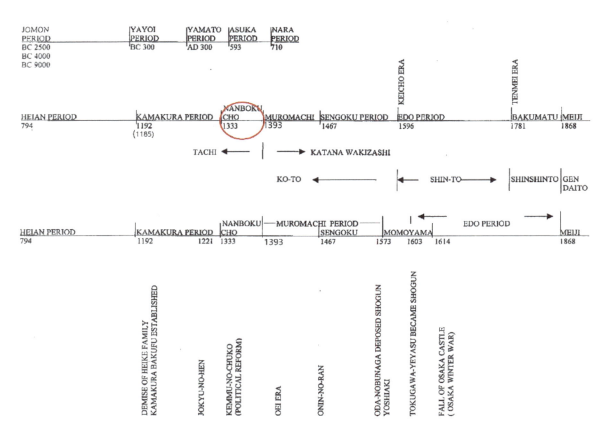

The circle above indicates the time we discuss in this section.

After *Jokyu-no-Ran* (Chapter 10 Jokyu-no-Ran), the power of the Imperial Court declined significantly. The successor, the *Hojo* clan with a dominant power during the *Kamakura* period, also began to have financial difficulty and started to lose control over the regional lords. One of the reasons was the cost incurred by the Mongol invasion. The *Kamakura Bakufu* (government) could not reward well to the *Samurai* who worked hard during the war. As a result, they were very dissatisfied with the *Bakufu*. Seeing this as a chance, Emperor *Go-Daigo* attempted to attack the *Kamakura Bakufu* two times but failed both times. He was exiled to *Oki* Island. Meantime, *Ashikaga Takauji* (足利尊氏) and several groups of anti-*Kamakura Samurai* gathered armed forces and succeeded in destroying the *Kamakura Bakufu* (1333). This war ends the *Kamakura* period.

Emperor *Go-daigo,* who had been exiled to *Oki* Island, returned to *Kyoto* and attempted political reforms. This reform was called *Kenmu-no-Chuko* (or *Kenmu-no-Shinsei,* 建武の中興). His reform, however, failed to satisfy most of the ruling class. Taking advantage of this situation, *Ashikaga Takauji* attacked the Imperial Court in *Kyoto,* deposed Emperor *Go-daigo,* and placed a member from the other branch of the Imperial family on the throne.

Emperor *Go-daigo*, however, insisted upon his legitimacy, moved to *Yoshino* in the South of *Kyoto*, and established another Imperial court. Thus began the Northern and the Southern Dynasties. With much strife between these rival courts and their problems within each court, more *Samurai* groups began moving to the Northern Dynasty. About 60 years later, the Southern Dynasty was compelled to accept the Northern Dynasty's proposal. Consequently, the Northern Dynasty became the legitimate imperial court. These 60 years are called *Nanboku-cho* or *Yoshino-cho* period.

During the *Nanboku-cho* period, *Samurai* demanded larger and showy yet practical swords. *Soshu Den* was the height of its prominence. However, the *Soshu* group was not the only group that made the *Soshu Den* style swords. Other schools and provinces of the different areas also made *Soshu Den* style swords.

<u>Late Kamakura Period Swordsmiths (Early Soshu-Den time)</u>

Tosaburo Yukimitsu (藤三郎行光)
Goro Nyudo Masamune (五郎入道正宗)
Hikoshiro Sadamune (彦四郎貞宗)

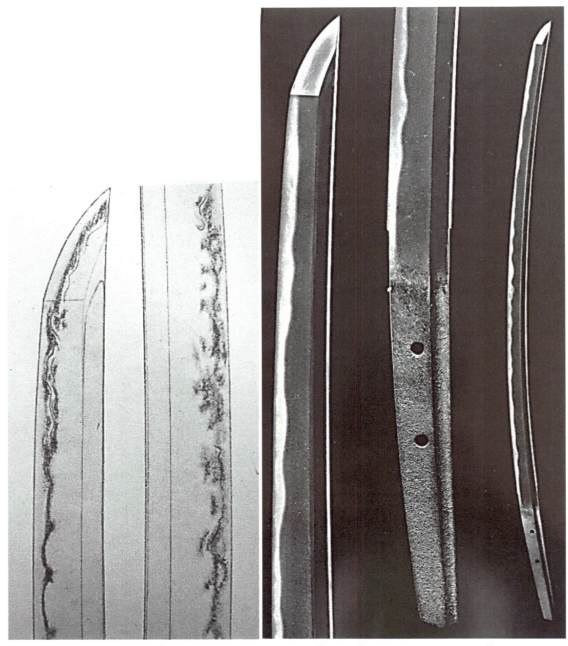

Masamune from Sano Museum Catalogue (permission granted)

Nanboku-cho Period Swordsmiths (Middle Soshu Den time)
Hiromitu (広光)
Akihiro (秋広)

Muromachi Period Swordsmiths (Late Soshu-Den time)
Hiromasa (広正)   Masahiro (正広)

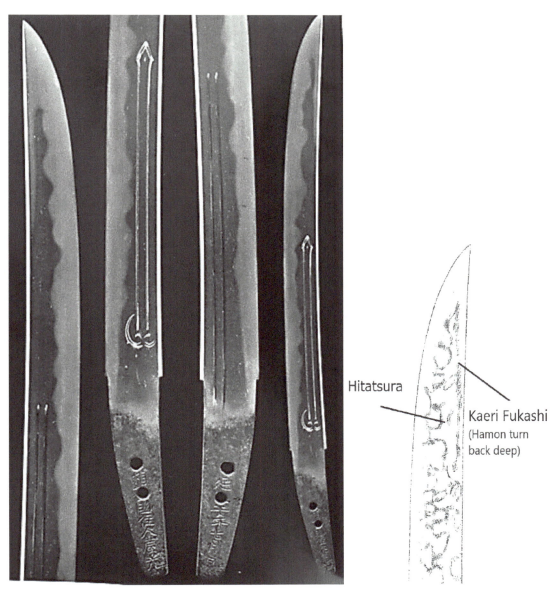

Hiromits (広光) from Sano Museum

18| Nanboku-cho Period Sword (南北朝太刀)

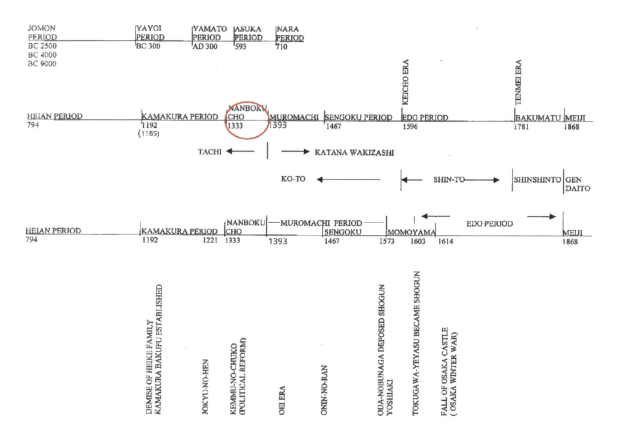

The circle above indicates the time we discuss in this section

During the *Nanboku-cho* period, *Samurai* demanded large, elaborate, and impressive, yet practical sword. The *Soshu Den* style sword in *Nanboku-cho* time was just that. This type was the most popular style then. The *Nanboku-cho* period was the height of the *Soshu Den*. Many swordsmiths moved from other provinces to the *Kamakura* area and forged the *Soshu Den* style swords. Other schools and provinces outside the *Kamakura* area also made the *Soshu Den* style swords in their own places.

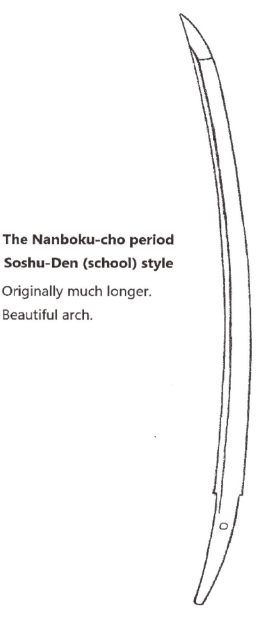

The Nanboku-cho period Soshu-Den (school) style

Originally much longer. Beautiful arch.

Sugata (姿: Shape)------------------The original length of a sword was 3, 4, or 5 feet long, but shortened to approximately two and a half feet long at a later time. A greatly shortened blade is called *O-suriage*.

The *Nanboku-cho* style sword has a shallow *Kyo-zori* (also called *Torii-zori*). Refer to Chapter 5 Heian Period Sword. The highest curvature comes around the middle of the body. A wide-body, high *Shinogi*, narrow *Shinogi-Ji* (Refer to Chapter 3, Names of parts). The thin *Kasane* (thickness of the body) is a distinctive feature for the *Nanboku-cho* style. High *Gyo-no-mune* or *Shin-no-mune*, sometimes *Maru-Mune* (round back).

Gyo-no-Mune   Shin-no-Mune   Maru-Mune

Hi (樋: groove) and Horimono (彫刻: engraving) -------- Often, a single *Hi* (*Bo-hi*), double *Hi*, *Suken* (dagger), *Bonji* (Sanscrit), and/or Dragon are engraved on *Shinogi-Ji* area. Refer to Chapter 3 Names of parts.

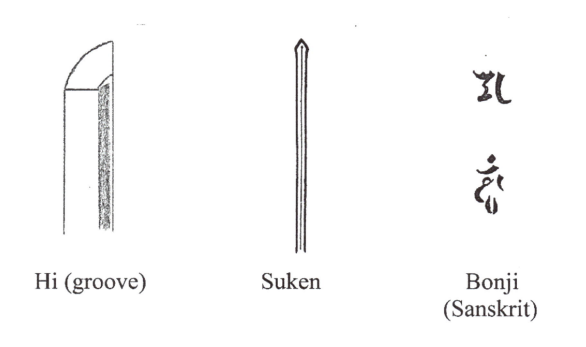

Hi (groove)   Suken   Bonji (Sanskrit)

Hamon (刃: Tempered line) ---- The lower part of the body shows a narrow-tempered line; gradually, the tempered line becomes wider and showy. Course *Nie*. *O-midare* (large irregular wavy *Hamon*), *Notare-midare* (wavy, irregular *Hamon*), *Gunome-midare* (a mix of repeated half-circular and irregular *Hamon*). *Inazuma*, *Kinsuji* (refer to Chapter 14 Late Kamakura Period Sword) sometimes appears.

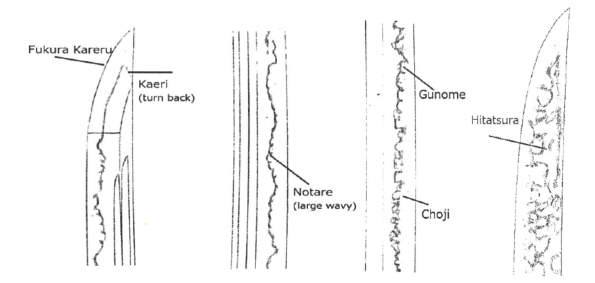

From Sano Museum Catalogue (Permission granted).

Ji-hada (地肌**:** Area between *Shinogi* and tempered line) ----------------------Wood-grain pattern (*Itame* 板目). Sometimes *Tobiyaki* (patchy tempered spots) appears on *Ji-hada*. For *Ji-hada,* refer to Chapter 3 Names of parts.

Kissaki (切っ先**) and Boshi (Tempered line at *Kissaki* area)** ---------- *O-kissaki* (long and large *Kissaki)*. *Fukura kareru* (less arc *Kissaki)*. *Midare-komi* (body and boshi have a similar tempered pattern), with *Kaeri-fukashi* (*hamon* deeply turns back), sometimes *Hitatsura* (entirely tempered). See the above illustration.

Soshu Den Sword-smiths during Nanboku-Cho Period

From Soshu--Hiromitsu (広光) Akihiro (秋広)
From Yamashiro --Hasebe Kunishige (長谷部国重)
From Bizen (called So-den Bizen)-------------Chogi (長儀)group Kanemitsu (兼光) group
From Chikuzen ---Samoji (左文字) group

Chogi (長義) From Sano Museum Catalog, Permission to use granted

The distinctive characteristics of the Nanboku-cho period sword on the photo above

- The trace of an engraving of *Suken* inside *Nakago* indicates that this area was once a part of the main body.
- Large and Long *kissaki*

19 | Nanboku-cho Period Tanto (南北朝短刀)

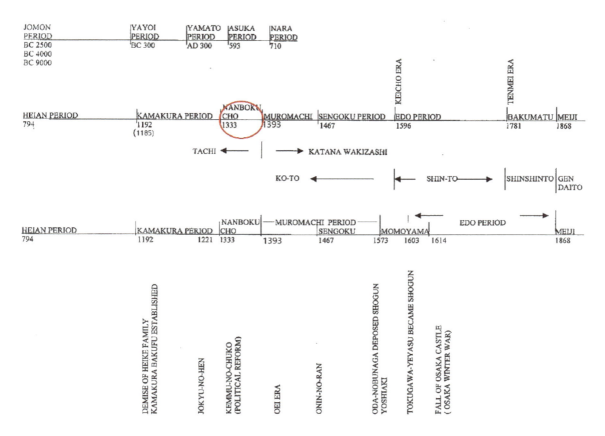

The circle above indicates the time we discuss in this section

During the *Nanboku-cho* period, a type of *Tanto* called *Hirazukuri Ko-wakizashi Sun-nobi Tanto* was made. *Hirazukuri* means a flat sword without the *Yokote* line and *Shinogi*. *Ko-wakizashi* means a shorter sword. *Sun-nobi Tanto* means longer than standard *Tanto*. This is also called *Enbun Jyoji Ko-wakizashi Tanto*. It is called this way because the majority of this type of *Tanto* were forged around the *Enbun* and the *Jyoji* imperial eras. In Japan, a new imperial period starts when a new emperor ascends to the throne. The *Enbun* era was from 1356 to 1361, and the *Jyoji* period was from 1362 to 1368.

Nanboku-Cho Period

Enbun jyoji Kowakizashi Tanto

Sugata (姿: shape) ---------------The length of a standard size *Tanto* is approx. one *Shaku*. *Shaku* is an old Japanese measurement unit for length, and one *Shaku* is very close to 1 foot.

8.5 *Sun* (the *Sun* is another old Japanese measurement unit for length) is approximately 10 inches. Ten inches is the standard size *Tanto* called *Josun Tanto*. Anything longer than *Josun Tanto* is called *Sun-nobi Tanto*. Anything shorter than *Josun* is called *Sun-zumari Tanto*.

Most of the *Nanboku-cho tantos* are longer than *Josun Tanto,* approximately 1 foot 2 inches long. Therefore, they are called *Hirazukuri Ko-wakizashi Sun-nobi Tanto*. *Saki-zori* (curved outward at the top. See the illustration above). Wide width and thin body. *Fukura Kareru* (no *Fukura* means less arc). *Shin-no-mune*. See the drawing below.

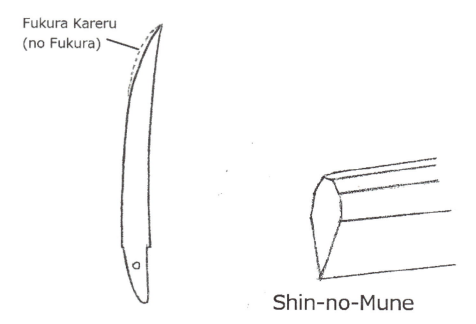

Hi, (樋: Grooves) and Horimono (彫り物: Engraving) ------- A groove or grooves on the *Mune* side. *Bonji* (Sanscrit, see Chapter 16 Late Kamakura Period (Early Soshu-Den Tanto), *Koshi-bi* (Short groove), *Tumetuki Ken*, *Tokko-tsuki Ken* (see below) appear. *Ken* (dagger) is curved widely and deeply in the upper part and shallower and narrower in the lower part. This is called *Soshu-bori* (*Soshu* style carving).

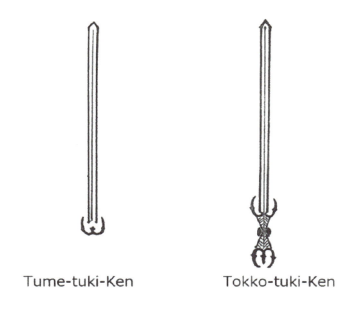

Hamon (刃: Tempered line) ------- The narrowly tempered at the lower part gradually becomes wider toward the top. Then a similar wide *Hamon* goes into the *Boshi* area. *Hamon* in the *Kissaki* area is *Kaeri-fukashi* (turn back deep). See the illustration below. Coarse *Nie*. *O-midare* (large irregular *Hamon* pattern).

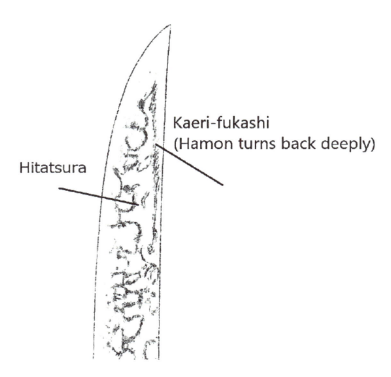

From Sano Museum Catalogue

Ji-hada (地肌: Area between *Shinogi-ji* and tempered line) ---------Loose wood grain pattern called *Itame*. *Yubashiri* (refer to Chapter 16 Late Kamakura Period), *Tobiyaki* (Irregular patchy tempered spot) appear. Crowded *Tobiyaki* is called *Hitatsura* (drawing above).

Nakago (茎: Tang) ---- Short *Tanago-bara*. *Tanago-bara* means the shape of the belly of a Japanese fish *Tanago* (bitterling).

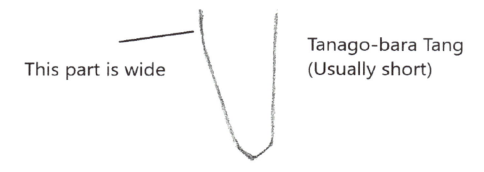

Tanto Sword-smiths during Nanboku-Cho Period

Soshu Den ---Hiromitsu (広光) Akihiro (秋広)
Yamashiro Den ---Hasebe Kunishige (長谷部国重)
Bizen Den --Kanemitsu (兼光) Chogi (長義)

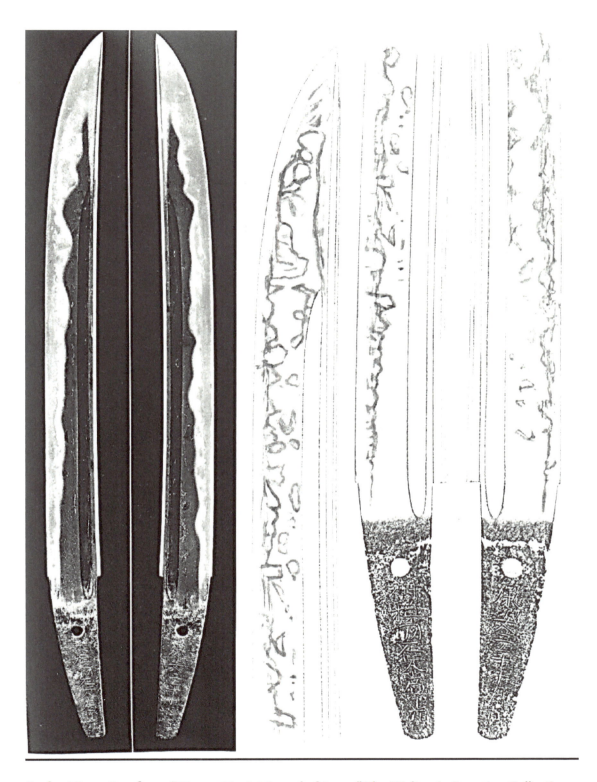

Soshu Hiromitsu from "Nippon-To Art Sword of Japan" The Walter A. Compton Collection

20|Muromachi Period History (室町時代歴史)

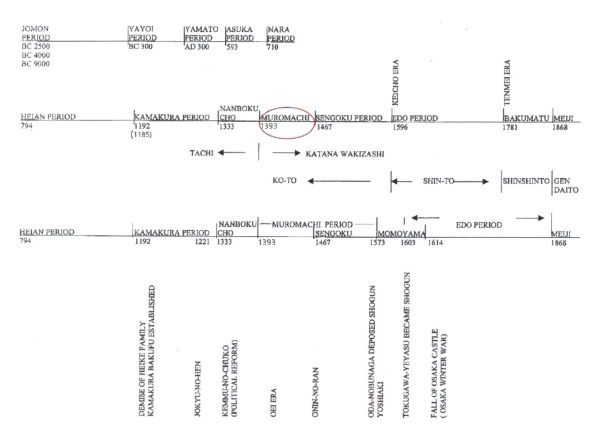

The circle above indicates the time we discuss in this section

The *Muromachi* period began after *Ashikaga Takauji* (足利尊氏) and several other prominent leaders ended the *Nanboku-cho* period. Discussed in 17|Nanboku-cho Period History (1333-1393).

The grandson of *Ashikaga Takauji*, *Ashikaga Yoshimitsu* (足利義満：often called *Shogun Yoshimitsu*), built a new beautiful palace at *Muromachi* (室町) area in *Kyoto*. The palace became the center of the government called the *Muromachi Bakufu* (室町幕府: *Muromachi* Government). This is the beginning of the *Muromachi* period. *Ashikaga Yoshimitsu* built the famous "*Kinkaku-ji Temple** (Golden Pavilion)" in *Kyoto* as his second house.

Kinkaku-ji Temple* (金閣寺: Golden Pavillion) ---------------*Ashikaga Yoshimitsu* (足利義満) built *Kinkaku-Ji Temple* in 1397. Later, it became *Rinzai-shu* (臨済宗) school Buddhist temple, but it was initially built as the second house for *Ashikaga Yoshimitsu* as well as a state guesthouse. Today, it is designated as a world heritage site. This temple was burnt down by an arsonist in 1950 but was rebuilt in 1955. The novelist *Mishima Yukio* wrote the novel "*Kinkaku-ji*" related to the Golden Pavillion and the arsonist. The famous quote in the book is, "The *Ho-oh* (A mythic golden bird, a Chinese version phoenix) on the roof of the *Kinkaku-ji Temple* is stationary, but it flies through the time eternally."

In the *Muromachi* period, the Emperor's power became weaker. The *Shogun* (将軍) held all the political power. Little by little, several groups of *samurai* who were officially appointed as *Shugo Daimyo* (守護大名: high-ranking officials) started to gain political and economic power by holding the critical positions in the *Muromachi Bakufu*. They also owned a large land. A couple of powerful *Shugo Daimyo* were *the Hosokawa* (細川) family and the *Yamana* (山名) family.

The *Ashikaga* family made a great effort to make the *Muromachi Bakufu* sound and powerful through politics. The beginning of the *Muromachi* period was peaceful and prosperous. Yet by the time *Ashikaga Yoshimasa* (足利義政) became the 8th *Shogun,* the *Muromachi Bakufu* was corrupted very severely. *Shogun Yoshimasa* did not pay much attention to his job, governing the country as a *shogun*. Instead, he was chasing women (his mother had to scold him for that), spent a large amount of money on building the Silver Pavilion called "*Ginkaku-ji Temple* (銀閣寺)," and retreated himself there. *Shogun Yoshimasa* did not have an heir. Therefore, his brother, *Yoshimi* (義視), was named to the next *Shogun*.

However, later, *Yoshimasa's* wife *Hino Tomiko* (日野富子)* had a son, *Yoshihisa* (義尚). Now, brother *Yoshimi* (義視) allied with a family of high-ranking official, the *Hosokawa's* (細川) while the son, *Yoshihisa,* allied with another powerful family, the *Yamana's* (山名), and several other smaller groups of *Samurai* allied with either side and the war broke out. This war is called *Onin-no-Ran* (応仁の乱) in 1467. It spread out all over the country and continued for 11years.

Hino Tomiko (日野富子)*----------------------------The wife of *Shogun Yoshimasa*. She took advantage of her political privileges to make a large amount of money by investing in the rice commodity market to control rice prices and sold with a high profit. Then she loans the money to the high-ranking officials at a high-interest rate. The corruption reached an uncontrollable level.

As a result of *Onin-no-Ran*, beautiful *Kyoto* was burnt down to ashes. The authority of the *Muromachi Bakufu* only reached the vicinity of the small surrounding area of *Kyoto*. *Onin-no-Ran* caused the next period called the *Sengoku* period (戦国時代), that is the Warring States period. During the *Sengoku* period, Japan was divided into 30 or so small independent countries and fought each other until *Oda Nobunaga, Toyotomi Hideyoshi, Tokugawa Iyeyasu* united them again.

Kinkaku-ji Temple (Golden Pavilion)   My family trip in 2019

21| Muromachi Period Sword (室町時代刀)

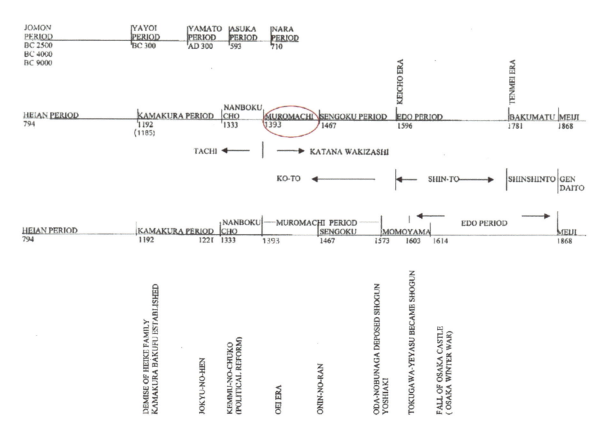

The circle above indicates the time we discuss in this section

The *Muromachi* period was a relatively peaceful and prosperous time until a little before "*Onin-no-Ran*," which happened at the end of the *Muromachi* Period. Refer to Chapter 20 Muromachi Period History (室町時代歴史). The *Nanboku-cho* style long sword became useless; thus, they were shortened. The shortened blade is called *Suriage*. In general, the *Muromachi* period was the declining time for sword making.

Tachi and Katana

Until the end of the *Nanboku-cho* period or the beginning of the *Muromachi* period, *Samurai* suspended swords from one's waist, the blade side down. When a sword was worn this way, the swordsmith inscribed his name to the side that faces outward, which means that the blade comes on your right when you see the inscription. In this case, the sword is called *Tachi*.

Yet, around the *Muromachi* period, a sword was worn between one's belt, with the blade side up. The swordsmiths inscribed his name to face outward when it was worn. Therefore, when you see the inscription, the cutting edge comes on your left. Then it is classified as *Katana*.

Around the beginning of the *Muromachi* period, *Samurai* started to wear a pair of swords called *Dai-sho* (大小), meaning large and small. The long one is *Katana,* and the short one is *Wakizashi*. In general, *Tachi* is longer than *Katana*. *Katana is longer than Wakizashi, and Wakizashi* is longer than *Tanto.* Here is the order of the length.

Tach > Katana > Wakizashi > Tanto

The difference between *Tachi* and *Katana* comes from the way it was worn, not the length.

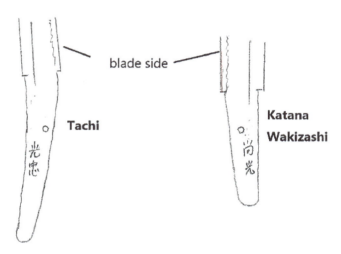

O-suriage (大磨上: Katana shortened by great length)

How much the sword should be shortened depends on the sword's original length and how much the owner wants it shortened. *O-suriage* is a kind of sword that is shortened by a great length. Once a blade is shortened that much, the inscription of the maker's name is cut off. When *Hon'ami* family (本阿弥家, a sword connoisseur family who have appraised Japanese swords for generations since the *Muromachi* period till today) appraised such a *Suriage* sword, they wrote the make of the sword and the swordsmith's name on the front side of the hilt, and the connoisseur's name with his *Kaou* (similar to signature) on the back. There are several ranks of writings. Which level it should be done is depending on the quality of the sword and how an owner wants it. Below are the classes (highest to lower).

Kin Zougan (金象嵌)--The name is inlaid in gold
Gin Zougan (銀象嵌)--The name is inlaid in silver
Kinpun Mei (金粉名)--The name is lacquered in gold powder
Shu-mei (朱明)--The name is written in vermilion

Sugata (姿: Shape) ------------------ The average length is usually 2 feet and 3 to 4 inches (68~71cm). The shape of the *Muromachi* period *Katana* is somewhat similar to the *Heian* period *Tachi* style. However, *Muromachi Katana* is not as grand or graceful as the *Heian* period sword. The curvature is usually the *Koshizori* shape. *Koshizori* means the highest curvature comes at the lower part of the blade. The length and shape are suitable for wearing between the body and the belt. The width and the thickness are well balanced with the size of the sword. Small *Kissaki*.

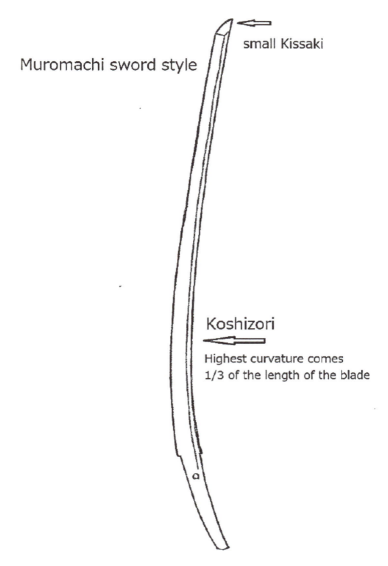

Hirazukuri-Wakizashi------------*Hirazukuri* means a flat surface with no *Shinogi* and Yokote line. Usually, one foot and 1 to 2 inches long. No curvature. *Hirazukuri-Wakizashi* appeared during the *Muromachi* time.

Hamon (刃文: tempered line) ---------------------- *Nioi* base. The tempered area is well balanced to the width of the blade. *Koshi-hiraita-midare* mixed with *Choji-midare*.

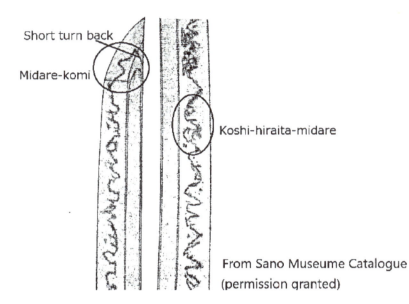

From Sano Museume Catalogue (permission granted)

Boshi (鋩子: Tempered line at *kissaki* area) --------------- *Midare-komi,* short turn back. See the illustration above. *Midare* is an irregular wavy pattern.

Ji-hada (地肌: Area between *Shinogi* and tempered line) -------------------Soft look, large wood grain pattern, *Ji-utsuri* (faint smoke or cloud-like effect) shows.

Horimono (彫物: Engravings) ------------ *Bo-hi* (single groove), *Soe-hi* (*Hi* accompanied with a thin groove), *Futasuji-hi* (double narrow groove), Sanskrit, *Tokko-tsuki ken*, *Tsume-tsuki Ken,* name of God, and dragon. Carvings became elaborate.

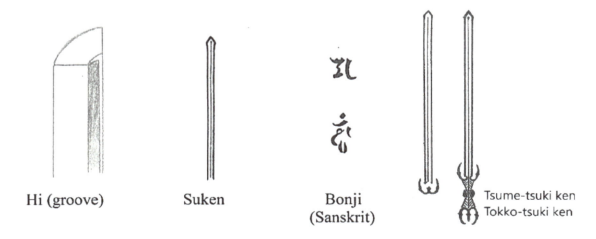

Hi (groove)   Suken   Bonji (Sanskrit)   Tsume-tsuki ken / Tokko-tsuki ken

Swordsmiths during the Muromachi Period

Bizen Den ---------------Osafune Morimitsu (長船盛光), Yasumitsu (康光), Moromitsu (師光)
Yamashiro Den--Yamashiro Nobukuni (山城信國)

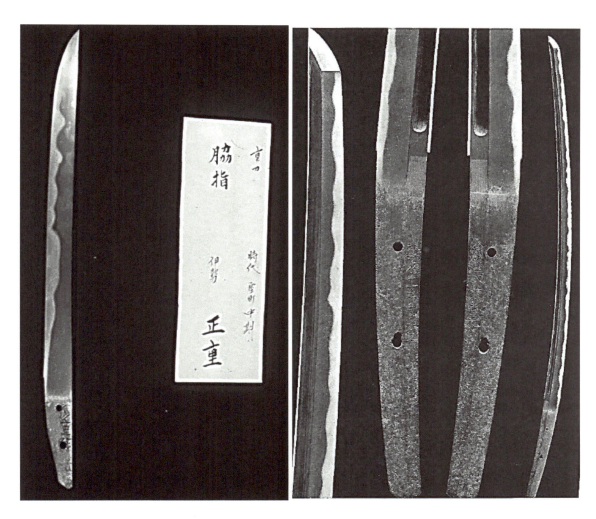

Ise Masashige (伊勢正重), classified as
Juyo Token(重要刀剣: Important Sword)
Once my family sword

Bozen Osafune Naomitsu (備前長船尚光)
Sano Museum Catalogue (permission granted)

22 | Sengoku Period History (戦国時代歴史)

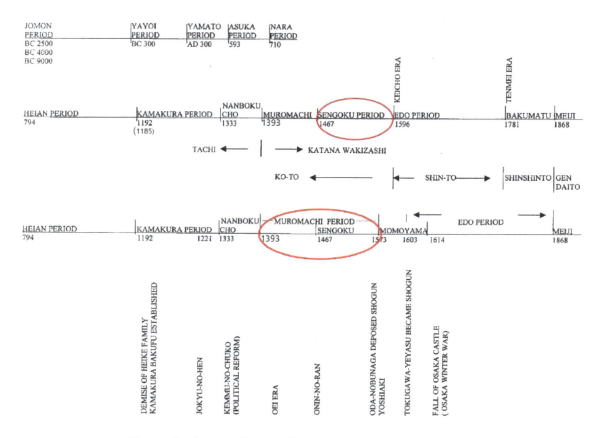

The circle above indicates the time we discuss in this section

The above timeline shows two circles. In political history, the *Sengoku* period (戦国時代) is a part of the *Muromachi* (室町) period, which is the lower circle. However, in the sword history, we separate the *Muromachi* period and the *Sengoku* period (Warring States period), the top circle. In sword history, we divide the time this way because, in those two periods, the sword style changed, and the environment of sword making also changed.

After the *Onin-no-Ran* (応仁の乱) had started (discussed in 20|Muromachi Period History), the beautiful capital city, *Kyoto* (京都) was in a devastating condition. The *Shogun's* (将軍) power reached only to the very limited small area. The rest of the country was divided into 30 or so small independent states. The heads of those independent states were called *Shugo Daimyo* (守護大名). They were initially government officials who had been appointed and sent there by the central government.

Also, powerful local *Samurai* often became the head of those states. They fought against each other to take over the other's land. During the *Sengoku* period, vassals would kill his master and stole his domain, or farmers would revolt against their lords. A state like this is called "*Gekoku-jo* (lower class *Samurai* overthrow the superior)."

This is the time of the Warring States called the *Sengoku* period. The head of a state was called *Sengoku Daimyo* (戦国大名: War-lord). The *Sengoku* period lasts about 100 years. Little by little, powerful states defeated less powerful ones after long hard battles and gained more territory. Thirty or so small countries became 20, then ten and so on. Eventually, a few dominant *Sengoku Daimyo* (War-lord) were left. Each *Daimyo* of those states tried to fight his way up to *Kyoto* and tried to be the country's top. The first one who almost succeeded was *Oda Nobunaga* (織田信長). However, he was killed by his own vassal, *Akechi Mitsuhide* (明智光秀), and soon *Akechi* was killed by his colleague, *Toyotomi Hideyoshi* (豊臣秀吉).

After *Toyotomi Hideyoshi* defeated *Akechi Mitsuhide* and his troop and a few more significant war-lords, he almost completed uniting Japan. Yet, *Hideyoshi* had one more rival to deal with to complete his job. That was *Tokugawa Iyeyasu* (徳川家康). Now, *Toyotomi Hideyoshi* and *Tokugawa Ieyasu* were the last contenders for the top position. Both knew that their opponents were smart and able. Any wrong move on either part would be a fatal mistake. So, they decided to keep an amicable co-existing relationship on the surface for a while. Though *Toyotomi Hideyoshi* tried to make *Tokugawa Ieyasu* his vassal, *Tokugawa Ieyasu* somehow maneuvered to avoid that. In the mind of *Tokugawa Iyeyasu*, since he was younger than *Toyotomi Hideyoshi*, he knew that he could just wait until *Hideyoshi*'s natural death. And that happened eventually.

After *Hideyoshi's* death, *Tokugawa Ieyasu* fought *Hideyoshi's* vassals and won at the *Battle of Sekigahara* (関ヶ原の戦い) in 1600. Then, in 1615, at the battle of the *Osaka Natsu-no-Jin* (*Osaka Summer Campaign*: 大阪夏の陣), *Tokugawa* won against *Hideyoshi's* son, Hideyori's army. After this, the *Toyotomi* clan ceased to exist entirely, then the *Edo* (江戸) period started. The time is called the *Edo* period because *Tokugawa Ieyasu* lived in *Edo*, current Tokyo (東京).

*The *Sengoku* period is often depicted in TV dramas and movies. People who lived through the *Sengoku* period had a very hard time, but it is the most exciting time for making TV shows and movies. The life of *Oda Nobunaga, Toyotomi Hideyoshi* and, *Tokugawa Ieyasu* are the most favorite story in Japan. Especially the story of *Toyotomi Hideyoshi* is one of the most popular ones. His background was a poor farmer, but he eventually became the top ruler of Japan. That is one fascinating success story.

Portrait of *Toyotomi Hideyoshi* (豊臣秀吉) by *Kano Mitsunobu*, owned by *Kodai-Ji* Temple. From Wikimedia Commons, the free media repository

23 | Sengoku Period Sword (戦国時代刀)

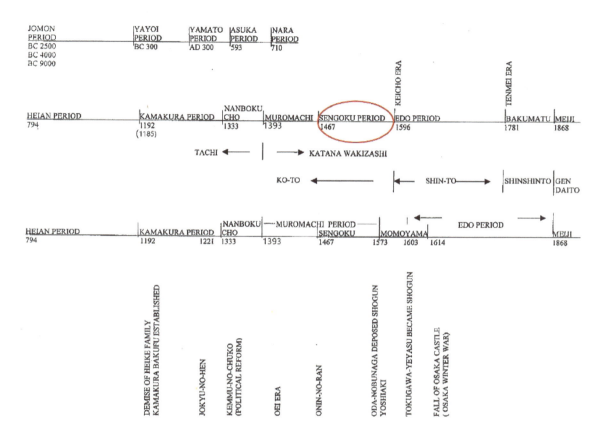

The circle above indicates the time we discuss in this section

After the *Onin-no-Ran*, *Kyoto* was in a devastating condition. Distinguished swordsmiths in the *Kyoto* area were almost all gone. *Sengoku Daimyo* (war-lord or feudal lord) needed a large number of swords from nearby. *Mino* and *Bizen* areas were the active sword-making places during the *Sengoku* time. It was because the *Mino* province was located in a convenient location from many feudal lords. Also, the *Shizu* group from *Yamato Den* (school) moved to *Mino* province. *Tegai Kaneyoshi* from *Yamato Den* moved to *Mino,* and many swordsmiths from *Yamashiro* and *Yamato* areas moved to *Mino*. Thus, *Mino* could supply the high demand for a large number of swords. During this wartime, *Samurai* demanded a very practical sword that wouldn't bend or break but cut well. Together with swordsmiths in the *Mino* area, *Bizen Osafune* swordsmiths fulfilled the high demand also.

Kazu-Uchi-Mono and Chumon-Uchi

Kazu-uchi-mono was a sword made just good enough for one battle. They were not made for permanent preservation.

Chumon-uchi was a custom-made sword. Good shape, good forging, often engraved the swordsmith's name and the name of a person who ordered it.

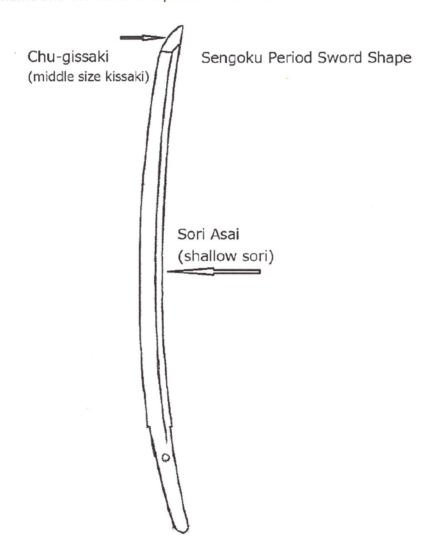

Characteristics of Mino-Den Swords

Sugata (姿：shape) -------------- Shallow curvature, low *Gyo-no-mune*, *Chu-kissaki* with *Fukura*. The width and the thickness are not too wide, not too thick. Engraving is rare with the *Mino Den* swords. On the *Bizen Den* swords, the bottom of the *Bo-hi* (single groove) shows a round end (see the last photo below) just above the *Machi* area (*for Machi,* see the diagram in 3 Names of parts).

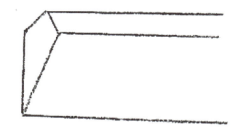

Gyo-no-Mune
(行の棟)

Hamon (刃文: Tempered line)

Mino Den --------Mostly *Nioi*. *Sanbon-sugi* (pointed *Gunome*), *O-notare*, *Yahazu-midare*, *Hako-midare* (box shape), *Chu-suguha* with *Katai-ha*. See the drawings below. Also, *Mino Koshi-ba* appeared. *Mino Koshi-ba*: approx. 1-inch *Sugu-ha* at the bottom, followed by irregular *Hamon*, then *Chu-suguha* at the top.

Mino-Den Hamon

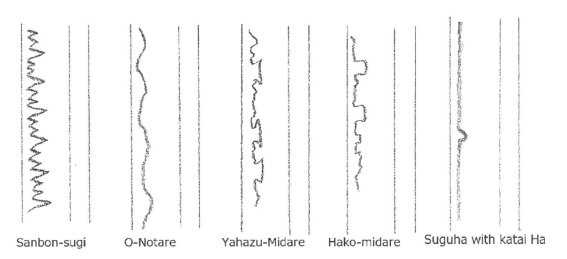

Sanbon-sugi   O-Notare   Yahazu-Midare   Hako-midare   Suguha with katai Ha

Bizen-Den ----------Mostly *Nioi*. Wide tempered line. *Koshi-hiraita-midare*. See the drawings below.

Bizen-Den Hamon

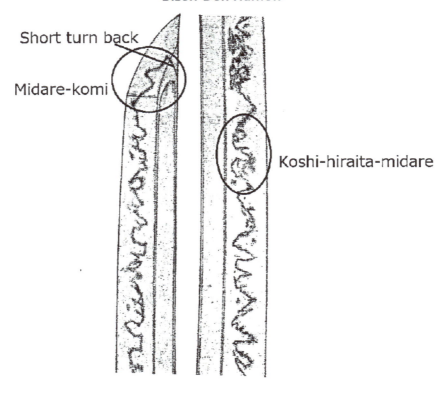

Sano Museum Catalogue

Boshi (鋩子: Tempered line at *kissaki* area) --------------------Turn back deep. *Jizo-boshi* (side view of a monk's head), *Ko-maru* (small round), *Kaeri-yoru* (lean)

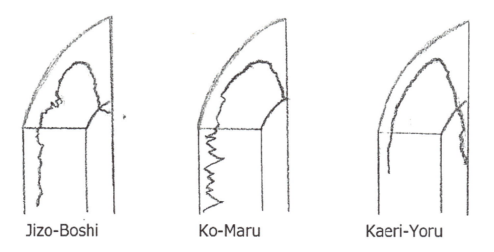

Ji-hada (地肌: Area between *shinogi* and tempered area) ------------*Mokume* (wood burl) mixed with *Masame* (straight grain). Often shows *Masame* in the *Shinogi* area. Sometimes, *Mokume* stands out.

Swordsmiths during Sengoku Period

Mino-Den -- Magoroku Kanemoto (孫六兼元)
- Izuminokami Kanesada (和泉守兼定)
Bizen-Den --Yosouzaemon Sukesada (興三左衛門祐定)
Norimitu (則光) Tadamitsu (忠光)

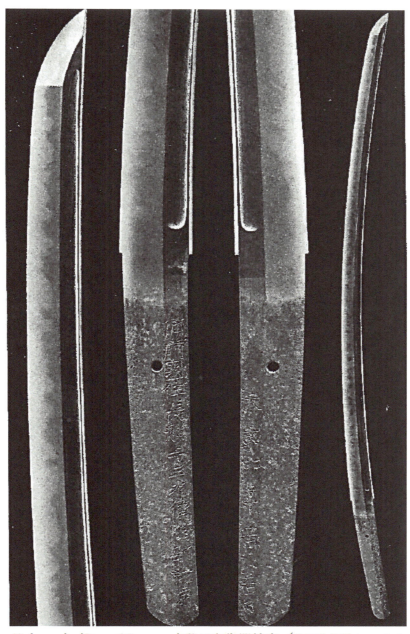

Yosozaemon Kukesada (Sano Museum) 興三左衛門祐定 （佐野美術館 Permission granted）

24 | Sengoku Period Tanto (戦国時代短刀)

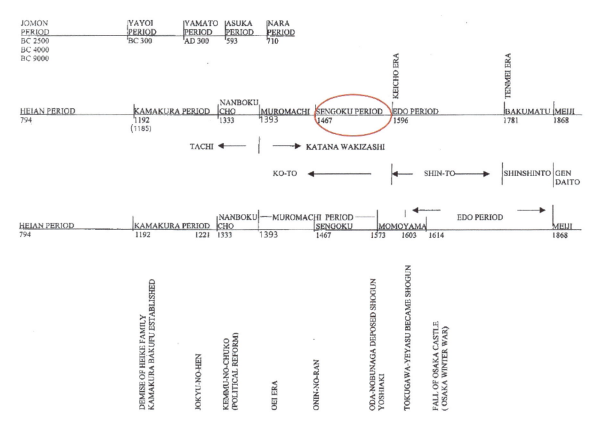

The circle above indicates the time we discuss in this section

Chukan-zori

Chukan-zori (中間反り) ---------------- *Chukan-zori Tanto* has a straight *Mune*(back). Its back does not curve either inward or outward.

Hamon (刃文: Tempered line) --------------------------*Sanbon-sugi* (三本杉), O-*notare* (大湾), *Yahazu-midare* (矢筈乱), *Hako-midare* (箱乱), *Gunome-choji* (互の目丁子), Chu-*suguha* (中直刃). See below.

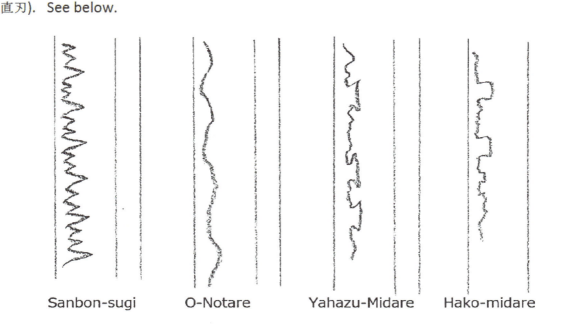

Horimono (彫物: Engraving) --------------------- Often *Hi* (groove) is curved.

Tanto Length ------------------------- Standard *Tanto* length should be no longer than one *Shaku*[*1] (approx. 12 inches, 30.5cm). The standard size *Tanto* is called *Jo-sun Tanto,* which is 8.5 *Shaku* (approx. 10 inches, 25.7cm). Longer than *Jo-sun* is called *Sun-nobi Tanto* (寸延). Shorter than *Jo-sun* is called *Sun-zumari Tanto* (寸詰).

Sun-nobi Tanto > *Jo-sun Tanto* (approx. 10 inches) > *Sun-zumari Tanto*

[*1] *Shaku* is a Japanese old measurement unit for length.

Takenoko-zori Jo-sun Tanto (筍反定寸短刀) --------------- *Takenoko-zori Jo-sun Tanto* was made during the *Sengoku* period. It resembles the swords made by *Rai Kunimitsu* of *Yamashiro Den*. (Illustration below)

Hamon (刃文: Tempered line) --------------- *Hoso-suguha* (細直刃: Narrow straight *Hamon*). *Katai-ha* (illustration below) shows somewhere on the blade. *Masame-hada* (Straight grain pattern) may appear on the *Mune* side.

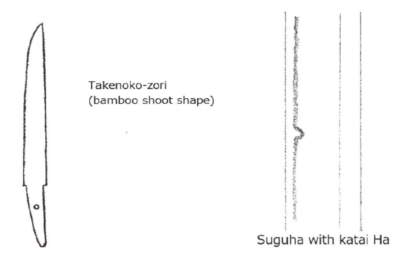

Takenoko-zori (bamboo shoot shape)

Suguha with katai Ha

Ji-hada (地肌: Area between *shinogi* and tempered line) ---------------- Some *Shirake* (白け: a whitish surface) sometimes appears. Some *Utsuri* (a light, whitish, cloud-like effect) on *Ji-hada* appears.

Sun-nobi Tanto (寸延短刀)----------------This type of *Tanto* is similar to the *Sakizori Tanto* of the late *Soshu Den* time. You may see *Hitatsura* type *Hamon*. (Illustration below). Unlike the *Soshu Den* style, the *Hitatsura* shows more on the lower part and less on the upper part of the *Tanto*.

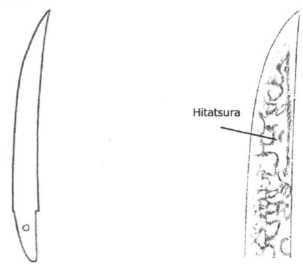

Hitatsura

Hirazukuri Takenokozori Sunzumari Tanto (平造筍反寸詰短刀)

This is a unique *Tanto* in the *Sengoku* period. *Hirazukuri* means a flat surface sword without *Shinogi, Yokote* line, or obvious *Kissaki*. *Takenoko-zori* means bamboo shoot shape (back of the sword curves inward). *Sun-zumari* means shorter than 10 inches long (shorter than 8.5 *Shaku,* or 25.7 cm). The lower part of the blade is wide and thick, and the tip is narrow and thin. It has a piercing sharp look.

- **Horimono** (彫物: **Engraving**) ------------- Deeply carved *Ken-maki Ryu* (a dragon wrapped around a spear).
- *Hamon* (刃文: **Tempered line**) --------- Wide tempered line, *Nioi* base. Irregular *Hamon*, wide *Suguha* (straight), and *Chu-suguha* (medium straight). The *Hamon* in the *Boshi* area turns back long.
- **Ji-hada** (地肌)----------- fine and wood burl pattern.

Moroha-tanto (諸刃短刀: Double-edged sword)

Double-edged sword with a *Hamon* on both cutting edges. Often *Bonji* (Sanscrit) is curved.

- **Hamon** (刃文: **Tempered line**) ---------- Wide tempered line. *Nioi* base. Irregular *Hamon*, wide *Suguha* (straight tempered line), and *Chu-suguha* (medium straight tempered line). *Hamon* turns back deeply.
- **Ji-hada** (地肌 : **Area between *shinogi* and tempered line**)------- Fine and wood burl pattern.

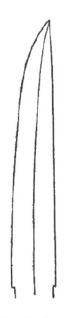

Moroha Tanto

The Swordsmith for Tanto during the Sengoku Period

The *Bizen* swords during the *Sengoku* period are called *Sue-bizen*. *Sue* is pronounced "su" and "e" as egg. *Bizen Osafune Yoso Zaemon Sukesada* (与三左衛門祐定) is the most regarded swordsmith during the *Sengoku* period. He also forged *Tantos*. One thing to point out is that there were many swordsmiths called *Sukesada*. *Yoso-Zaemon Sukesada* is the one who represents the era.

25 | Edo Period History 1603 - 1867 (江戸時代歴史)

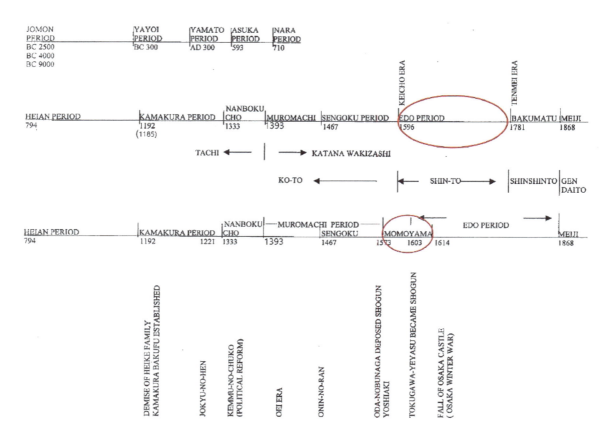

The circle above indicates the time we discuss in this section

Between the *Sengoku* period (戦国時代) and the *Edo* period (江戸時代) on political history, there was the time called the *Azuchi Momoyama* period (安土桃山). It was from around 1573 to 1614, as shown in the third (bottom) timeline above. This was the time when *Oda Nobunaga* (織田信長), *Toyotomi Hideyoshi* (豊臣秀吉) and *Tokugawa Ieyasu* (徳川家康) played central roles in politics.

After *Tokugawa Ieyasu* (徳川家康) won the *battle of Sekigahara* (関ヶ原の戦い) in 1600 and defeated *Toyotomi's* vassals (*Toyotomi Hideyoshi* had already been deceased by then), *Tokugawa Iyeyasu* became the *Shogun* (将軍) in 1603. This is the beginning of the *Edo Period* (江戸). In sword history, as you see in the middle timeline above, the *Edo* period comes right after the *Sengoku* period.

At the end of the *Sengoku* period and during the *Azuchi Momoyama* period, the economy grew a lot, and new culture flourished. The gorgeous and spectacular art, such as paintings, architecture, interior designs, and handicrafts, were created. The tea ceremony was developed by *Sen No Rikyu* (千の利休), and *Kabuki* also began to be performed around this time. It was somewhat similar to the European Renaissance. Strangely, this new art emergence happened at the same time in Japan and Europe.

Around this time, many Europeans came to Japan. That was the time of the exploration to the East by Europeans. They were from England, Spain, Holland, and Portugal. The novel "*Shogun*" by James Clavell was based on the real people's stories, William Adams and Jan Joosten Van Londersteyn[1] at the time. You can see Jan Joosten's statue in *Tokyo* Station today. On my yearly visit to Japan, I stay at a hotel near *Tokyo* Station. I often pass in front of "*Yan Yoosten's*" statue. It is located inside the *Tokyo* Station, underground in the middle of the bustling shopping area. It can be very easily missed unless you look for it. There is another statue of him outside the Station.

Shogun Tokugawa Iyeyasu hired William Adams and Jan Joosten (Japanese call him Jan Joosten, not his full name) as his advisers, and he acquired information on Europe from them. *Shogun Tokugawa Iyeyasu* treated them well. The area where Jan Joosten lived is now called *Yaesu* (八重洲) after his name, Jan Joosten. William Adams changed his name to *Miura Anjin* and lived in the *Miura* area. This place is approximately one hour and a half south by train from Tokyo today. The records of these two people are well kept and can be found easily.

Europeans brought many European goods and ideas. Although Christianity became popular and widely spread in the early *Azuchi Momoyama* period, *Toyotomi Hideyoshi* banned it later. After the *Meiji* Era (1868), a religious restriction was lifted.

The *Edo* period began when *Tokugawa Iyeyasu* became the *Shogun* (1603). It lasted until the *Meiji* (明治) *Restoration* in 1868. *Tokugawa Bakufu* (*Tokugawa* government) was the only entity that governed the country during the *Edo* period. The emperors existed, but the political power was shifted to the *Tokugawa Bakufu*.

Gradually, ports for the European ships were limited. Eventually, Spaniards were not allowed to come to Japan, then Portuguese. Japanese were forbidden to travel abroad. By around 1640, a port town called *Dejima* in *Hirato* in *Nagasaki* prefecture was the only place in Japan that opened for foreigners to do some business with Japanese. From Europe, only the Dutch were allowed to come. Japan closed the country to the outside world until the *Meiji Restoration* (1868).

During the *Azuchi Momoyama* period and the early part of the *Edo* period, many European ships visited Japan. Strangely, many of them shipwrecked near the shores around Japan. One of the reasons is that Japan is a volcanic island. Even if the sea's surface does not show anything sticking up from the water, there are many obstacles underneath, such as underwater mountains and massive hidden reefs. The Europeans did not have the waterway information that was common to the Japanese seamen.

Additional stories to share just for a fun

Another reason why many ships were wrecked was that those ships were looking for gold. When Marco Polo traveled to China, he heard from Chinese people that there was a small island country further to the east. The land was wealthy, and the emperors' palace was made of gold and silver. After Marco Polo went back to Italy, he wrote a book (in late 1300) about his journey and published it. In his book, he mentioned what he heard in China about the island country, Japan, even though he had never visited Japan himself. The book was widely read in many countries in Europe. When traveling to the East became possible for Europeans, they came to Japan to find gold.

Yes, Japan produced a large amount of gold. But for the Europeans, it was too late. By then, most of the gold was mined by the Fujiwara family in the *Oh-shu* area (奥州 Northern part of Japan). The area includes today's *Aomori*, *Akita*, *Fukushima*, and *Miyagi* prefectures, where the big *Tsunami* hit in 2011. *Toyotomi Hideyoshi* also owned many gold mines but already mined as much as possible with the skills they had then. Japan used to have many gold and silver mines all over the country. Those mines were already exhausted, and only a few were left for mining today.

Throughout history, there have been facts and rumors about "*Maizo-kin*: 埋蔵金." *Maizo-kin* is the gold buried or hidden by the people like *Tokugawa Shogun, Toyotomi Hideyoshi,* and wealthy *Daimyo* and merchants. Without having today's banks' vault, burying in secret places was the only way to store gold then. Several *Maizo-kins* have been found, including one in the middle of *Tokyo, Ginza*. There are still several big ones that haven't been found yet. Those are said to be *Hideyoshi Maizo-kin, Tokugawa Bakufu Maizo-kin,* and a few more big ones. Although several maps indicated the locations of the *Maizo-kin*, those maps were fake, of course. Today, whenever the ground is dug to build a large building structure, people start talking about a possible discovery of a big *Maizo-kin*.

Gold flowed out to outside Japan little by little over the centuries until the *Meiji Restoration* time. Because the exchange rate between gold and silver was much cheaper in Japan compared to the rest of the world. Today, we still mine gold on a small scale.

It is said that the name of the country, Japan, comes from Marco Polo's book. He called Japan "*Chipangu,*" which means "gold country" in his book. *² "From "*Chipangu*" to "*Zipang*" to "*Jipang,*" it eventually evolved to "Japan." Japanese don't call the country Japan but "*Nihon*" or "*Nippon*" (日本).

*¹ヤン ヨーステン 【Jan Joosten van Lodenstijn 】 https://www.weblio.jp
　　　　　　Or Jan Joosten van Londensteyn

*² Wikipedia "Names of Japan" or Check (Click) right to go to the link Jipangu

Cipangu described in the 1492 Martin Beham globe
From Wikimedia Commons, the free media repository (Names of Japan)

26 | Overview of Shin-to: Ko-to and Shin-to Difference (新刀概要)

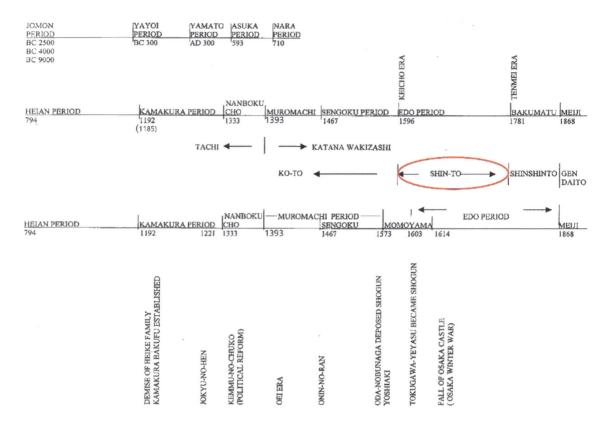

The circle above indicates the subject we discuss in this section

The previous chapter 25 stated that the *Edo* period was from 1603 to 1868. This is for political history. As seen in the third timeline above, the *Momoyama* period overlaps the *Edo* period. Some people think the *Momoyama* period was from 1573 to 1600. In terms of general history, there are several opinions on how to divide these transitional periods. For sword history, it is clear-cut. The swords made between approximate 1596 (慶長: *Keicho* era) and 1781 (天明: *Tenmei era*) are called S*hin-to*. The swords made between the *Tenmei* era and the *Meiji* are called *Shin Shin-to*.

After *Toyotomi Hideyoshi* almost completed to unite the country, people could enjoy a peaceful time. This quiet time changed the geographic distribution of swordsmiths where they lived. There were three major areas where the sword forging took place. Those were *Kyoto, Osaka,* and *Edo* (*Tokyo* today) areas. The rest of the swordsmiths gathered around near major *Daimyo's* (大名: feudal lord) castles.

Kyoto---- *Umetada Myoju* (梅忠明寿) group thrived, followed by the swordsmiths like *Horikawa Kunihiro* (堀川国広)*, Kunimichi* (国路)*, Kunisada* (国貞)*,* and *Kunisuke* (国助).

Osaka--------- *Osaka* was established as a commercial city and became the center of commerce. They produced swords and distributed them to the other regions in the country. The well-known Swordsmiths in *Osaka*: *Tsuda Sukehiro* (津田助広)*, Inoue Shinkai* (井上真改).

Edo-------------Many swordsmiths gathered in *Edo* (江戸: current Tokyo) where *Shogun Tokugawa Iyeyasu* lived. The well-known swordsmiths in *Edo*: *Nagasone Kotetsu* (長曽祢虎徹)*, Yasutsugu* (康継)*, Noda Hannkei* (野田繁慶).

By the time the grandson of *Tokugawa Iyeyasu*, *Tokugawa Iyemitsu,* became the *shogun* (寛永：*Kan'ei* era 1624 – 1643), swordsmiths spread out to other provinces than three areas mentioned above. In each significant *Daimyo* territory, swordsmiths had their shops near the castle and fulfilled the demand for *Daimyo* and subjects. By the *Genroku* era (元禄: 1695), the swords-making declined, and people demanded more picturesque *Hamon* designs*,* such as *Kikusui* (菊水: flower design) and *Fujimi* (富士見: *Mount Fuji*).

Fujimi   Kikusui

Difference between *Ko-to* and *Shin-to*

The next section describes the difference between *Ko-to* and *Shin-to*. But keep in mind, there are always exceptions to these rules.

1. The length of the *Shin-to Katana* is usually about 2 feet and 3 inches ± a little. *Wakizashi* is about 1 foot and 6 inches. Shallow curvature. Wide width. Thick body. *Gyo-no-mune*. *Chu-gissaki* with a slightly stretched look.

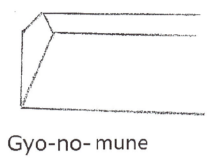

Gyo-no-mune

(行の棟)

2. *Ko-to* sword feels light. *Shin-to* feels heavy.

3. The bottom of *Hi* is rounded at above *Machi*. *Shin-to's Bo-hi ends* a little below the *Yokote* line

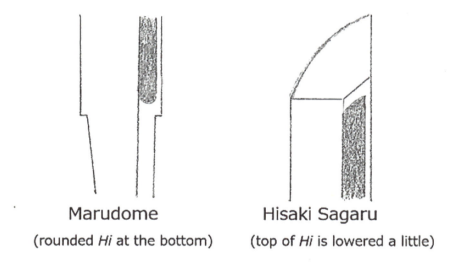

Marudome (rounded *Hi* at the bottom)   Hisaki Sagaru (top of *Hi* is lowered a little)

4. In general, for *Shin-to*, carvings are less common. Except, some swordsmiths are famous for their carvings. The design is refined and in detail. *Umetada Myoju* (埋忠明寿) is famous for his carvings.

5. For *Shin-to,* if it is mainly *Nie,* it is usually coarse *Nie*

6. Around the *Machi* area, *Hamon* starts with a straight tempered line (the bottom part of the blade in the illustration below), then *Midare,* or different types of *Hamon* comes in the middle, and it finishes with *Suguha* (straight *hamon*) in the *Boshi* area (the top

part). In general, this is the standard *Hamon* style of *Shin-to*, but there are always exceptions.

7. For *Shin-to,* the blade had the same kind of iron throughout Japan. Not many variations of iron were used throughout Japan. Very hard, dark color, and glossy look.

8. The *Nakago* is in a properly balanced shape. The bottom of the *Nakago* narrows down gradually. The type of *Yasuri-me* (file mark) is often a *Kesho-yasuri.* Engraved inscriptions show the swordsmith's name, the location, and the province, with the year it was made.

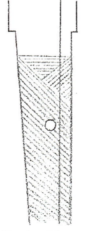

Kesho Yasuri

27 | Shinto Sword -- Main Seven Regions (Part A: 主要 7 刀匠地)

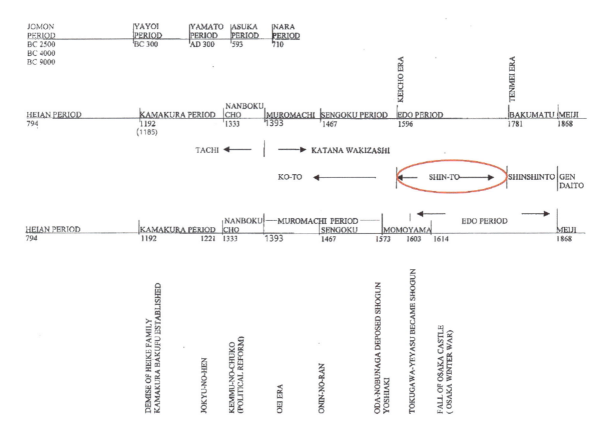

The circle indicates the subject we discuss in this section

In *Shin-to* time, there were seven main prosperous areas where many swordsmiths gathered and actively made swords. Those are *Yamashiro* (山城) in *Kyoto*, *Settsu* (摂津) in *Osaka*, *Musashi* (武蔵) in *Edo*, *Hizen* (肥前) in *Saga*, *Satsuma* (薩摩) in *Kagoshima*, *Echizen* (越前) in *Fukui*, and *Kaga* (加賀) in *Kanazawa*. Swordsmiths of each area shared their own common regional characteristics of these places. Knowing each of these characteristics is the easiest way to understand *Shin-to*. But keep it in mind that each swordsmith in one group also has his own unique way of sword making. The followings are only the general descriptions of these characteristics.

Below is a map of Japan. *Hokkaido* is omitted from the map because swords were not made there at that time.

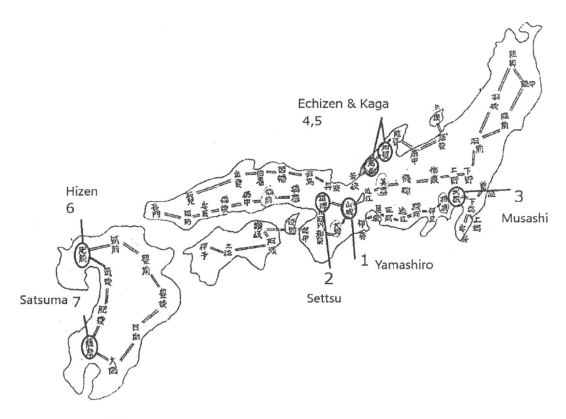

1. *Yamashiro* (山城) in Kyoto

Yamashiro Shin-to sword has a solid and strong look. *Hamon* at the lower part of the blade right above the *Machi* (区) area shows *Suguha* (straight hamon). This is called *Kyo-yakidashi* (京焼出), which means starting with a straight *Hamon*. Then it shows a sudden change to the design of *O-midare* (大乱). *O-midare* (irregular waviness) becomes less wavy at one or two inches below the *Yokote* line, then continues into the *Boshi* as a wavy *Hamon*. The design in the *Boshi* is *Komaru-boshi*. See the illustration below.

Ji-hada ------------ Somewhat rough (this depends on the swordsmith). *Masame-hada* (straight grain pattern) may show on *Shinogi-Ji* (the area between ridgeline and back).

Among the *Yamashiro Shin-to* group, there was a group called *Mishina* Group (三品). They were *Mino Den* (美濃) related. Therefore, their *Boshi* was often *Jizo-boshi* (地蔵鋩子). This is called *Mishina-boshi* (三品鋩子). *Jizo-boshi* is an image of the side of a man's head.

The well-known swordsmiths in the Yamashiro area ----------Umetada Myoju (梅忠明寿)
Horikawa Kunihiro (堀川国広)
Dewadaijyo Kunimichi (出羽大掾国路)

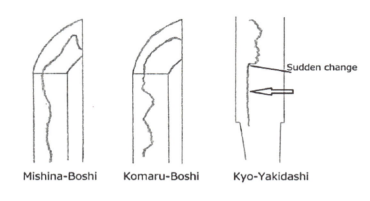

Mishina-Boshi   Komaru-Boshi   Kyo-Yakidashi

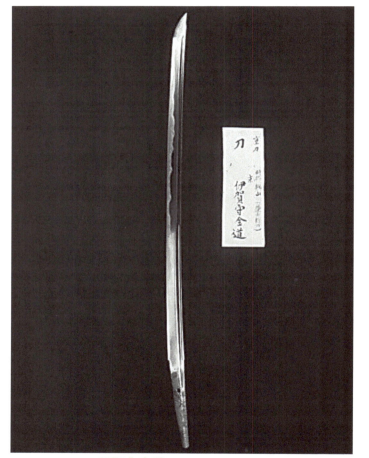

Iganokami Kinnmichi (伊賀守金道) Yamashiro Den   Once my family sword

2. *Settsu* (摂津) Osaka

Settsu (Osaka) created more *Wakizashi* than *Katana*. They tend to make it slightly *Sakizori* (top half curves outward) and slightly stretched *Boshi*. *Settsu* sword also has *Yakidashi* the same way as the previous *Yamashiro* sword. Yet, unlike *Yamashiro'* sword, in the area where *Suguha* changes into *Notare* (wavy pattern), the transition is not sudden but relatively smooth. This is called *Osaka Yakidashi*.

Osaka Boshi -------*Hamon* continues up to the *Yokote* line, then *Komaru* with a turn back.
Ji-hada-------------Very fine, almost no pattern, solid surface like especially, *Shinogi-ji* (between ridgeline and back). This is called *Osaka-tetsu* (iron).

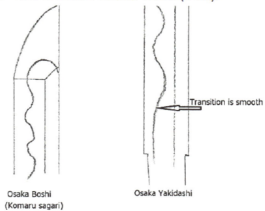

Osaka Boshi (Komaru sagari)   Osaka Yakidashi

Well known smiths in *Settsu* --------Tsuda Sukehiro (津田助広) Tsuda Sukenao (津田助直)
                                     Ikkanshi Tadatsuna (一竿子忠綱)

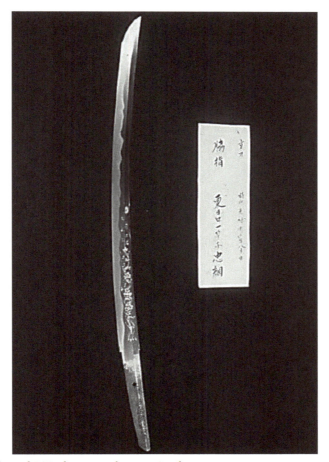

Ikkanshi Tadatsuna (一竿子忠綱) Once my family sword

28 | Shin-to Sword -- Main Seven Regions (Part B: 主要７刀匠地)

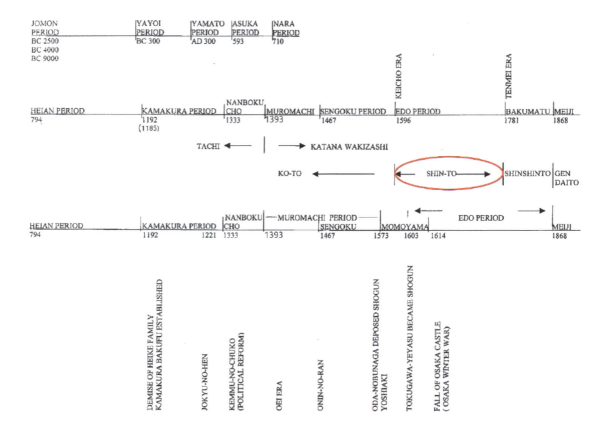

The circle indicates the subject we discuss in this section.

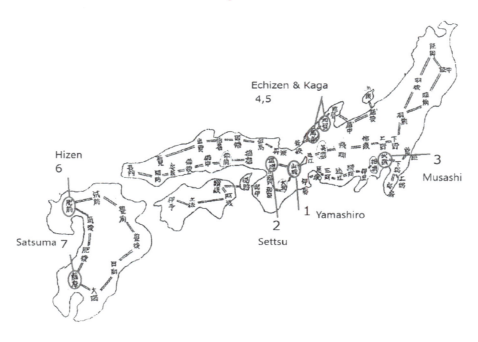

3. Musashi (武蔵) in Edo (江戸)

The *Katana* and *Wakizashi* made in the *Musashi* area have shallow *Sori* (curvature). Often the width of the upper part of the body tends to be narrow. Usually, the *Hamon* starts with a small irregular pattern, gradually becomes a bigger irregular pattern, then a few inches under the *Yokote* line, it becomes a small irregular pattern again. The *Boshi* is usually *Komaru-boshi*. The *Ji-hada* is somewhat rough. *Masame-hada* shows on *Shinogi-ji*.

Well-known swordsmiths in *Musashi* ---------------------------------- Noda Hankei (野田繁慶)
　　　　　　　　　　　　　　　　　　　Nagasone Okisato Nyudo Kotetsu (長曽根興里入道虎徹)

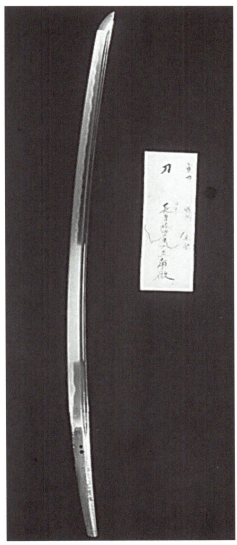
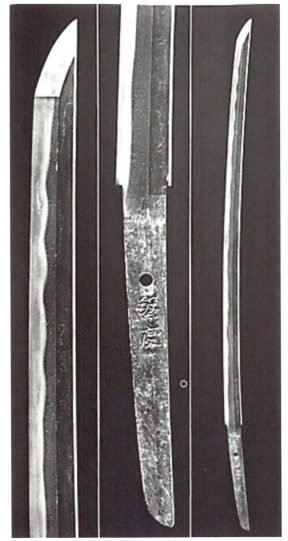

Nagasone Okisato Nyudo Kotetsu
(長曽根興里入道虎徹) Once my family sword

Noda Hankei (野田繁慶)
from Compton's collection "Nippon-to."

4. Echizen (越前) and 5. Kaga (加賀)

Many swordsmiths from *Mino* (美濃) area moved to *Echizen* and *Kaga* area (#4 & #5 on the map above). Therefore, the swords made in this area are called *Echizen-seki* and *Kaga-seki*. Refer to Chapter 23 Sengoku Period (戦国) Sword for *Mino Den*. The style of *Echizen Yasutsugu* (越前康継) is similar to the one of *Mino Den*.

Well-known swordsmith in Echizen -------------------------------Echizen Yasutsugu (越前康継)

6. Hizen (肥前)

Both *Katana* and *Wakizashi* in *Hizen* have a well-balanced shape. *Hizen* area tends to make swords with *Chu-suguha-hotsure* (a medium-width straight *Hamon* that looks like frayed fabric.) with fine *Nie* (沸). The *Boshi* has a regular clean line with uniform width tempered line, as shown in the illustration below. If you see a *Shin-to* sword which has *Chu-suguha Hamon* and a *Boshi* that looks like the one below, it is often made by *Hizen Tadayoshi* (肥前忠吉). Very fine *Ji-hada* (surface), sometimes called *Nukame-hada*.

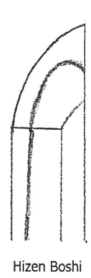

Hizen Boshi

Well-known swordsmith in Hizen -------------------------------Hizen Tadayoshi (肥前忠吉)

7. Satsuma (薩摩)

The swords made in *Satsuma* have a solid look for both *Katana* and *Wakizashi*. *Kissaki* (the top pointed area) is a little stretched. *Yakidashi* (a few inches above *Machi*) shows a small irregular *Hamon*. *Hamon* is *O-midare* with coarse *Nie* called *Ara-nie.* The *Ara-nie* forms *Togari-ba* (pointed pattern, see the drawing below). One of the characteristics of this region is *Satsuma-nie*. That is, the *Ara-nie* around *hamon* continues and blends into the *Ji-hada* area. Therefore, the border between *Ha-nie* and *Ji-nie* is unclear. Inside the *Hamon,* sometimes shows a thick line shaped like lightning. This line is called *Satsuma-no-imozuru* (sweet potato vine), less favorable than *Inazume* and *Kinsiji.* This is the most prominent feature of the *Satsuma* sword. *Boshi* has a narrow-tempered line with a small irregular pattern. This is called *Satsuma-boshi.* On the *Ji-hada* surface, *Chikei* (a long dark line-like) appears. This is called *Satsuma-gane* (薩摩金).

Togari-ba

Well-known swordsmiths in Satsuma ------------------------- Izunokami Masafusa (伊豆守正房)
Ichinohira Yasuyo (一平安代)
Mondonosho Masakiyo (主水正正清)

29 | Bakumatu Period History   1781 – 1867   (幕末歴史)

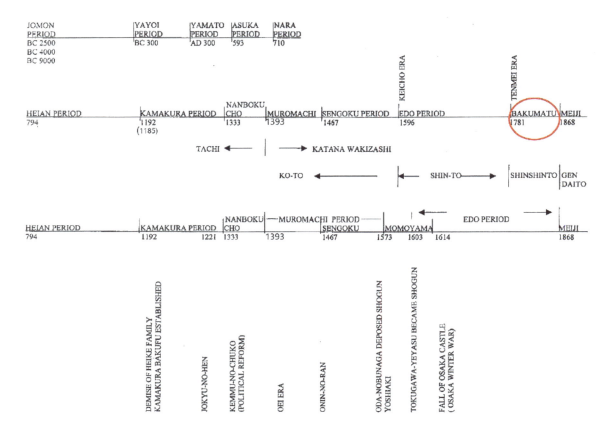

The circle indicates the subject we discuss in this chapter.

The *Bakumatsu* period is the last part of the *Edo* period on sword history. See the circle on the middle timeline above. However, political history does not divide the *Edo* period and the *Bakumatsu* period. There is not a clear-cut date for the *Bakumatsu* period.

The *Azuchi-Momoyam* period (安土桃山) is between the time when *Oda Nobunaga* (織田信長) deposed *Shogun Ashikaga Yoshimasa* (将軍足利義昭) in 1573 and the time when *Tokugawa Iyeyasu* became the shogun in 1603 or when *Tokugawa Iyeyasu* won the battle against *Toyotomi Hideyori* (*Hideyoshi's* son) at *Osaka Summer campaign in 1615*. The *Azuchi-Momoyama* period was a short period when *Oda Nobunaga*(織田信長), *Toyotomi Hideyoshi* (豊臣秀吉), and *Tokugawa Iyeyasu* (徳川家康) were maneuvering the intricate political struggles. During this time, the country flourished culturally and economically. After a long wartime period, people finally saw the country getting reunited and the peaceful life waiting ahead.

The stories of *Oda Nobunaga*, *Toyotomi Hideyoshi*, and *Tokugawa Iyeyasu* have been the most popular stories for the Japanese. Often the stories around this time are depicted on TV programs and in movies. The *Edo* period was the time when the *Tokugawa* family ruled Japan.

The *Tokugawa* government was called the *Tokugawa Bakufu*. Throughout the *Edo* period, the *Tokugawa* family's direct line, usually the firstborn sons, became the *shogun*. Yet, the emperors co-existed at the same time. Even though they did not have political power, the emperor's family still held imperial status.

During the *Edo* period, it was a very peaceful time. Unlike the previous period, there were no wars. Yet, later in the time, the long-last *Edo* period (last approximately 260 years) became stagnated and began showing structural and financial problems in the ruling. This is the *Bakumatsu* (幕末) time, which means the last part of the *Edo Bakufu*.

In the previous chapter, Chapter 25, Edo Period History explained that the *Edo Bakufu* closed the country to the outside world for most of the era. The only place in Japan with access to foreign countries was *Dejima* in *Nagasaki* (Southern part of Japan). During the *Bakumatsu* period, several European ships came to Japan asking (more like demanding) Japan to open ports for water and other whaling ships' supplies. Also, some countries wanted to trade with Japan. Those countries were England, Russia, America, and France, etc.

In 1792, the Russian government sent an official messenger to Japan demanding it to open up for trades. In 1853, Commodore Perry from the U.S. appeared with four massive warships at a port called *Uraga* (浦賀: Kanagawa prefecture now) and demanded Japan to open ports for water, fuel, and other supplies for the U.S. whaling ships.

At the end of the *Bakumatsu* time, the *Tokugawa Bakufu* faced political and financial difficulties governing the country. Also, intellectual people were afraid that Japan might get into trouble like China, the Opium War (1840 -1842), with England. The pressures to open the county were building up. It became apparent that Japan could no longer continue to close the country. In such a time, Commodore Perry appeared at *Uraga* with four huge black warships and demanded Japan to open the country. These warships scared the Japanese and excelled the big wave of the anti-*Bakufu* movement. The *Meiji* Revolution was ready to happen, and Perry's warships were the last blow.

Tokugawa Bakufu made treaties with several foreign countries and opened a few ports for trades. The *Bakufu's* authority was lost, and Japan was divided into several different political groups. While they fought chaotically, the *Meiji* Restoration movement continued. In 1868, the *Tokugawa Bafuku* moved out of the *Edo* Castle in *Edo* (now *Tokyo*), and the *Meiji* Emperor moved in. The *Meiji Shin Seifu* (Meiji new government) was established centering the *Meiji* Emperor, and the *Tokugawa Bakufu* ended.

From ja.wikipedia.org/wiki/黒船   Public Domain
File: Commodore-Perry-Visit-Kanagawa-1854.jpg

Commodore Matthew C. Perry's visit of Kanagawa, near the site of present-day Yokohama on March 8, 1854. Lithography. New York: E. Brown, Jr.

30 | Bakumatsu Period: Shin Shin-to 1781 – 1867 (新々刀)

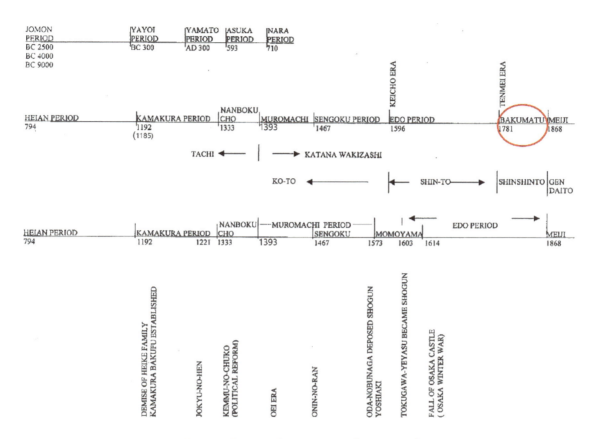

The circle above indicates the time we discuss in this section

The later part of the *Edo* period is called *Bakumatsu*. See the circled area of the timeline above. Swords made during this time are called *Shin Shin-to*. They are also called *Fukko-to* (復古刀: revived sword). *Fukko-to* copied the shape, *Hamon*, *Boshi*, and other features of the *Ko-to* and *Shin*-to swords. The characteristics of *Shin Shin-to* (新々刀) and well-known swordsmiths are those below.

The Characteristics of Shin Shin-to

- *Katana, Wakizashi,* and *Tanto* all tend to be similar to or copy of the *Ko-to* and *Shin-to* in shape.

- Many swords often have *Hi* or detailed engravings.
- One swordsmith would make more than one style swords like *Soshu Den, Bizen Den*, and *Shin-to* style together.
- Often shows *Katai-ha*.

Katai-ha

- Weak (not tight) *Nioi*.
- *Yakidashi* (2 to 3 inches above *Machi*) is often *Suguha* (straight line *Hamon*), even though the rest is irregular *Hamon*. *Boshi* is often irregular *Midare*.
- Detailed engravings, but more realistic than the previous times.

Well known swordsmiths of Shin Shin-to

Settsu (Osaka area) -------------Gassan Sadayoshi (月山貞吉)　Gassan Sadakazu (月山貞一) *Gassan* family is famous for detailed carvings.

Musashi no Kuni (Tokyo area) ------Suishinshi Masahide (水心子正秀)　Minamoto Kiyomaro (源 清麿) Taikei Naotane (大慶直胤) Taikei Yoshitane (大慶義胤) *Yoshitane* is famous for his carvings.

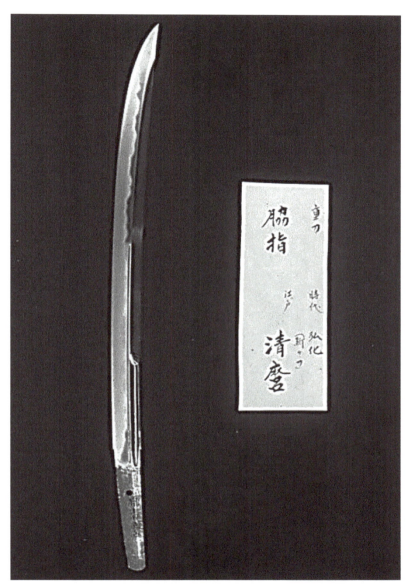

Minamoto Kiyomaro(源清麿) Once my family sword

Tosa (四国: Shikoku area) -- Sa Yukohide (左行秀)
Satsuma (鹿児島: Kagoshima) --------------------- Oku Motohira (奥元平) Naminohira (波平)

Meiji Ishin-To

Right before the *Meiji* Restoration, long swords (approx. 3 feet) with no curvature were made. *Sa Yukihide* (from *Tosa*) forged this type of sword. *Saigo Takamori* (西郷隆盛)、*Sakamoto Ryoma* (坂本龍馬) owned swords like this. Both are famous historical characters during the *Meiji* Restoration. Both of them were a part of the *Kin'no-to* (勤党 group, which supported the Emperor and renewed the political system.

31 | Sword Making Process

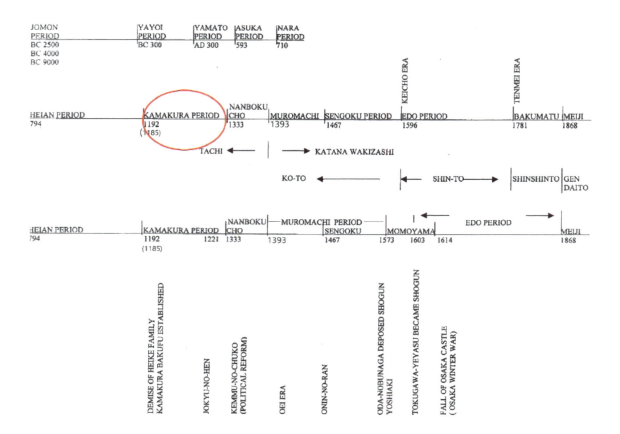

As a part of the sword study, it is necessary to describe the process of making a sword. This chapter explains only a very basic procedure of sword-making. It is a simple outline of the sword-making process since I lack expertise in the field.

When I was small, I used to see the process of metal being heated up in the furnace in my father's factory. He owned a machine tool company and a forging factory. It was fascinating to see the metal was heated up, taken out of the furnace, pounded by two men, then put back in the furnace, and pounded again and again. To this day, I can still remember the exact color of the metal when it should be taken out of the fire. That was a strange thing to learn for a small girl. Not only that, it was dangerous for children to be close to the furnace when the metal was being heated. But those days, people's idea for safety was different. I think the factory workers enjoyed seeing my brother and me being so impressed, so amazed and regarded them as heroes. We kept going to the shop until my father moved the factory to a larger place. Today, I would never allow my grandchildren to be near a furnace.

The sword-making involves very many detailed processes, and each swordsmith has his secrets. Anybody interested in more detailed explanations, please refer to a book written by a famous swordsmith, Mr. *Yoshihara Yoshindo,* and a DVD made by his son. Their information is below. Mr. *Yoshihara's* book is sold on Amazon. DVD is sold on Japan Amazon. DVD may be necessary to go through the proxy service; Zen Market since it is sold on Amazon Japan.

Book: The Art of the Japanese Sword -----The Craft of Sword Making and its Appreciation by Yoshihara Yoshindo, Leon and Hiroko Capp   Published by Saviolo Edizioni

DVD: Katana/On Ko So Shin (温故創新)-------Katana project by Yoshihara Yoshikazu (吉原義一). Use proxy service-Zen Market, since only Amazon Japan sell it.

Tamahagane (玉鋼)

In the old days, the early sword-making time, swordsmiths extracted iron from iron sand and refined it by themselves for sword material. By the *Kamakura* period (refer to the timeline above), ironmaking was done by separate entities. Swordsmiths buy iron called *"Tamahabane"* from ironmakers. *"Tamahagane"* is the essential part of sword-making. *"Tamahagane"* is the iron made with the *Tatara* process, a unique Japanese smelting process.

Tamahagane from Mr. Yoshihara

Kawa-gane (側鉄) and Shin-gane (芯鉄)

The Japanese sword is made from steel of two different hardness. *Kawa-gane* is for outer steel. *Shin-gane* for inner steel. *Kawa-gane* is harder steel, which contains about 0.6% carbon contents. *Shin-gane* is softer steel that has about 0.25% carbon content. Japanese swords are made with softer steel inside, wrapped around by harder steel; this way, it is hard to bend and hard to break.

Kawa-gane (側鉄: outer steel) ------ Shita-gitae (下鍛: Base forging)

Heat a block of *Tamahagane* → Hit with a hammer and make flat pieces → While *Tamahagane* is still hot, quench in water quickly → Break into small pieces.

Separately forge a rectangle plate with *Tamahagane* → Connect this plate with a handle or a lever to create a *Teko* → Stack up the previously broken metal pieces on the *Teko* carefully and closely.

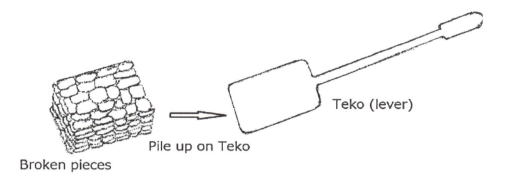

→ Cover the stacked up *Tamahagane* with ashes and clay for protection → Heat this in the furnace → Take it out from the furnace, and hit with a hammer → Repeat this process many times to stretch out *Tamahgane* about twice as long.

While *Tamahagane* is still hot, make a notch in the center and fold in half → Continue the same process of heating up, hammering to stretch, and folding half (widthwise and lengthwise alternatively approximately 6 or 7 times depending on the original carbon level in *Tamagahane*). This process reduces the carbon content to the desired level.

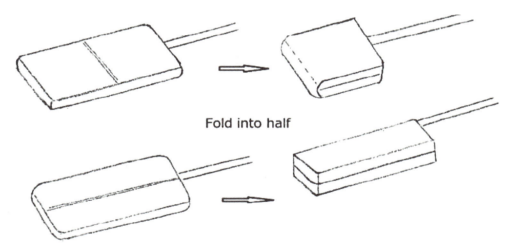

Fold into half

Kawagane (側鉄: Outer steel) -----Age-gitae (上鍛: Finish forging)

At the end of *Shita-gitae,* chisel the block of *Tamahagane* so that it can be separated into two or three sections → Quench in water → Cool down → Break it into pieces along with the markings → Combine these pieces and repeat the heating, hammering, and folding processes.

Usually, the folding process is done 6 to 7 times for *Shita-gitae* (base forging) and 6 to 7 times for *Age-gitae* (finish forging). Total 12 times or so depending on the original carbon contents in the *Tamahagane* used. This process is for *Kawa-gane* (側金)

Purpose of heating hammering and folding

- Each time the heating and folding process is done, *Tamahagane* loses carbon content. For outer steel, the ideal carbon content should be approximately 0.6%. If the carbon content is too high, steel is hard, and as a result, the sword can crack. If it is too low, the sword will be too soft and can bend. Swordsmiths judge by their eyes to determine the right amount of carbon content. This is the professionalism and the art of sword-making.
- Removing slags and impurities from *Tamahagane*.
- Each heating and folding processes create many layers of thin steel that create the *Ji-hada* pattern (surface patterns like wood grain, burl look, straight grain, or a mixture of those)

Shin-gane (inner steel 芯鉄)

Shin-gane is the inner metal that is softer steel with less carbon. By having softer inside, the sword has flexibility. Having hard outer steel with higher carbon with softer steel inside prevents the sword from cracking or breaking. To make the *Shin-gane* steel, mix softer steel with *Tamahagane*. Repeat the same process as *Kawa-gane*.

Tsukuri Komi (造り込み)   Sunobe (素延)

Wrap the *Shin-gane* with the *Kawa-gane,* then weld two pieces together by heating, hammering, and stretch out to make a steel bar. There are several ways to wrap the *Shin-gane*, but the most common way is called *Kobuse* (甲伏). The illustration below is the cross-section.

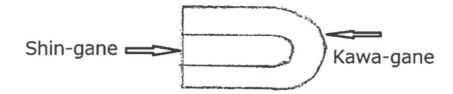

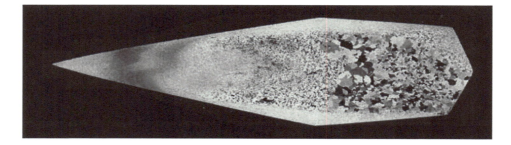

The above photo (taken by my husband) shows a cross-section of a sword. Many years ago, a member of our sword club gave us a very rusty, damaged sword. My husband cut the blade and took the micro photo of the cross-section. This sword has a more complicated construction than the usual *Kobuse* method. It looks like it has 3 (4?) different hardness of steel. This sword seems it was once one of the top swords made by a top sword-maker.

Hizukuri (火造)

Hizukuri is to make the final shape of the sword from *Sunobe* by heating and hammering. At this point, *Ha* (cutting edge) gets thinner, the *Shinogi* side gets higher, and it starts to form a sword's shape.

Arashiage (荒仕上げ)

This process is rough finishing.

Tsuchitori (土取)

Mix clay, pine tree ash, ground stone, and water. Coat the sword with this muddy mixture. Scrape off a thin layer of the mix a little around the *hamon* area, then dry out. By doing the *Tsuchitori* process, *hamon* is created, and cutting-edge hardens at the same time.

Yaki-Ire (焼入れ)

After the muddy paste is dried, heat the sword evenly in the furnace. Judging by the heated sword's color, pull it out from the furnace, quickly quench it in the water. Usually, this process is done after the sun goes down so that the swordsmith can see the color of the metal and can judge the temperature of the heated sword more accurately. This is the most crucial process since all the work done up to this point may be ruined if he fails to judge the heated sword's precise color, water temperature, and quenching timing.

The final process is to send the sword to a polisher. The polisher called *Togishi* polishes and sharpens the blade. He brings out the beauty of the surface and the sharpness of the sword. This completes the whole process of sword-making. Every step is essential, but the polishers' final process is as important as the rest of the work.

32 | Swords after WWII

While I was growing up in *Azabu* and *Mita* in Tokyo, and later in *Kamakura*, my father was heavily involved in a Japanese sword museum called "*Nihon Bijutsu Token Hozon Kyokai*." At that time, the head of the organization was Dr. *Honma* and Dr. *Sato*.

Initially, Dr. *Honma* and Dr. *Sato* were at the Tokyo National Museum's sword department in *Ueno*. Later, a separate Nonprofit Organization for the Japanese Sword Museum was built in *Yoyogi* in *Shibuya*. Though the address was *Yoyogi* in *Shibuya*, it was almost in *Shinjuku*. To build this Museum, my father, Mr. *Watanabe* (owner of the *Wataki*, an apparel company), and Mr. *Suzuki Katei* (owner of the construction company) were heavily involved. Those two friends used to come to our house all the time (literally all the time) and stayed hours talking and gossiping. At present, the Museum moved to a new location, *Sumida-Ku* (*Sumida* Ward), *Tokyo*, near the *Sumo* arena in *Ryogoku*. Refer to the website below.

Dr. *Honma* and Dr. *Sato*, who used to come to our house in *Tokyo* and all other people involved, were deceased many years ago, but they were in their prime time then. I am talking about the late 1960s to 1970s. I was in my teens, then.

Many people told me that a few very prominent people and Dr. *Honma* and Dr. *Sato*, visited General MacArthur's headquarter during the occupation after World War II, and they convinced MacArthur that the Japanese swords were not weapons but art objects. They did so because MacArthur ordered all Japanese to turn in their swords and forbade them to own one. After a great effort, Dr. *Honma*, Dr. *Sato*, and other high-rank people changed MacArthur's mind. Yet, many swords had already been turned in at *Akabane* (a place in *Tokyo*), though some people hid valuable ones. Those swords turned in are called *Akabane* swords.

A huge number of Akabane swords were taken by American soldiers and brought to the U.S. as a souvenir from Japan. Those soldiers didn't know if they took a valuable one or an ordinary kind. Approximately 25 years after the war, in the late 1960s and 1970s, Japanese sword dealers went to the U.S. and started to buy back many Japanese swords. I have a few sword-dealer friends who did that. They advertised in local newspapers that they would buy Japanese swords. As you can imagine, many swords were in bad shape. Some people had used the wrong chemicals to take the rust off. Only a few were recovered in good condition.

Among those recovered, one of the very famous missing National Treasure swords was found by Dr. Compton. He was the chairman of the board of Miles Laboratories in Elkhart, Indiana. Miles Laboratories was a pharmaceutical company that produced many kinds of products, including Alka- Seltzer. He had good knowledge of Japanese swords. When he saw this sword in Atlanta's antique store, he realized it was not just an ordinary sword. He contacted *Nihon Bijutsu Token Hozon Kyokai* (日本美術刀剣保存協会) for consultation. During the process, my father became a good friend of his. My father and I visited his house several times, and they visited ours back and forth. Dr. Compton returned this sword to the *Terukuni Shrine* (照国神社) in *Kagoshima* prefecture without compensation. The story of Dr. Compton continues in the last part of Chapter 45 Part 2 of -- 11 Ikubi Kissak (猪首切先). Even though Japanese swords dealers bought and took many swords back to Japan, it seems like there are many Japanese swords still left in the U.S.

Nonprofit organization: Nihon Bijutsu Token Hozon Kyoukai (日本美術刀剣保存協会)
1-12-9 Yokozuna Sumida-Ku Tokyo Japan 130—0015
Tel: 03-6284-1000
https://www.touken.or.jp/

*The above website explains the access to the Museum.

33 | The Information on Today's Swordsmiths

In the present time, there are many serious swordsmiths in Japan. I am a good friend of two of them. One is Mr. *Yoshihara Yoshindo* (吉原義人), and the other is Mr. *Yamamura Tsunahiro* (山村綱廣). I met them when we were in our 20s, still single.

I met Mr. *Yoshihara* at one of the sword meetings I attended with my father. That was in the early 1970s. Since then, we have encountered each other at different sword gatherings here and there. His son, *Yoshihara Yoshikazu* (吉原義一), is also a well-known swordsmith. His grandson also decided to be a swordsmith. Naturally, my friend *Yoshihara* was very excited to train him.
Whenever we meet at the different sword meetings, he often tells me fascinating stories. Here are some of them.

Mr. *Yoshihara* once had an apprentice from a Middle Eastern country who was sent by his king. The apprentice lived in *Yoshihara*'s house with other Japanese apprentices. He was a very quiet good apprentice and had no problem with food, and he ate Japanese food with other Japanese apprentices.

Mr. *Yoshihara* also told me that a king from a European country once visited his studio. The king gave *Yoshihara* his photo, which had his autograph on it as a gift. Another story was that a famous Hollywood movie director ordered a couple of swords and visited his house. It seems that it was about the same time I ordered him a sword for myself. The photo below is my sword made by him at that time.

Yamamura-kun (we put "*kun*" at the end for male friends and "*san*" for female friends) and I were students at *Mori Sensei*'s sword class together. He was the top student; I was almost the last. He is the direct line of *Goro Nyudo Masamune* (五郎入道正宗), the 24th generation. He now has a studio near Kamakura Station. But back then, he had a store almost in front of the *Hachiman-gu* Shrine (八幡宮) in *Kamakura*.

We had one more person, Mr. *Kurokawa* (黒川), in our group. He is the owner of a big sword store in *Tokyo*, "*Soken-do* (霜剣堂)." We were all *Kamakura* residents then. We used to get together at *Yamamura-kun's* store in front of the *Hachiman-gu* Shrine, having a good time and joking around in the store.

Below is the information about their stores.

To order a sword, you can contact
Yoshihara Yoshindo (吉原義人)
8-17-11 Takasago, Katsushika-Ku, Tokyo 125-0054 Japan   Tel (03) 3607 - 5255

Masamune Kougei (正宗工芸)
13-29 Onari-cho, Kamakura-shi, Kanagawa, 248-0012 Japan   Tel (0467) 22- 3962

Soken-Do (霜剣堂)
28-1, 6-Chome, Jingu-mae, Shibuya-ku, Tokyo 150-0001 Japan
Tel (03) 3499 - 8080

My sword made by Mr. Yoshihara

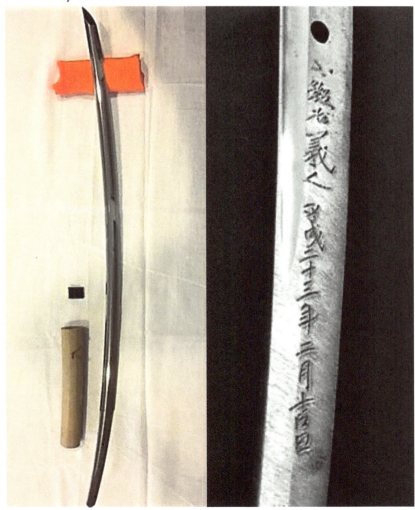

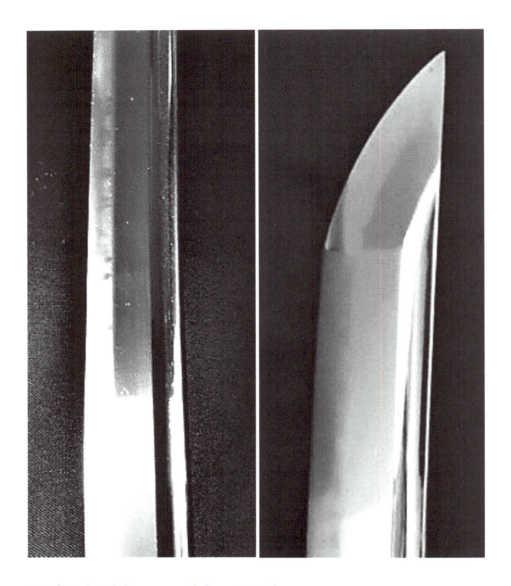

吉原新刀 (Yoshihara sword description)
- Shape: *Koshizori Chu-gissaki, Bo-hi* (one groove)
- Boshi: *Midare-komi* and *Komaru-kaeshi* (round with turnback)
- Hamon: *Komidare Nioi*
- Hada: very fine *Komokume* almost *Muji*
- Mei: *Kaji Yoshindo Heisei* 二十三 *nen* 二月 *Kichijitu*
  ＊It means: Sword smith *Yoshindo Heisei* year 23 (2011) February good day

34| Part 2 of -- 1 Timeline

Chapter 34 is a continued part of Chapter 1 Timeline. Please read Chapter 1 before reading this section.

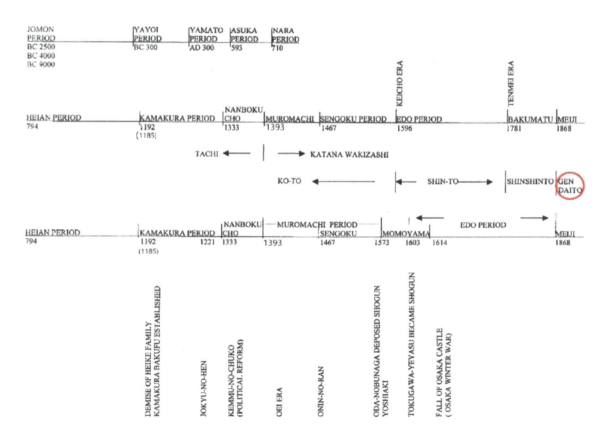

The circle above indicates the time we discuss here

In the "Chapter 1 Timeline", I mentioned that *Gendai-to* (現代刀) is the swords made between the *Meiji Restoration* (明治維新 1868) and now. It has been about 150 years since the *Meiji Restoration*. Even though all swords made after the *Meiji Restoration* are categorized into one *Gendai-to* group, there are quite a few differences in quality and kind. The very different one is *Gun-to* (軍刀). Those are military swords that were forged to use in World War I and World War II. Some of them have a saber-like handle. With some exceptions, those were made not using the traditional sword-making method of heat and fold technique. Among the *Gendai-to, Gun-to* is usually considered much less value. The *Gun-to* sword made around during World War II is called *Showa-to*.

It often has a brown leather scabbard. *Gun-to* is not a part of the study of the Japanese sword.

*Refer to" https://en.wikipedia.org/wiki/Gunt%C5%8D" for Japanese military sword.

Gun-to from Wikimedia Commons, the free media repository

At the time of the *Meiji Restoration* (明治維新), swords called *Meiji-ishin-to* (明治維新刀) or *Kin'no-to* (勤王刀) were made. These swords were owned by famous historical figures like *Saigo Takamori* (西郷隆盛), and *Sakamoto Ryoma* (坂本龍馬). They are important historical figures who pushed the *Meiji Restoration* forward. These swords are long, and some of them are almost 3 feet long and have no curvature.

Today, many famous swordsmiths are forging great swords. Some are recognized as Living National Treasure. *Gendai-to* is the sword made after the *Meiji Restoration* till now, but please keep in mind that there is a wide range of differences in quality, variety, and purposes among them.

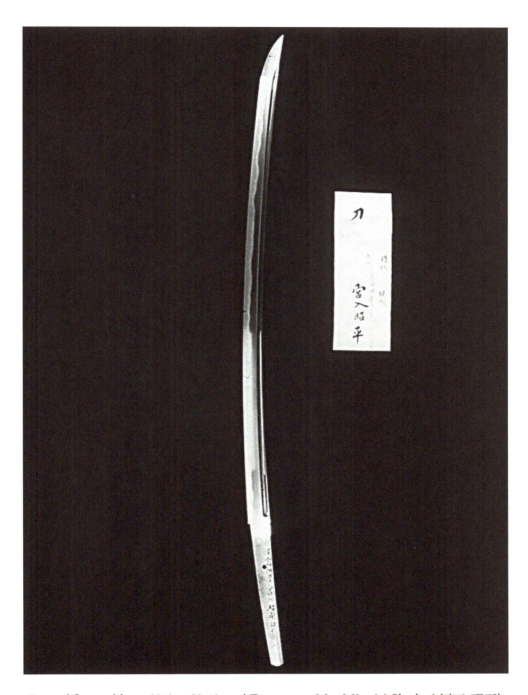

Sword forged by a Living National Treasure, Mr. Miyairi Shohei (宮入昭平)
My brother's sword

35 | Part 2 of -- 2 Joko-to (上古刀)

Chapter 35 is a continued part of 2 Joko-to (上古刀). Please read chapter 2 before this section.

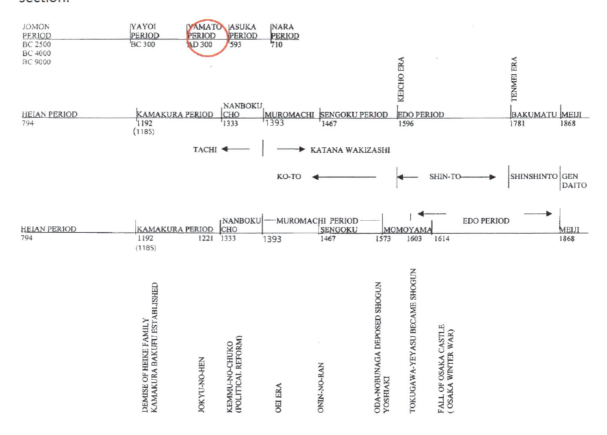

The circle above indicates the time we discuss here.

The *Kofun* (古墳) culture appeared around the 4th, 5th, and 6th centuries. *Kofuns* are massive burial places for powerful rulers. *Kofun* are often *Zenpo-koen-fun* (前方後円墳) which is, the front part is a square and the back is round. If you look at it from the sky, it shapes like a keyhole. The largest *Kofun* is the *Nintoku Tenno Ryo* (仁徳天皇陵) in *Osaka*. This is the tomb of Emperor *Nintoku*. The size is 480 m X 305 m, and the height is 35 m. Inside the *Kofun*, we found swords, armors, bronze mirrors, jewelry, iron, and metal tools. Sometimes, iron itself was found. Only the ruling class possessed the iron since it was considered a very precious item then. Outskirts of the *Kofun*, a large number of *Haniwa*[*1] were placed. There are several theories for the purpose of *Haniwa*. One is as a retaining wall, and another is as a dividing line between the sacred area and the common area. And there are several more theories.

Originally, *Haniwa* were just simple tube shapes. Eventually, they became interesting clay figurines such as smiling people, smiling soldiers, dogs with a bell around the neck, women with a hat, farmers, houses, monkeys, ships, birds, etc. Some of them were very elaborately made and very cute. From the looks of them, people in those days seem to have been wearing elaborate clothes. The *Haniwa* figurines are very popular among children in Japan. We used to have a children's TV program, a *Haniwa* is the main character.

*Haniwa*s suggest to us what people's life was like then. Their facial expressions are all happy and smiling. According to the old Japanese history book, "*Nihon Shoki*" (日本書紀: The oldest Japanese history book completed during the *Nara* period.), *Haniwa* were the replacement of martyred, but it hasn't been proven yet.

From another huge *Kofun, Ogonzuka Kofun* (黄金塚古墳) in *Osaka*, they found a sword and bronze mirrors among other items. Refer Chapter 2|Joko-to. The writing below is from my college day notebook.

The professor explained how to determine the time a particular item had been made by reading half-disappeared characters on the items such as a bronze mirror or a sword. For example, there was a sword, the hilt of it was made in Japan, and the blade was made in China. It had a round hilt and, on it, showed some Chinese characters. It said, "中平 [ ] 年." The third letter was not legible. But we knew 中平 year was between 184 to 189 AD, and "年" indicated "year." Therefore, it was made sometime between 184 to 189. And this sword came out from the 4th-century tomb.

Also, he explained that many nested *Doutaku* (銅鐸)*² had* been excavated from many places. They were nested inside one another. *Doutaku* was a musical instrument for rituals. Therefore, scholars believe that the people then hid *Doutaku* in a hurry and escaped quickly when they were being attacked by their enemies.

In many countries, excavation may be time-consuming, tedious work, and often takes a long time to find anything. But in Japan, it is not as hard as in other countries. We often find things. It may not be what you are looking for, but we excavate artifacts quite often.

*¹腰かける巫女 (群馬県大泉町古海出土) 国立博物館蔵　Sitting Shrine Maiden
(Excavated from Gunma Prefecture) owned by National Museum, Public domain photo

*² 滋賀県野洲市小篠原字大岩屋出土突線紐５式銅鐸　東京国立博物館展示　Public domain photo
Dotaku:　Excavated from Shiga Prefecture　Displayed at Tokyo Nationa Museum.

36 | Part 2 of -- 3 Names of the Parts

This chapter is a continued part of Chapter 3, Names of Parts. Please read Chapter 3, Names of parts, before reading this section.

This chapter is about how to find the *Koshi-zori* or *Chukani-zori*. *Chukan-zori* is also called *Torii-zori* or *Kyo-zori*. *Chukan-zori* means the most curved part of the sword body comes around the middle, and for *Koshi-zori,* the most curved part comes lower than the center of the blade, approximately 1/3 of the lower body. Every sword looks to have its curvature around the middle part, especially when you look at photos of a sword in books. It is because those swords are placed to fit nicely in a given rectangle photo space.

The correct way to look for the curvature is to stand the *Nakago* (茎) vertically. In this way, you can see the location of the curvature more precisely. If the *Nakago* is not vertical, the curvature looks to be in every swords' middle area. When you look at a sword, the first thing to do is to hold a sword and make sure that the *Nakago* stands vertically. When you look at a sword in a book, rotate (shift or slide) the book slightly so that the *Nakago* is perpendicular. You can see the precise location of the curvature in this way. Keep in mind; sometimes it is subtle.

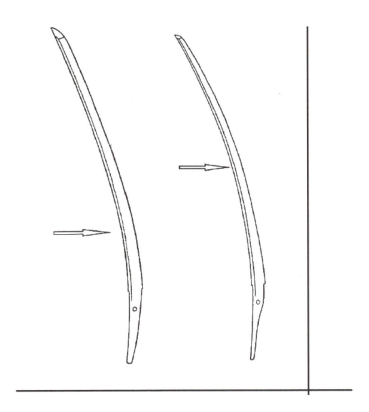

37 | part 2 of -- 4 Heian Period History 794-1192 (平安時代歷史)

This chapter is a continued part of Chapter 4 Heian Period History. Please read Chapter 4 before reading this section.

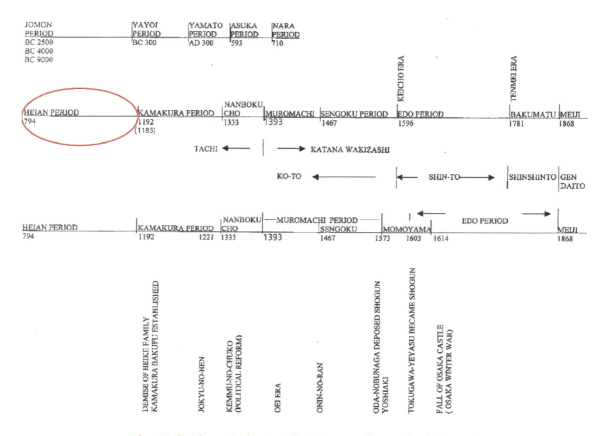

The circle above indicates the time we discuss in this section

Around the middle *Heian* period, a novel, "*Genji Monogatari*" ("The *Tales of Genji*": 源氏物語) was written by a female author, *Murasaki Shikibu* (紫式部). She was an aristocrat court lady. Her father was *Fujiwara Tametoki* (藤原為時), a scholar. There were several novels and essays written by female authors around that time, but "*The Tales of Genji*" is the worldly known literature as the greatest Japanese literature. "*The Tales of Genji*" is a treasure for the Japanese. We love this novel so much that the Japan Mint issued 2000-yen bill[*1] with a scene from the novel. See the photo below. The author herself is printed at the lower right corner on the back of the bill. The bill is very beautiful that, instead of using it, people just keep it. Therefore, it does not circulate much. I have four bills, but I cannot bring myself to use them. It is too nice to use.

The novel is about *Hikaru Genji's* (the hero, 光源氏) love history (yes, history) from when he was about 16 years old until he died. There are ten more chapters after his death, called "*Uji Jyu- jyo.*" This section is a story of his son and grandson. When he died, the title of the chapter is "Vanishes into the cloud (雲隠れ)," a very poetic title. The *Tales of Genji* depicts the aristocratic society's daily life, customs, lifestyle, and how people think in those days. Surprisingly, though they did not have the technology we have now, the way they thought was not significantly different from us. The description of the process of courting is in Chapter 4, Heian Period History.

The author created *Hikaru Genji* (光源氏), the main character, a high-level aristocrat, an emperor's illegitimate son. He was depicted as a most charming, good-looking, smart, and sophisticated aristocrat, and all the women fell for him. He would go around all kinds of women one after another; a beautiful woman, not so good-looking but very smart, very young, older, even including his stepmother, wealthy or not so wealthy, etc. It sounds like the story from the tabloid magazine. Still, *Murasaki Shikibu* depicted the hero's and heroines' thoughts, emotions, daily lives, and how the men thought about the women and vice versa, with her excellent writing skill. The author, *Murasaki Shikibu,* wrote this novel to entertain the female audiences in the court where she was living. It became so popular then that it is said that even the emperor at the time asked her how the next story would develop. "*Genji Monogatari*" is translated into English. You can buy the translated book on Amazon or go to YouTube and search for "*Genji Monogatari*" or "*The Tales of Genji.*" You will find many "*Genji Monogatari*" in *Anime,* old TV programs, and old movies in full or short clips.

Another female author, *Sei Sho-nagon* (清少納言), wrote an essay called "*Makura no Soshi* "(枕草子) *around* the same time. In it, she described the court ladies' daily lives. In one chapter, she mentioned *kakigori* (shaved ice: かき氷). High-class people then must have had a chance to eat shaved ice, though the ice was not easy to come by during summer in the middle *Heian* period.

Once you have the general idea of how the *Heian* aristocrat's life was like, you may realize why the *Heian* sword is shaped like the way it is. And it becomes easier to identify a *Heian* sword from amongst other swords that were made in different times and other provinces than *Kyoto*. All sword styles reflect the society where the swordsmiths lived. During the *Heian* period, the *Yamashiro Den* style represented sword style. In the next chapter, the subject matter is centered around the *Yamashiro Den,* though there were other sword groups in different regions.

* 1   The back of the 2000-yen bill

Murasaki Shikibu

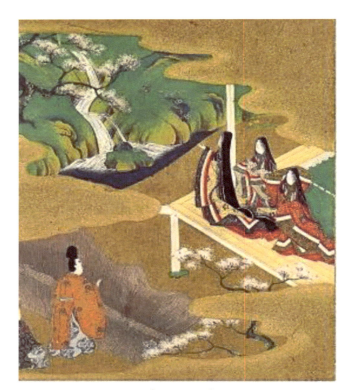

Wakamurasaki
Part of the Burke Album, a property of Mary Griggs Burke (Public Domain). Paintings by Mitsukuni (土佐光国), 17 centuries.   The scenes are based on "*The Tales of Genji*."

38 | Part 2 of -- 5 Heian Period Sword 794 – 1192 (平安時代太刀)

This chapter is a continued part of Chapter 5 Heian Period Sword. Please read Chapter 5 before reading this section. More sword terminologies will be used in the coming chapters. They were explained between chapters 1 to 31. For unfamiliar sword terminologies, please read Chapters 1 to 31.

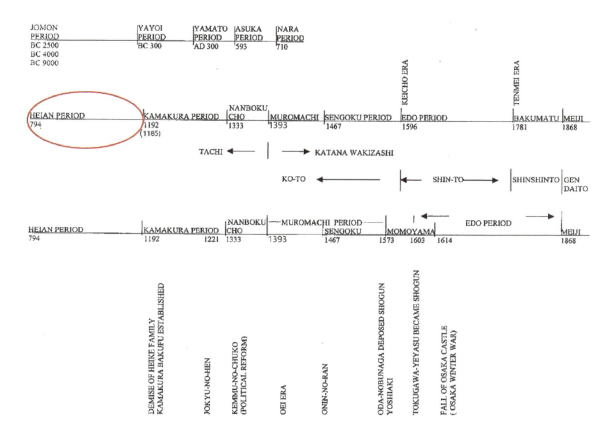

The circle above indicates the time we discuss in this section

There are several active schools of swordsmiths during the *Heian* period. We use the word *"Den"* for school. They are *Yamashiro Den* (山城伝), *Yamato Den* (大和伝), *Bizen Den* (備前伝). Also, the following areas are other active groups during the *Heian* period: *Houki-no-Kuni* (伯耆の国), and *Oo-U* (奥羽). *Oo-U* is pronounced "Oh," and "U" as uber.

Yamashiro Den (山城伝)

During the *Heian* period, among *Yamashiro Den* swords, the most famous sword was "*Mikazuki Munechika* " (三日月宗近) by *Sanjo Munechika* (三条宗近). *Mikazuki* means crescent. It was named *Mikazuki Munechika* because the crescent-shaped *Uchinoke* (collection of *Nie*) pattern appears in *Hamon*. It has a graceful shape, narrow-body, *Koshi-zori*, *Funbari*, and small *Kissaki*. It shows the wood grain pattern surface and *Suguha* with *Nie* mixed with small irregular, sometimes *Nijyu-ha* (double *Hamon*:二重刃) appears. *Sanjo Munechika* lived in the *Sanjo* area in *Kyoto*. His sword style was carried on by his sons and grandsons: *Sanjo Yoshiie* (三条吉家), *Gojo Kanenaga* (五条兼永), and *Gojo Kuninaga* (五条国永). *Gojo* is also an area in Kyoto.

三日月宗近　Mikazuki Munechika　東京国立博物館蔵 Tokyo National Museum
Photo from "Showa Dai Mei-to Zufu 昭和大名刀図譜," published by NBTHK

Houki -no-Kuni (伯耆の国)

Houki-no-Kuni is today's *Tottori* Prefecture. It is known as the place to produce good iron. The sword, "*Doujigiri Yasutsuna*" (童子切安綱) made by *Houki-no-Yasutsuna* (伯耆の安綱) was one of the famous swords during the time.

The characteristics of *Yasutsuna*'s sword----------It has a graceful shape with small *Kissaki*, narrow *Hamon* (often *Suguha* with *Ko-choji*), coarse *Nie* on *Hamon* area, large wood grain pattern mixed with *Masame* on *Ji-hada*. *Hamon* area often shows *Inazuma* and *Kinsuji*. *Boshi* area is *Yakizume*, *Kaen* (pronounced *ka* as a calf, *en* as engineer) with a small turn back.

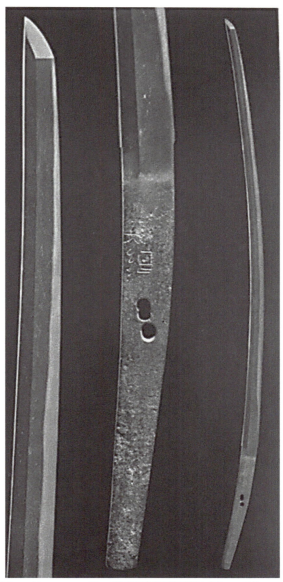

伯耆の安綱 (Houki no Yasutsuna)　佐野美術館図録 (Sano Museum Catalogue)

Bizen Den (備前伝)

Bizen is today's *Okayama* Prefecture. It is known as the place to produce good iron. From the *Heian* period until now, *Bizen* has been famous for the sword-making tradition. The sword-making group in this area during the *Heian* period was called the *Ko-bizen* group. The most famous swordsmith in the *Ko-bizen* group was *Bizen Tomonari* (備前友成), *Bizen Masatsune* (備前正恒), and *Bizen Kanehira* (備前包平).

<u>Ko-bizen group's characteristics</u> --------- A graceful narrow body, small *kissaki*, narrow tempered line with *Ko-choji* (small irregular) with *Inazuma* and *Kin-suji*. *Ji-hada* is a small wood grain pattern.

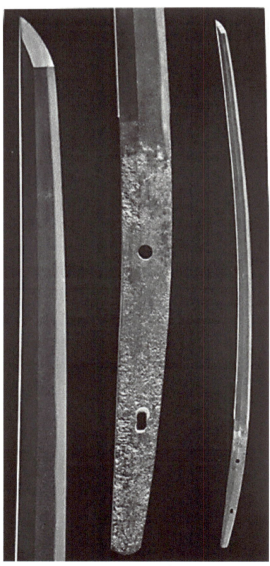

Bizen Kanehira (備前包平) Sano Museum Catalogue (Permission to use granted)

I saw *Ko-bizen Sanetsune* (真恒) at *Mori Sensei's* house. That was one of the *Kantei-to* of that day. I received *Douzen*[1]. The book written by *Hon'ami Koson* was used as our textbook. Each time I saw a sword at *Mori Sensei's* house, I noted the date on the swordsmith's name in the book we used. It was Nov. 22, 1970. It had a narrow body line, small *kissaki* (that was *Ko-bizen Komaru*), *Kamasu*[2] (no *fukura*), and *Suguha*. *Kamasu* is the condition where the *fukura* (arc) is much lesser than usual. Thinking back then, it is amazing we could see famous swords like this as our study materials.

Kantei-Kai

Kantei-kai is a study meeting. Usually, several swords are displayed, with the *Nakago* part being covered. The attendees guess the name of the sword maker and hand in the answer sheet to the judge. Below are the grades.

Atari ----- If the answer is right on the exact name, you get *Atari*. That is the best answer.

Dozen ------ The second best is *Dozen*. It means almost the correct answer. The subject sword was made by the family or the clan of the right *Den*. *Dozen* is considered very good. It indicates the student has a good knowledge of the particular group.

Kaido Yoshi ----- This means correct about the line, but not about the family.

Jidai Yoshi------- It means the time or period is correct. Each *Kantei-kai* has different grading systems. Some may not have a "*Jidai Yoshi*" grade.

Hazure-------- the wrong answer.

Once all answer sheets are handed in, the answer sheets are graded and returned. The judge reveals the correct answer and explains why.

[1] *Dozen*: Almost the same as the correct answer.
[2] *Kamasu*: The name of a fish. It has a narrow and pointed head.

39| Part 2 of -- 6 Kamakura Period History 1192-1333 (鎌倉歴史)

This chapter is a continued part of Chapter 6 Kamakura Period History 1192 – 1333. Please read Chapter 6 before reading this section. Some of the information here may overlap with Chapter 6 since this is the continued part.

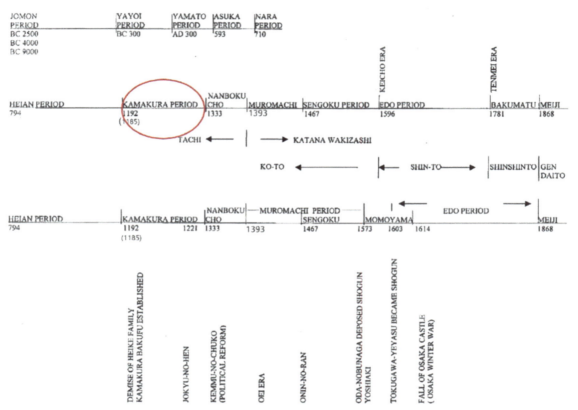

The circle above indicates the time we discuss in this section

Taira no Kiyomori (平清盛)

Chapter 6 Kamakura Period History described there were two major samurai groups, the *Genji* (源氏) and the *Heishi* (平氏) at the end of the *Heian* period. The head of the *Genji* was *Minamoto no Yoshitomo* (源義朝), and the head of the *Heishi* (or *Heike*) was *Taira no Kiyomori* (平清盛). They were childhood friends. Yet, because of the political situation and circumstances, they became enemies by the time they grew up to adulthood. After their several power struggles, the *Genji* side lost, and *Taira-no-Kiyomori* became very powerful. He favored his men and gave high positions to them, and had his daughter married to the emperor. As a result, *Kiyomori's* power went even beyond the emperor. This was the time people would say, "if you are not a part of the *Heishi* family, you are not a human being."   A situation like this created too many opponents against him. Eventually, the suppressed *Genji* and other *samurai* groups gathered and raised an army, fought against the *Heishi*, and defeated them.

While *Taira-no-Kiyomori* was in power, he started trading with China, contributing to Japan's economic prosperity.   The picture below is the *Itsukushima Jinja Shrine* (厳島神社) built by *Taira no Kiyomori*. It is registered as a UNESCO World Heritage Site.

From Wikipedia. The photo is in the public domain. Author: Rdsmith4
File Itsukushima Floating Shrine.jpg 8 /05/04

Minamoto no Yoritomo (源頼朝)

Minamoto no Yoritomo (源頼朝) was a son of *Minamoto no Yoshitomo*(源義朝). After *Yoshitomo* was defeated by *Taira no Kiyomori* (平清盛), the direct bloodline of *Genji*, *Minamoto no Yoritomo* was sent to *Izu* Island. He was in his early teens.

Yoritomo grew to be a young man in *Izu* Island and eventually met *Hojo Masako* (北条政子) there. She was a daughter of *Hojo Tokimasa* (北条時政) who was a local government official. While *Tokimasa* was on a business trip to Kyoto, *Yoritomo* and *Masako* had a baby. *Tokimasa* was afraid that if the *Heishi* found out about his daughter and *Yoritomo*, the *Hojo* family would get into trouble. So, he planned to have *Masako* marry somebody else. But she eloped with *Yoritomo* the night before the wedding. It is said that this story was written in the famous Japanese history book called "*Azuma Kagami*:

吾妻鏡" and in a few other books. People started to believe this is how it happened between them. However, some say the story may not be exactly how it happened. In the meantime, in Kyoto, the *Heishi* became very powerful and tyrannical in the central government called *Chotei* (朝廷) and suppressed the opponents. All the angry, dissatisfied groups formed an army to attack the *Heishi*. *Minamoto no Yoritomo* was the head of those opposing groups, and his army grew bigger and stronger with the help of *Masako*'s father, *Hojo Tokimasa*. By this time, *Hojo Tokimasa* had realized he would have had a better chance if he had sided with his son-in-law. The *Genji*'s army pushed the *Heishi* all the way to the southern part of Japan. The *Heishi* was defeated in a place called *Dan no Ura* (壇ノ浦) near *Kyushu* (九州) in 1185.

Yoritomo set up *Kamakura Bakufu* (*Kamakura* government) in Kamakura. After *Yoritomo*'s death, his wife *Masako* proved herself as an able leader, and she saved *Kamakura Bakufu* when it was attacked by *Chotei,* the central government.

Here is one famous story about her. When *Yoritomo* used to go around to see other women in the town of Kamakura, *Masako* sent her men to follow her husband and had them set fire on the house of the woman whom her husband was after. In her mind, the *Hojo* was the one who made *Yoritomo* the head of the *Kamakura Bakufu*. Without aid from the *Hojo family*, *Yoritomo* had no chance to be what he became.

Tsurugaoka Hachimangu in Kamakura (鶴岡八幡宮) Author: Urashimataro from Wikipedia   Photo is public domain

Tsurugaoka Hachimangu is one of the major shrines in *Kamakura*. It is a walking distance from *Kamakura* train station. In the photo above, there is a big shrine at the top of the long steps. Every year on Dec 31, a large number of people come to the shrine to listen to the *Joya-no-Kane* (除夜の鐘: the night watch bells on New Year's Eve)

Minamoto-no-Yoshitsune (源義経)

Minamoto-no-Yoritomo (源頼朝) had several half-brothers. *Taira-no-Kiyomori* (平清盛) saved those young boys' lives on the condition that they would become a monk when they grew up. For *Kiyomori,* they were childhood friend's sons, after all. One of them was *Ushiwak- maru* (牛若丸: later *Minamoto-no-Yoshitsune* 源義経) who was raised by *Taira-no-Kiyomori* while he was an infant, believing *Kiyomori* was his father. Later *Yoshitsune* was raised in *Kurama Yama* Temple.

He spent his life there until he became mid-teens. After that, he went to live with the *O-shu Fujiwara* (奥州藤原) family. They were in the northern part of Japan, quite some distance away from Kyoto. *O-shu Fujiwara* was a very wealthy clan. They had a luxurious culture there. Because of the distance from *Chotei* (central government), they behaved as if they were living in an independent country. They created great wealth by mining gold and trading it with some countries outside of Japan.

Yoshitsune lived there rather happily for a while, but when he heard his half-brother *Yoritomo* raised an army to attack the *Heishi*, he decided to join them. *Yoshitsune* was quite skillful in the battles. He won many famous battles, which were very critical for *Genji* to win the war.

Yoritomo had a big political plan on how to proceed to take over the *Heishi's* power. But *Yoshitusune* did not understand that. He was a good warrior but not a politician. That made *Yoritomo* irritated and angry at him. On top of that, *Yoshitsune* became very popular in Kyoto. That made *Yoritomo* anxious, and he decided to get rid of Yoshitsune.

Yoshitsune fled to *O-shu Fujiwara*. In the beginning, *O-shu Fujiwara* protected *Yoshitsune* but could not hold against *Yoritomo's* army. *Yoritomo* destroyed *O-shu Fujiwara* entirely at the end. Today, a grand architecture built by *O-shu Fujiwara* was restored. You can visit "*Konjiki-do:* 金色堂" inside the "*Chuson-ji* Temple: 中尊寺."

Chinese knew about the wealth of *O-shu Fujiwara*. Later, Marco Polo heard about the wealthy small country further into the East. He mentioned this wealthy small island in his book, "*The travels of Marco Polo*." In this book, he wrote, "All the houses are made of gold," this described *O-shu Fujiwara*. Of course, all the houses were not made of gold.

Marco Polo introduced Japan as "Zipangu" in his book. It means the golden country. The name "Zipangu" evolved into Japan. However, we, the Japanese, don't call our country Japan. We call it "Nihon" or "Nippon," and both are correct.

40|Part 2 of -- 7 Overview of the Kamakura Period Sword

This is the second part of Chapter 7, Overview of the Kamakura Period Swords. Please read Chapter 7 Overview of the Kamakura Period Swords before reading this section.

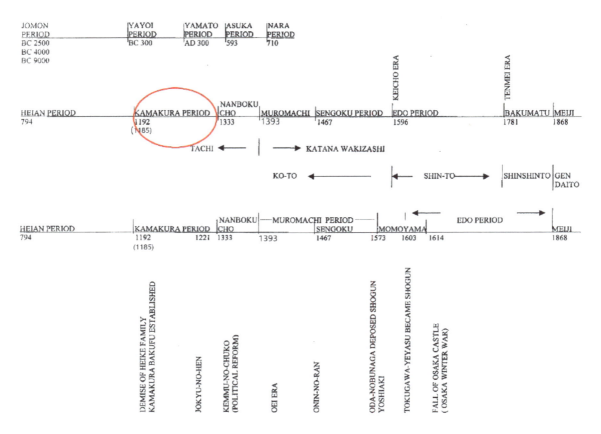

The circle above indicates the time we discuss in this section.

The *Kamakura* period was the golden age of sword making. Approximately half of the well-known swords at present were made during the *Kamakura* period. It is probably because the war between the *Genji* and the *Heishi* demanded many swords, and the swordsmiths improved their swords through the war experience. Also, Emperor *Gotoba* (後鳥羽) invited many skilled swordsmiths to his palace and treated them favorably, and encouraged them to create excellent swords by giving them high ranks. During the *Kamakura* period, the techniques of sword making improved significantly.

Middle Kamakura Period ---- Yamashiro Den (山城伝)

The Middle *Kamakura* period was the height of the *Yamashiro Den*. Among *Yamashiro Den*, there were three major groups (or families). They are *Ayanokoji* group (綾小路),

Awataguchi group (粟田口), and Rai group (来).

Among the Awataguchi group, six swordsmiths received the honor as the "Goban-kaji" from the Emperor Gotoba (後鳥羽上皇). Awataguchi is the name of an area in Kyoto.

Ayanokoji (綾小路) group lived in the Ayanokoji area in Kyoto. My sword textbook had a note that I saw Ayanokoji Sadatoshi (綾小路定利) on March 22nd, 1972. My note was only a few words; it said O-suriage, Funbari, narrow-body, and Ji-nie.

Rai group started from Rai Kuniyuki (来国行). Rai Kuniyuki and Ayanokoji Sadatoshi are said to have had a close friendship. Rai Kuniyuki created many well-known swords. His famous Fudo Kuniyuki (不動国行) was owned by Shogun Ashikaga Yoshiteru (足利義輝), then changed hand to Matsunaga Danjo (松永弾正), then to Oda Nobunaga (織田信長) to Akechi Mitsuhide (明智光秀), then to Toyotomi Hideyoshi (豊臣秀吉). They were all historically famous powerful Daimyo. It is said that Toyotomi Hideyoshi held this sword for the memorial service of Oda Nobunaga. Rai Kuniyuki's son was Niji Kunitoshi. He also created well-known swords.

Middle Kamakura Period ----- Bizen Den (備前伝)

The Bizen Den during the Heian period was called Ko-bizen. They are similar to the one in the Yamashiro Den style. The true height of the Bizen Den was in the Middle Kamakura period. The Bizen area (today's Okayama prefecture) had many ideal aspects for sword making: the good climate, the good production of iron, the abundant wood for fuel, and the convenient location. Naturally, many swordsmiths moved there, and it became a major place to produce swords.

The Bizen region produced many swords whose quality level was higher than other sword groups and more famous swordsmiths.
Fukuoka Ichimonji Norimune (則宗) and his son Sukemune (助宗) received the honor of the Goban-kaji from the Emperor Gotoba. Among the Osafune group (長船), famous Mitsutada (光忠) and Nagamitsu (長光) appeared. My father owned four Mitsutada. Three Tachis and one Tanto. He was so proud of owning four Mitsutada that he asked his tailor to monogram Mitsutada on the inside pocket of his suit jacket.

From Hatakeda group (畠田), Hatakeda Moriie (畠田守家), and from Ugai (鵜飼) group, Unsho (雲生) and Unji (雲次) appeared. The famous Kunimune (国宗) also appeared around this time. Because there were many swordsmiths in the Bizen Den, a large number of Bizen swords exist today. Each swordsmith showed his own characteristics on their swords. Therefore, kantei on Bizen swords can be complex.

The classification of the sword ranking from the top
1. Kokuho (国宝: National Treasure)
2. Juyo Bunkazai (重要文化財: Important Cultural Property)
3. Juyo Bijutu-hin (重要美術品: Important Artwork)
4. Juyo Token (重要刀剣: Important Sword)   more to follow

Below are my father's four *Bizen Osafune Mitsutada*. He took those pictures many years ago at home. You can see he was not much of a photographer. He wrote the name of the swordsmith, the period the sword was made, the name(s) of *Daimyo* who owned it in the past, and the classification on a rectangular white paper.

　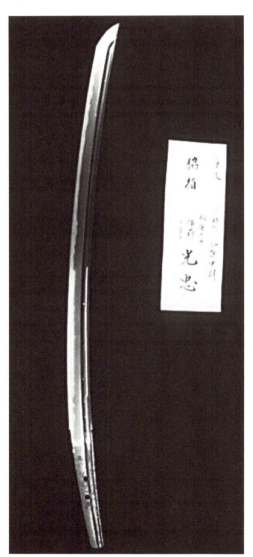

Osafune Mitsutada (長船光忠: Juyo Bunkazai)　　Osafune Mitsutada (長船光忠: Juyo Bunkazai)

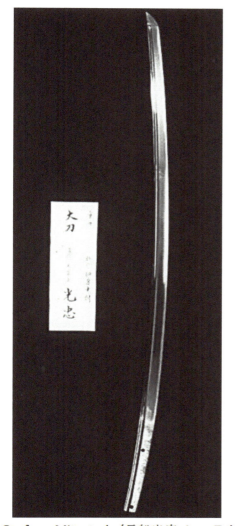 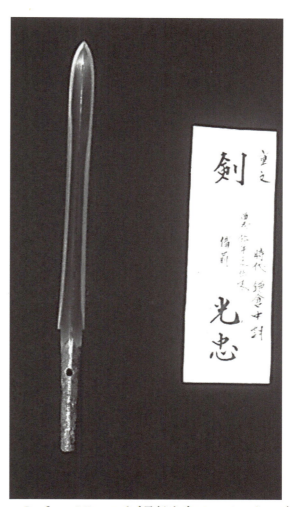

Osafune Mitsutada (長船光忠: Juyo Token)   Osafune Mitsutada (長船光忠: Juyo Bunkazai)

Late Kamakura Period ----- Soshu Den (相州伝)

Yamashiro Den started to decline in the latter part of the *Kamakura* Period. At this time, many swordsmiths moved to the *Kamakura* area under the new power of *Kamakura Bakufu* (鎌倉幕府) by the *Hojo* clan. The new group, *Soshu Den* (相州伝), started to emerge. *Fukuoka Ichimonji Sukezane* (福岡一文字助真) and *Kunimune* (国宗) from *Bizen* moved to *Kamakura*. *Toroku Sakon Kunitsuna* (藤六左近国綱) from *Awataguchi* group of *Yamashiro Den* moved to Kamakura. Those three are the ones who originated the *Soshu Den* in Kamakura. *Kunitsuna's* son is *Tosaburo Yukimitsu,* and his son is the famous *Masamune* (正宗). Outside of Kamakura area, *Yamashiro Rai Kunitsugu* (来国次), *Go-no-Yoshihiro* (郷義弘) from *Ettshu* (越中) province, *Samoji* (左文字) from *Chikuzen* province (筑前) were the active swordsmiths.

41 | Part 2 of -- 8 Middle Kamakura Period: Yamashiro Den (山城伝)

This chapter is a detailed part of Chapter 8. Please read Chapter 8 before reading this section.

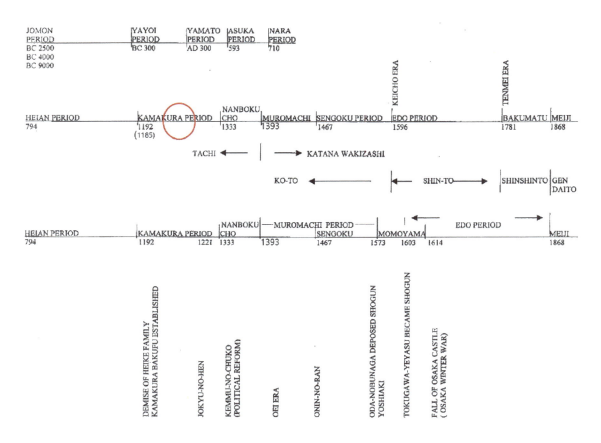

The circle indicates the time we discuss in this section

During the middle *Kamakura* period, there were three main groups among the *Yamashiro Den*. They were *Ayano-koji* (綾小路) group, *Awataguchi* (粟田口) group, and *Rai* (来) group.

When we refer to a particular group, we call it *"xxx ha," "xxx ippa,* "or *"xxx ichimon."* We use those three terms interchangeably. They all basically mean "group." For example, when we say *Ayano-koji ippa*, we mean *Ayano-koji* group.

<u>Ayano-Koji Ippa (綾小路)</u>

Sugata (shape) -----------------In general, gentle or graceful *Kyo-zori* shape. The difference in the width between the *Yokote* line and *Machi* is not much. The sword is slender yet thick. Small *Kissaki*.

Hi and Engraving ------------------------ *Bo-hi* (single groove) or *Futasuji-hi* (double grooves)

Hamon ---------------------- *Nie* base with *Ko-choji* (small clove shape) and *Ko-midare* (small irregular). Small *Inazuma* (lightning-like line) and *Kinsuji* (golden streak) may show. Double *Ko-choji* (two *Ko-choji* side by side) may appear.

Boshi (tempered line at kissaki area) ------------------------ *Ko-maru* (small round), *Yakizume* (refer to the illustration below), and *Kaen* (flame-like pattern)

Ji-hada --------------- Small wood grain with a little *Masame* (straight grain). *Ji-nie* shows.

Nakago (hilt) --------------------------- Long, slightly fat feeling

Ayano-koji Ippa swordsmiths ----------Ayano-koji Sadatoshi (綾小路定利) Sadanori (定則)

Awataguchi Ichimon (粟田口)

Many swordsmiths from the *Awataguchi Ichimon* (or *Awataguchi* group) received the honor of the *Goban Kaji* (best swordsmith) from *Gotoba Joko* (Emperor *Gotoba* 後鳥羽上皇). Their general characteristic is as follows.

Sugata (Shape) ------------------ Elegant *Torii-zori* (or *Kyo-zori*) shape

Hi and Engraving -------------- The tip of the *Hi* comes all the way up and fill in the *Ko-shinogi*. The end of the *hi* can be *Maru-dome* (the end is round), *Kaku-dome* (the end is square), or *Kakinagashi*.

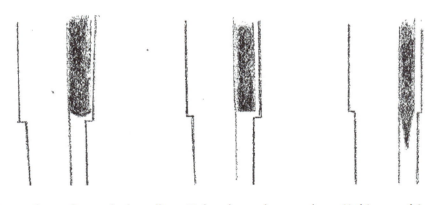

Maru-dome (rounded end)   *Kaku-dome* (square)   *Kakinagashi*

Hamon ------------- The slightly wider tempered line at the bottom, then it becomes narrower at the top. *Nie* base (this is called *Nie-hon'i*). Straight tempered line mixed with *Ko-choji* (small cloves) *or* wide straight line mixed with *Choji*. *Awataguchi-nie* appears. *Awataguchi-nie* means a fine, deep, and sharp, shiny *Nie appears* around the tempered line area. Fine *Inazuma* (lightning-like line) and *Kinsuji* (golden streak) appear.

Boshi (tempered line at kissaki area) ------------ Both *Ko-maru* (small round) and/or *O-maru* (large round). The return is sharrow. *Yakizume, Nie-kuzure,* and *Kaen* (flame).

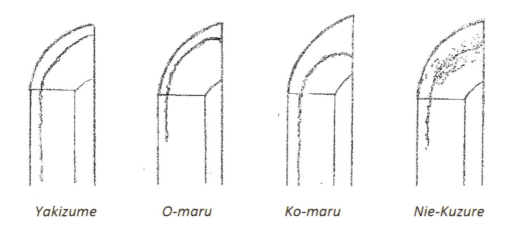

Yakizume   O-maru   Ko-maru   Nie-Kuzure

Ji-hada -------------- Fine *Ko-mokume* (wood swirls) with *Ji-nie*. *Ji-nie* is *Nie* on *Ji-hada*. *Yubashiri* and/or *Chikei* appear.

Nakago ------------------ Often two-letter inscription

Awataguchi Ichimon swordsmiths------------------ Awataguchi Kunitomo (粟田口国友), Hisakuni (久国), Kuniyasu (国安), and Kunikiyo (国清)

Rai Ha (来)

The general characteristics of the *Rai* group are as follows. However, each swordsmith has his own characteristics.

Sugata (shape) --------------- Graceful with dignity. Thick body. *Rai* forged *Ikubi Kissaki*.

Hi and Engravings ------------------------- Wide and shallow *Hi*.

Hamon --------------------------- *Nie* base. *Suguha* (straight). Wide *suguha* with *Ko-midare* (small irregular) and *Choji* (cloves). Sometimes large *Choji* at the lower part and narrow *Suguha* at the top. *Inazuma* and *Kinsuji* appear around the *yokote* area.

Boshi ----------------------------------- *Komaru, Yakizume* (refer to the illustration above)

Ji-hada --------------------- Finely forged *Itame* (small wood grain). Sometimes mixed with *Masame* (parallel grain). Fine *Nie*. *Rai* group's swords sporadically show *Yowai Tetsu* (weak surface), which may be the core iron.

Rai Ha swordsmiths---------------------- Rai Kuniyuki (来国行), Rai Kunitoshi (来国俊) or Niji Kunitoshi (二字国俊), Ryokai (了戒). *Rai Kunitoshi* is said to be *Rai Kuniyuki's* son. *Ryokai* is said to be *Rai Kunitoshi 's* son.

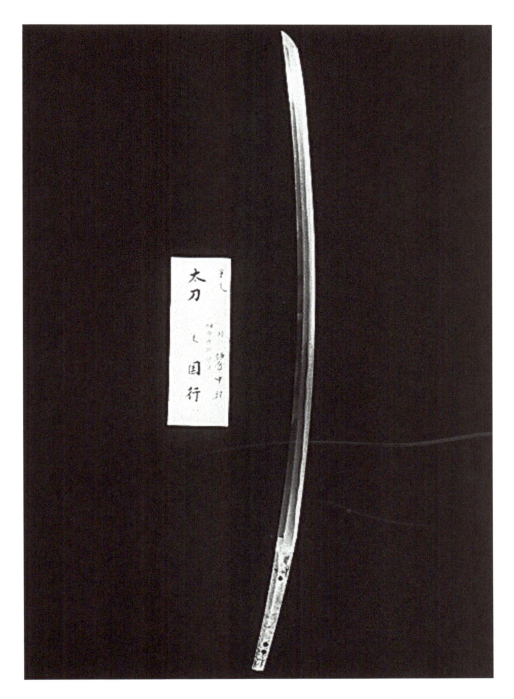

Rai Kuniyuki (来国行)　Once my family sword, photo taken by my father with his writing.

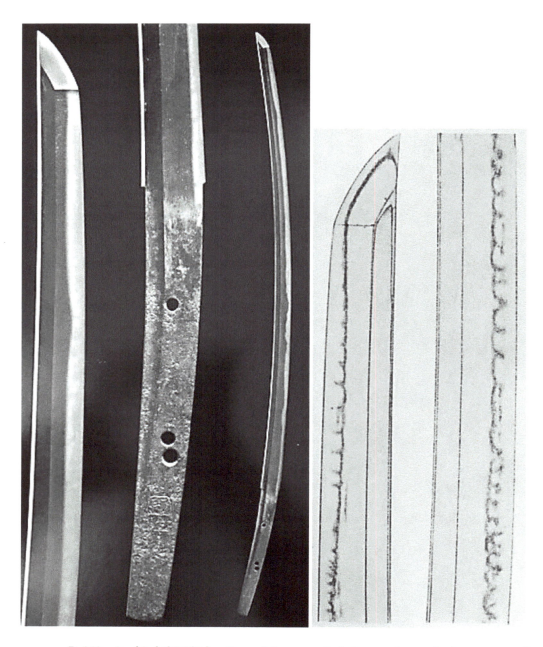

Rai Kuniyuki （来国行） Sano Museum Catalogue (permission granted)

42 | Part 2 of -- 9 Middle Kamakura Period: Bizen Den (備前伝)

This chapter is a detailed part of Chapter 9. Please read Chapter 9 Middle Kamakura Period (Bizen Den) before reading this section.

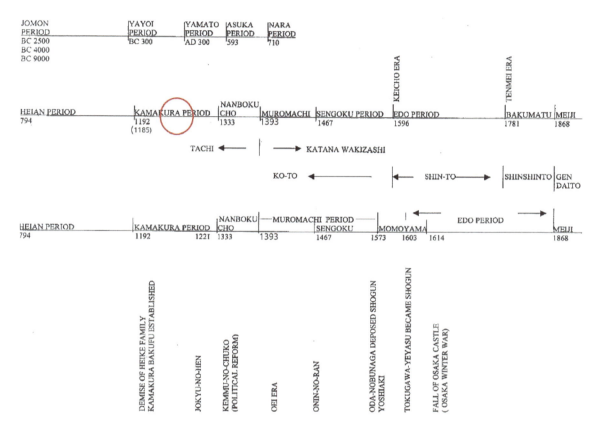

The circle above indicates the time we discuss in this section

The middle *Kamakura* period was the height of the *Bizen Den*. In different regions other than *Bizen,* swords styles often reflected people's preferences and politics in the particular area. But the *Bizen* sword had its own style and was not affected much by those elements throughout the time. The clients of *Bizen* swords came from all over the country. Therefore, the *Bizen* swordsmiths created the swords liked by everybody.

The general style of Bizen Den

- In general, their style is likable by everybody.
- The shape, the width of the blade, the thickness of the body, and the tempered line are a standard size or usual design, seldom out of the ordinary.

- *Nioi* base
- Soft feeling *Ji-gane* (steel)
- *Utsuri* (cloud-like shadow) appears.
- The tempered line tends to have the same width, not too wide, not too narrow.

Fukuoka Ichimonji group

Names of swordsmiths among *Fukuoka Ichimonji* group
Fukuoka Ichimonji Norimune (福岡一文字則宗), *Fukuoka Ichimonji Sukemune* (福岡一文字助宗). Those two were the main swordsmiths among the *Fukuoka Ichomonji* group (福岡一文字). From this group, six swordsmiths including *Norimune* and *Sukemune* received the honor as the "*Gobankaji*" from Emperor *Gotoba* (後鳥羽上皇). I saw *Fukuoka Ichimonji Muneyoshi* (福岡一文字宗吉) at *Mori Sensei's* class on June 25, 1972. My note pointed out a lot of *Utsuri* (shadow) on the blade.

Sugata (shape) -------------------- Graceful and classy shape. Generally, well-proportioned shape. The difference between the top width and bottom width is not much. Sometimes stout-looking *Kissaki* like *Ikubi-kissak* (refer Chapter 11 Ikubi Kissaki (猪首切先)) appears.

Hi and Engraving -------------The tip of *Hi* may follow the *Ko-shinogi* line. See below. The end of *Hi* goes under *Machi* ending with square, or *Kakinagashi* (refer to Chapter 41)

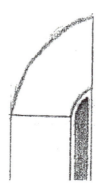

Hamon ---------- Wide *Ichimonji-choji* tempered line. It means the same width tempered line from the bottom to the top. The same *Hamon* front and back. *O-choji-midare* (large clove-like pattern), *Juka-choji* (overwrapped-looking *Choji*). *Nioi* base. *Inazuma* and/or *Kinsuji* appear.

Boshi -------------- Same *Hamon* continues into the *Boshi* area and ends with *Yakizume* or turn slightly. Sometimes *O-maru*.

Jihada ----------- Fine and a soft look. *Itame* (woodgrain pattern). Lots of *Utsuri* (cloud-like shadow or reflection)

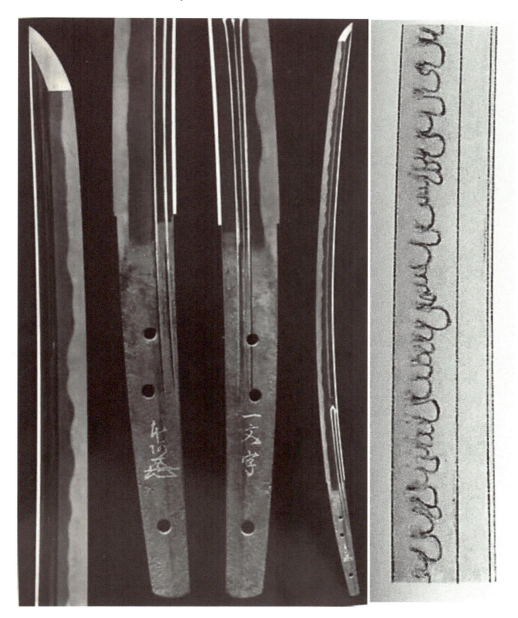

Ichimonji Sano Museum Catalogue (佐野美術館) (permission granted)

*The sword above is *O-suriage*. The end of the *Hi* is lower than the *Mekugi-ana* inside *Nakago*.

43|Part 2 of -- 10 Jokyu-no-Ran & Gotoba Joko (承久の乱)

This chapter is a continued part of Chapter 10, Jyokyu-no-Ran (承久の乱) 1221. Please read Chapter 10 before reading this section.

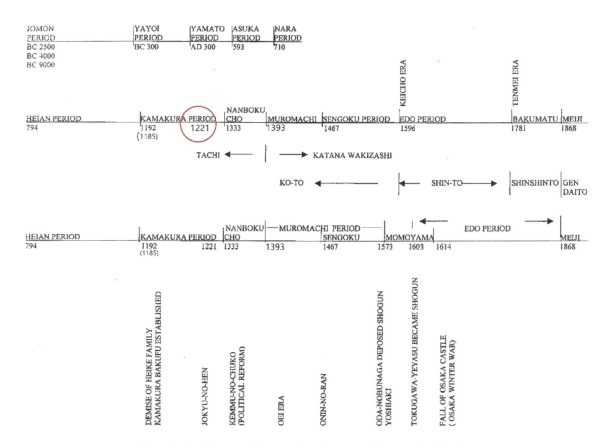

The circle above indicates the time we discuss in this chapter.

Chapter 10 described how *Jokyu-no-Ran* (承久の乱) had started. In the end, Emperor *Gotoba* (or *Gotoba Joko*) was exiled to *Oki* Island (隠岐の島).

Emperor *Gotoba* was a very talented man in many fields. He was very good at *Waka* (和歌), Japanese short poem.   To compose *Waka,* you are required to include several elements such as scenery, a season, one's inner feeling with the refined sentiment, or the surrounding state within the very limited number of words. It requires a literary talent. He was also good at equestrianism, *Kemari* (a ball game for upper-classmen at that time), swimming, *Sumo* wrestling, music, archery, swordsmanship, calligraphy painting, and even sword-making. His contribution toward the sword field created the golden age of sword making in the middle *Kamakura* period. Surprisingly, *Gotoba Joko* was not just good at things in many different areas, but he mastered them to the top level. Especially his *Waka* (poetry) was highly regarded. He edited *Shin Kokin Wakashu* (新古今集), which was a collection of 1980 *Waka* poems.

Emperor Gotoba, Enthroned at the Age Four

Emperor *Gotoba* was enthroned at the age of four (some say three). The problem was Emperor *Antoku* had already existed at the same time. They were both about the same age. Two emperors at the same time was a big problem. How did it happen?

To have a new emperor, the head of the emperor's family must appoint the next emperor. While the Emperor *Go-Shirakawa* (後白河天皇) was in jail, Emperor *Antoku* was set by *Taira no Kiyomori* (平清盛). Though *Kiyomori* was the head of the *Heishi*, the most powerful *Samurai* group, he was not from the emperor's family. That was against the tradition. This was not acceptable for Go-*Shirakawa* Emperor (後白河天皇). Emperor *Go-Shirakawa* was furious at *Taira no Kiyomori* and picked Emperor *Gotoba* and enthroned him. This is the reason why two emperors coexisted.

There was one more thing. To be an emperor, the emperor must have *Sanshu-no-Jingi* (三種の神器: Three imperial regalia); There are three items the emperor must have to be a legitimate emperor. They are a mirror, a sacred sword, and a *Magatama* (jewelry)*.

But *Sanshu-no-Jingi* were taken by the *Heike* family together with Emperor *Antoku* when they fled from the *Genji*. The *Heike* clan was pushed by the *Genji* all the way to *Dan-no-Ura* (壇ノ浦), and they were defeated there. *Dan-no-Ura* is a sea between *Kyushu* (九州) and *Honshu* (本州). When it became clear for the *Heike* family that they were defeated, all the *Heike* people, including the young Emperor *Antoku,* jumped into the sea and drowned. They took *Sanshu-no-Jingi* with them into the ocean.

Later, people searched for the *Sanshu-no-Jingi* frantically; however, they recovered only the *Jewelry* and the *Mirror* but not the Sword. Because of the tradition, the emperor must have *Sanshu-no-Jingi*; otherwise, he was not recognized as a legitimate emperor. *Gotoba Joko* was tormented for a long time for not having all three.

Today, the *Jewelry* is with the present Emperor family, and the *Mirror* is with *Ise Jingu* Shrine (伊勢神宮). The *Sword* is still missing somewhere in the ocean. Some say that the lost Sword down into the sea was a copy and one kept at *Atsuta Jingu* Shrine (熱田神宮) is the real one.

* *Sanshu-no-Jingi* (三種の神器)--------------- 1. The *Sword*; *Kusanagi-no-Tsurugi* (草薙の剣) 2. The *Mirror*; *Yata-no-Kagami* (八咫の鏡), 3. The *Magatama* (Jewelry); *Yasakani-no-Magatama* (八尺瓊勾玉) by Token World: www.touken-world.jp/tips/32747/

Politics by Emperor Gotoba

Emperor *Gotoba* wanted political power back from the *Kamakura Bakufu*. He was a very impulsive, passionate, unpredictable quick-tempered person. He tried to revive the *Chotei* (朝廷) power. The *Chotei* is the central government controlled by the emperor and aristocrats. Emperor *Gotoba* decided to rely on the armed forces to achieve this goal. He set up a *Saimen no Bushi* (armed forces directly under Emperor *Gotoba's* command).

When he saw *Minamoto no Sanetomo* was killed, he realized *Kamakura Bakufu* must have been in turmoil. Thinking this was a good chance, he sent out the emperor's order to all the *Daimyo* to fight against *Kamakura Bakufu*. He expected an easy victory, but *Kamakura Bushi* was united tightly and fought well under *Hojo Masako's* leadership, the "Nun Shogun." She organized one tightly united armed force, whereas the Emperor *Gotoba* side was not very organized. They were not used to fighting.

In the end, the Emperor *Gotoba* side lost. When he realized he had lost, he claimed it was not him, but his men did it independently. He insisted that it had nothing to do with him. Therefore, it was wrong to punish him. But of course, *Hojo Masako* and *Kamakura* Bakufu did not believe Emperor *Gotoba* and exiled him to *Oki* Island. Emperor *Gotoba* ended his life there. Although he was so smart and accomplished in so many different fields, he could not win against the grandma "Nun-*shogun*," *Hojo Masako*.

Sword-Making by Gotoba Joko

Gotoba Joko had a superior ability to evaluate swords, and he became the superior swordsmith himself. He invited many top-level swordsmiths from different sword groups to his court, gave them a title, and treated them respectfully. Also, he made them his instructors and assistants. *Gotoba Joko* brought in skilled swordsmiths from many different places in rotation. Those who were invited to the palace were called *Gobankaji* (御番鍛冶), an honorary title. On the Sword he created, he inscribed a chrysanthemum with 16 petals. The present emperor still uses this design as the emperor's crest. The Sword with the chrysanthemum design is called *Kiki Gosaku* (菊御作).

Today, you can visit the Emperor *Gotoba* Museum on *Oki* Island, and there are a few sites that are believed to be the emperor's sword-making site. Some people say it is debatable if the sites are real. Today, *Oki* Island is a beautiful resort island. It can be reached by ferries from *Shimane* Prefecture, which takes about 2 hours by boat. Also, it can be reached by airplane directly from Osaka.

Gotoba Joko, owned by Minase Shrine (This picture is Public domain)

44| Part 2 of -- 11 Ikubi-kissaki (猪首切先)

This chapter is a detailed chapter of Chapter 11, Ikubi Kissaki. Please read Chapter 11 before reading this section.

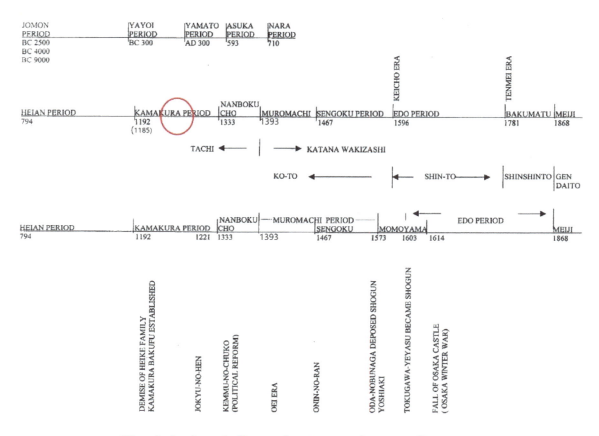

The circle above indicates the time we discuss in this section.

The middle *Kamakura* period was the golden age of sword making. We cannot deny it was because *Gotoba Joko* (refer to Chapter 10 and Chapter 43) honored the skilled swordsmiths highly. After the *Jokyu-no-ran*, *Samurai* began to prefer grand-looking swords. Those were *Ikubi-kissaki* swords. It is said that there were no mediocre swords among the *Ikubi -kissaki* swords. In this chapter, we discuss the swordsmiths who were famous for *Ikubi Kissaki.*

Bizen Osafune Mitsutada (備前長船光忠)

Bizen Osafune Mitsutada is one of the most famous swordsmiths for *Ikubi-kissaki.* His swords are the most sought-after swords among sword collectors. He was the founder of the *Osafune* group, followed by his son *Nagamitsu* (長光), then grandson *Kagemitsu*

(景光), and the rest of the descendants.

Sugata (shape) ------------------------- Grand look with *Ikubi-kissaki*. The body is relatively thick with *Hamaguri-ha* (refer to Chapter 11 Ikubi Kissaki). Often *suriage*.

Hi (engraving) ------------------------- Often *Bo-hi* (wide groove). The end of *Bo-hi* above *Machi* often shows *Kakudome* (square end).

Hamon (Tempered line) -------------------- *Yakihaba* (*the Hamon* width) is a mixture of wide and narrow *Hamon*. *Nioi* base. Large *Choji*, *Kawazuko-choji* (tadpole head shape, refer to the illustration below second from the last), *Inazuma,* and *Kinsuji* (refer to the drawing in Chapter 14 Late Kamakura Period Sword).

Boshi -------------------------------------- *Yakizume*. *Yakizume* with a short turn back.

Ji-hada -------------------------------------- Fine and soft look surface. *Chikei* appears.

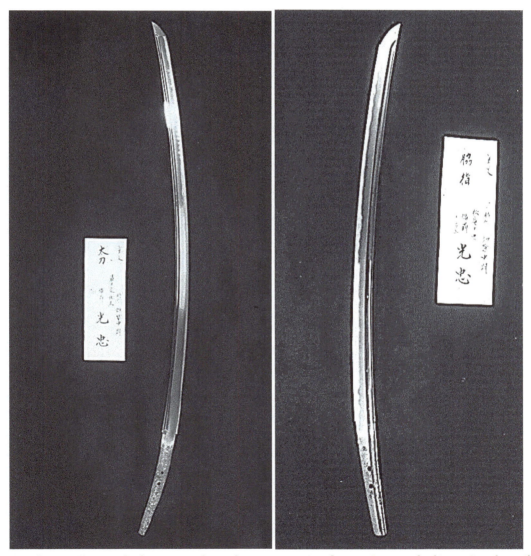

Osafune Mitsutada (Juyo Bunkazai)   Osafune Mitsutada (Juyo Bunkazai)

 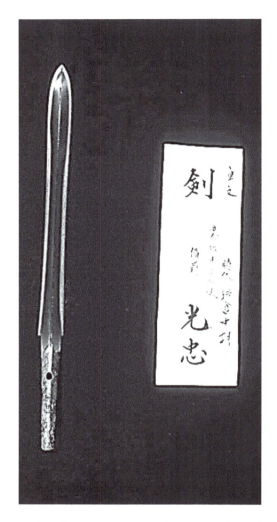

Osafune Mitsutada (Juyo Token) Osafune Mitsutada (Juyo Bunkazai)
Above 4, once my family sword

I displayed the above four photos several times on other pages. Those were *Mitsutada* swords that my father used to own. My father did the calligraphy and took these pictures for himself. He was very proud that he had collected four *Mitsutada* swords, and he had the name, "Mitsutada," monogrammed inside his suit jacket. It is said that *Oda Nobunaga* (織田信長), with his wealth and political power, collected 28 *Mitsutada* swords.

I know those photos are not so good. To avoid any possible infringement on copyrights or intellectual property rights, photos are limited to my father's photographs (not so wonderful, though), Sano Museum Catalog photos (permission granted), some public domain photos from Wikipedia, and a few sources. Please bear with me that I don't have good pictures.

Bizen Osafune Nagamitsu (備前長船長光)

Nagamitsu is *Mitsutada's* son.

Sugata --------------- Shape is similar to the early *Kamakura* period style, which is with *Funbari* and narrow at the top. This is called *Nagamitsu Sugata*.

Hamon -------------- Wide tempered line. *Nioi* base. *O-choji Midare* (large clove shape) mixed with *Kawazuko-choji* (see below). Many *Ashi* appear. Also, he does *Suguha-choji* (straight with *Choji* mixed). Works of *Inazuma* and *Kinsuji* shows.

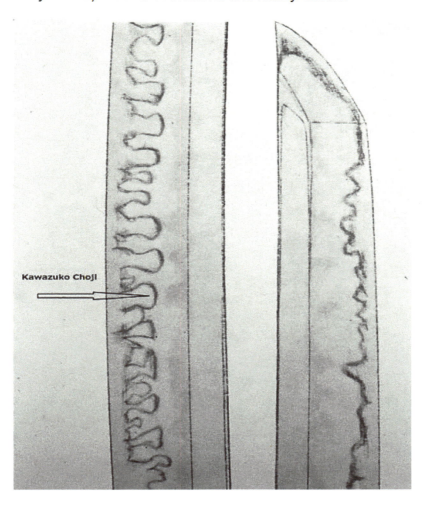

Kawazuko Choji (tadpole head like) Sano Museum Catalogue (permission granted) *Kawazuko Choji* on the sword above is very clear that it is almost a textbook-like example. But usually, they are not as apparent as this.

Boshi ---------------------- *Yakizume* or turn back a little.

Ji-hada --------------------- Fine wood grain pattern. Well known for *Utsuri* (shadow). *Choji Utsuri* (Shadow of *Choji*) or *Botan Utsuri* (resembles flower peony). *Choji Utsuri* shows in the above picture.

The next poster is for an exhibit of swords at the Museum of Tetsu (iron) in *Sakaki, Nagano*, in 2003. The center objects in the poster are *Nagamitsu's* sword and it's *Koshirae* (scabbard). It was our family sword then. *Toyotomi Hideyoshi* (豊臣秀吉), a great *Daimyo* in *the Sengoku* period, awarded this sword to his famous war strategist, *Takenaka Hannbei* (竹中半兵衛).

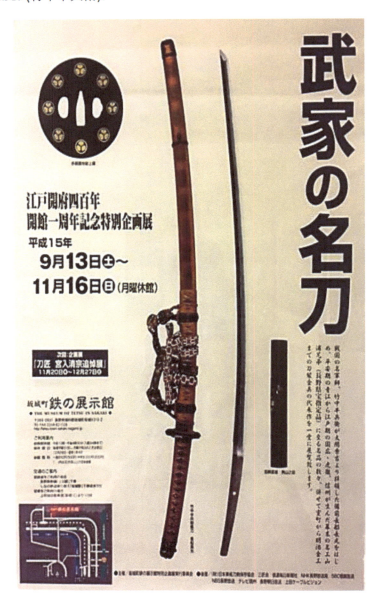

45| part 2 of -- 11 Ikubi Kissaki (猪首切先)
continued from Chapter 44.

This chapter is a detailed part of Chapter 11 Ikubi-kissaki and continued from Chapter 44|Part 2 of 11 Ikubi-kissaki Sword. Please read Chapter 11 and Chapter 45 before reading this section.

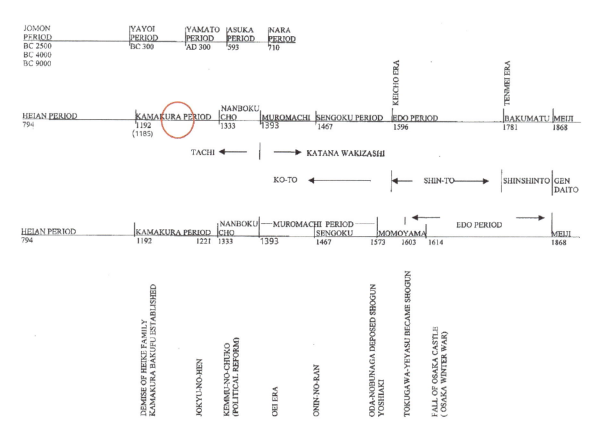

The circle above indicates the time we discuss in this section

Bizen Saburo Kunimune (備前三郎国宗)

Another swordsmith that should be mentioned in this section is *Bizen Saburo Kunimune* (備前三郎国宗). In the middle *Kamakura* period, the *Hojo* clan invited top swordsmiths to the *Kamakura* area. *Awataguchi Kunitsuna* (粟田口国綱) from *Yamashiro* of *Kyoto*, *Fukuoka Ichimonji Sukezane* (福岡一文字助真) from *Bizen* area, *Bizen Kunimune* (備前国宗) from *Bizen* area moved to *Kamakura* with their circle of people. Those three groups started the *Soshu Den* (相州伝). Refer to Chapter 14, Late Kamakura Period swords.

Sugata (shape) ---------------------------- *Ikubi-kissaki* style. Sometimes *Chu-gissaki*. Thick body. Narrow *Shinogi* width. *Koshi-zori*.

Horimono (Engravings) ----------------------------------- Often narrow *Bo-hi* (single groove)

Hamon (Tempered line) -------------*O-choji Midare* (irregular large clove shape) with *Ashi*. Or *Ko-choji Midare* (irregular small clove shape) with *Ashi*. *Nioi* base with *Ji-nie* (*Nie* in the *Hada* area). Some *Hamon* is squarish with less *Kubire* (less narrow at the bottom of the clove). *Hajimi* (刃染み rough surface) may show. Often the *Kunimune* swords are as follows; the lower part shows *Choji*, the upper part shows less work without *Ashi*.

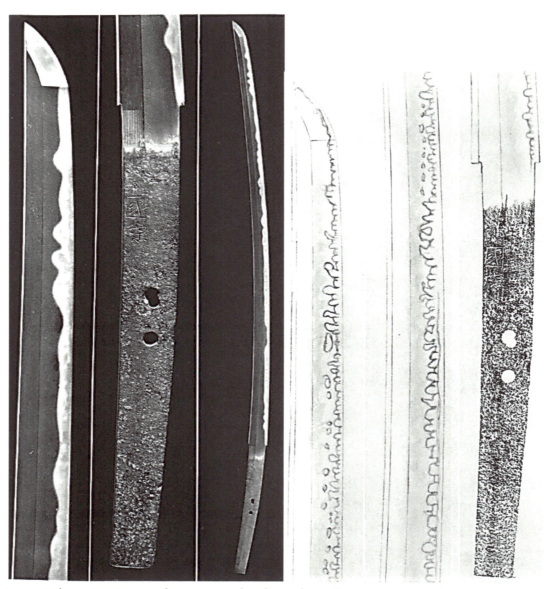

Bizen Saburo Kunimune (備前三郎国宗)   Photo from "Nippon-to Art Sword of Japan," The Walter A. Compton Collection.   National Treasure

Boshi ----- Small irregular. *Yakizume* or short turn back

Ji-hada -----Wood-grain. Fine *Ji-hada* with some *Ji-nie* (*Nie* inside *Ji-hada*). *Midare-utsuri* (irregular shadow) shows. A few *Hajimi* (rough surface).

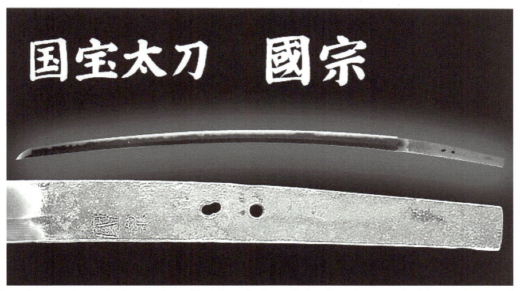

The above photo is from the official website of the *Terukuni Jinja* Shrine in Kyushu. http://terukunijinja.p-kit.com/page222400.html

This is the National Treasure, *Kunimune,* preserved at *Terukuni Jinja* Shrine in Kagoshima prefecture. See the photos on the previous page. This *Kunimune* sword was lost after WWII. Dr. Compton, the board chairman of Miles Laboratories in Elkhart, Indiana, found it in Atlanta's antique store. I mentioned Dr. Compton in Chapter 32 Japanese Swords after WWII. When he saw this sword, he realized this was not just an ordinary sword. He bought it and inquired to the *Nihon Bijutu Token Hozon Kyokai* (The Japanese Sword Museum) in Tokyo. It turned out to be the famous missing National Treasure, *Kunimune,* from *Terukuni Jinja* shrine. He returned the sword to the shrine without compensation in 1963.

My father became a good friend of his around this time through Dr. *Homma* and Dr. *Sato* (both were leading sword experts). Later, Dr. Compton asked Dr. *Honma* and my father to examine his swords he had in his house (he had many swords) and swords at The Metropolitan Museum of Arts in New York, Philadelphia Museum of Art, and Museum of Fine Arts, Boston. My father wrote about this trip and the swords he examined in those museums and published the book in 1965; the title was *"Katana Angya* (刀行脚)*."*

For Dr. Compton and my father, those days must have been the best time of their lives. Their businesses were doing well and they were able to spend a lot of time on their interests and had fun. It was the best time for me, too. One time, while I was visiting Compton's house, he showed me his swords in his basement for hours, almost all day. His house was huge, and the basement he built as his study had a fire prevention system, and the lighting system was perfect to view swords and other art objects.

Phoebe, his wife, said to him that he shouldn't keep a young girl (college student then) in the basement all day. He agreed and took me to his cornfield to pick some corn for dinner. From a basement to a cornfield, not much improvement? So, Phoebe decided to take me shopping and lunch in Chicago. Good idea, but it was too far. Compton's house was Elkhart, Indiana. The distance between Elkhart and Chicago was about two and a half hours by car. It was too far just for shopping and lunch. To my surprise, the company's employee flew us and landed on the rooftop of a department store, then did the shopping, had lunch, and flew back.

Miles Laboratories and a well-known large Japanese pharmaceutical company had a business tie-up then. Dr. Compton used to come to Japan quite often, officially, for business purposes. But whenever he came to Japan, he spent days with sword people, including my father, and I usually followed him. One of the female workers of this pharmaceutical company, her job description was to translate the sword book into English.

My parents' house was filled with Miles's products. Miles Laboratories had a big research institute in Elkhart, Indiana. I visited there several times. One day, I was sitting with Dr. Compton in his office, looking into a sword book with our heads together. That day, a movie actor, John Forsythe, was visiting the research lab. He was the host of a TV program Miles Laboratories was sponsoring. All female employees were making a big fuss over him. Then he came into Dr. Compton's room to greet him, thinking the chairman must be sitting in his big chair at his desk looking like a chairman. But he saw Dr. Compton looking into the sword book with his head against my head. The appearance of Dr. Compton was just like any chairman of the board of a big company one can imagine, and I was a Japanese college student looking like a college student. John Forsythe showed a strange expression on his face that he did not know what to think.

46|Part 2 of --12 Middle Kamakura Period:Tanto (鎌倉中期短刀)

This chapter is a detailed part of Chapter 12—the Middle Kamakura Period Tanto. Please read Chapter 12 before reading this section.

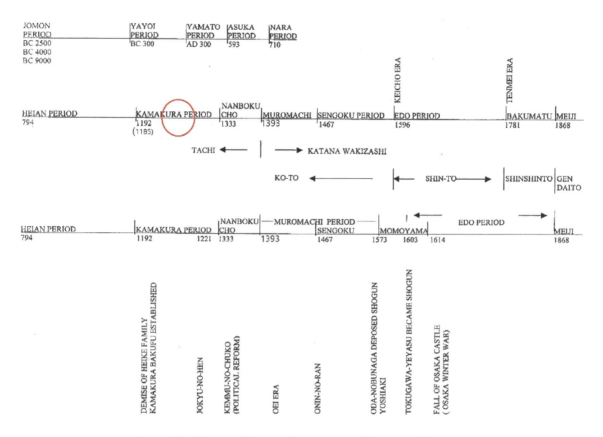

The circle above indicates the time we discuss in this section

In Chapter 12, Middle Kamakura Period: Tanto described that the shape of *Tanto* called *Takenoko-zori* had appeared during the middle *Kamakura* period. This style of *Tanto* curves inward a little at the tip. The drawing below may be a bit exaggerated to show the curve. The real *Takenoko-zori* curvature is not so apparent. Maybe a few millimeters inward.

Usually, the length of the *Tanto* is approximately 12 inches. *Tanto* are described as follows; a *Tanto* of approx. ten inches is called *Josun Tanto* (定寸短刀), longer than ten inches is called *Sun-nobi Tanto* (寸延び短刀), and less than ten inches is called *Sun-zumari Tanto* (寸詰短刀).

Takenoko-zori
(bamboo shoot shape)

Sun-nobi Tanto (寸延び)　>　Josun Tanto (定寸: standard size)　>　Sun-zumari Tanto (寸詰り)
(> 10 inches)　　　　　　　　(approx. 10 inches)　　　　　　　　(< 10 inches)

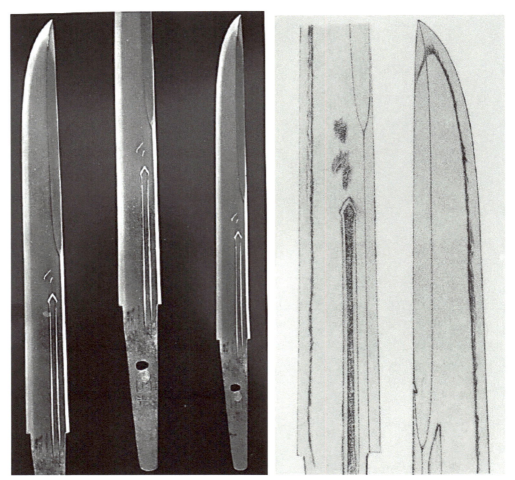

Shintogo Kunimitsu (新藤五国光) Sano Museum Catalogue, permission granted to use

The style above is called *Kanmuri-otoshi* (冠落し); the *Mune* side (opposite side of cutting edge) is shaved off. The length is approximately 10 inches. Woodgrain pattern surface, *Nie* on *Ji* (refer to Chapter 3 Names of parts). Very finely forged. *Hamon* is medium *Suguha* (straight). *Boshi* is *Ko-maru* (small round). Because of the *Kanmuri-otoshi* style, it may not be easy to see the *Takenoko-zori*; the *Mune* side bends inward very slightly. Among the *Tanto* producers, *Shintogo Kunimitsu* is considered as the top *Tanto* maker.

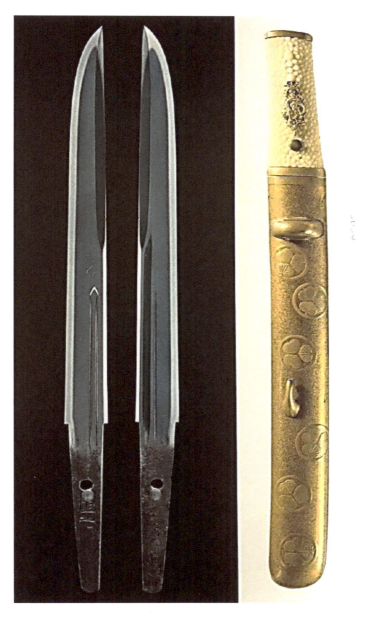

The above photo is also by *Shintogo Kunimitsu* (新藤五国光) with *Saya*. *Saya* is the scabbard. The handle of the scabbard (white part) is made with sharkskin. Both photos are from Sano Museum Catalog "Reborn". Permission granted.

47| Part 2 of --13 Late Kamakura Period: Genko (鎌倉末元寇)

This is a detailed part of Chapter 13 Late Kamakura Period, Genko(鎌倉末元寇). Please read chapter 13 before reading this section.

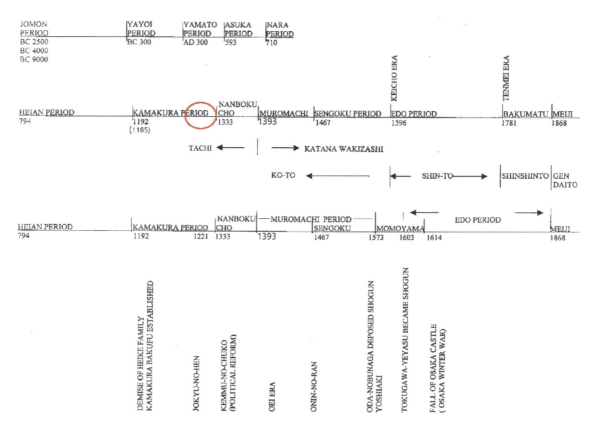

The circle above indicates the time we discuss in this section.

Genko (元寇): Mongolian Invasion

Chapter 13 described the Mongolian invasion simply. Here is a more detailed description. The Mongol Empire was a vast empire that spread between present Mongolia to Eastern Europe from the 13th to the 14th centuries. The grandson of Genghis Kahn, Kublai Kahn, sent several official letters to Japan demanding Japan to become a dependent state of the Mongol Empire (元: Yuan) and ordered to send a tribute to them. They threatened Japan that they would invade if Japan did not follow their demand. *Hojo Tokimune* (北条時宗), who was in power in *Kamakura Bakufu* (government) at the time, refused and ignored the letters many times. That led to the two-time invasions by the Mongol Empire. It is often said that the strong typhoon hit Japan on each occasion and Mongols were pushed away by the two big typhoons.

This is correct, but the real story had a lot more to it.

Bun'ei-no-eki (文永の役) 1274

The first Mongolian invasion was called *Bun'ei-no-eki*. In early October in 1274, Mongol troops (Mongols, Han people, and Koreans) of 40,000 men* departed from the Korean Peninsula on 900* large and small ships and headed to Japan. After they arrived on *Tsushima* Island (対馬), Mongol troops burnt villages and killed many people, including the island people. Village people were captured and sent to the top officials of the Mongols as their slaves. It was a sorrowful scene.

The Mongols moved to *Iki* Island (壱岐の島), to *Hizen* shore (肥前), to *Hirado* Island (平戸), to *Taka* Island (鷹島), then to *Hakata* Bay (博多). In each place, the disastrous sad scene was the same as everywhere. On each battlefield, Japanese soldiers and villagers were killed in large numbers. The *Kamakura Bukufu* sent a large number of *Samurai* troops to the battlefield. The Japanese forces sometimes won and pushed the Mongols back but mostly lost. Many Japanese wives and children near the battleground were captured.

Eventually, no soldiers dared to fight against the Mongols. Mongols' arrows were short and not so powerful, but they put the poison at the tip, and they shot the arrows all together at one time like rain. Also, this was the first time the Japanese saw firearms. The loud sound of explosions frightened horses and *Samurai*.
Japanese troops had to retreat, and the situation was awful for the Japanese. But one morning, there was a big surprise! All the ships disappeared from the shore. They were all gone on the morning of October 21st (on today's calendar, November 19th). All Mongols vanished from the coast of *Hakata*.

What happened was that the Mongols decided to quit the fight and went back to their country. The reason was that even though they were winning, they also lost many soldiers and one of the key person of the army. The Mongols realized that no matter how much they won, the Japanese kept coming more and more from everywhere. Also, the Mongols realized that they could not expect reinforcements from their country across the ocean. Their stocks of weapons were getting low. The Mongols decided to go back. Here was a twist. Around the end of October (November by today's calendar), the sea between *Hakata* (where Mongols were stationed) and Korea was very dangerous because of the bad weather. Only a clear day with the south wind made it possible to sail over the sea. The name of the sea where the Mongol soldiers had to sail back is called *Genkai Nada* (玄界灘), very famous for the rough water. For some reason, the Mongols decided to head back during the night. That was a mistake. They may have caught a moment of the south wind, but it did not last long. As a result, they encountered a usual severe rainstorm. Many ships hit against each other, against the cliff, capsized, and people fell into the ocean. Several hundred broken ships were found on the shores of Japan.

The Mongol invasion ended here. This war is called *Bun'ei-no-eki* (文永の役). The Mongols lost a large number of people, ships, soldiers, food, and weapons. Actually, it was Korea that lost a great deal. They were forced to supply people, food, weapons, etc., by the Mongols. After the war, in Korea, only older men and children were left to work on the farm. On top of it, they had a drought and prolonged rain.

Ko'an-no-eki (弘安の役) 1281

The second Mongolian invasion is called *Ko'an-no-eki* in 1281. After the first attempt to invade Japan, Kublai Khan kept sending messengers to Japan to demand it to become Mongol's dependent territory. The *Kamakura Bakufu* kept ignoring and killed messengers. Kublai Kahn decided to attack Japan again in 1281. The top advisers of Kublai Kahn tried to convince him not to do it because the ocean was too dangerous, the country was too small, the place was too far, and there would be nothing to gain even if they win. But Kublai Kahn still insisted on attacking.

This time they came in two groups. One was the East-route troop with 40,000* soldiers on 900 ships, and the other was the South-route troop with 100,000* soldiers on 3,500 ships. This was the enormous scale of forces in history. They planned to depart from each designated port, and they planned to join on the *Iki* Island (壱岐の島) by June 15th, then work together. The East-route troop arrived there before the South-route troop. Instead of waiting for the South-route troop to come, the East-route troop started to attack *Hakata* Bay (博多) on their own. But since the previous invasion of the *Bun'ei-no-eki*, Japan had prepared to fight and built a 20-kilometer-long stone wall. This stone wall was 3 meters high and 2 meters thick. The East-route troop had to give up to land from *Hakata* and moved to *Shiga-no Shima* Island (志賀島). In this place, the fight between Mongols and Japan was even, but in the end, the East-route troop lost and retreated to *Iki* Island and decided to wait for the South-route troop to arrive.
The South-route troop never came. They had changed their plan. On top of that, while the East-route troop was waiting for the South-route troop to arrive, they lost over 3,000 men over an epidemic. Some suggested going back home with difficulty like this,

but they concluded to wait for the South-route troop as long as their food would last. Meanwhile, the South-route troop decided to go to *Hirado* Island (平戸島), which was closer to *Dazaifu* (太宰府). *Dazaifu* was the final and most important place they wanted to attack. Later, the East-route troop found the South-route troop went to *Hirado* Island. Finally, two forces joined on *Hirado* Island, and each group was stationed on the nearby island called *Takashima* Island (鷹島). The problem was that since this island had very high tide and low tide, the ships were not easily maneuvered.

In the meantime, 60,000 Japanese men were marching toward the place where the Mongols were stationed. Before Japanese soldiers arrived to fight against the Mongols, a big typhoon came on July 30th, and Mongols were caught in a big typhoon. Their ships were hitting each other, and many sank. People fell from the boats and drowned. By this time, it had been about three months after the East-route troop left Mongol in early May. That means they were on the ocean for about three months or so. In the northern *Kyushu* area (九州), typhoons usually come, on average, 3.2 times between July and September. The Mongols were on the ocean and Japan's shorelines for about three months. They were bound to be hit by a typhoon sooner or later.

The Mongol Empire lost 2/3 of its naval forces in the event of *Ko'an-no-eki*. Even after the Mongols failed the two invasions, Kublai Khan still insisted on attacking Japan again, no matter how his advisers reasoned him not to. In the end, the plan was delayed and terminated because of many rebellions and upheavals, and no lumber was left to build ships. Soon later, Kublai died in 1294. The historical record of Mongols indicated that Mongolian officials highly praised Japanese swords. Some even say one of the reasons why it was not easy to defeat Japan was their long sharp swords. The experience of the Mongolian invasion changed the *Ikubi kissaki* (猪首切先) sword to the new *Soshu-Den* (相州伝) style sword. The next chapter describes a new style of sword, *Soshu-Den* swords.

The stone wall scene. Photo from Wikipedia. Public Domain
* Number of soldiers by https://kotobank.jp/word/元寇-60419. Referred to several different reference sources. They all have a similar number of soldiers and ships.

48 | Part 2 of --14 Late Kamakura Period Sword: Early Soshu Den
(鎌倉末太刀)

This chapter is a detailed part of Chapter 14| Late Kamakura Period Sword. Please read chapter 14 before reading this section.

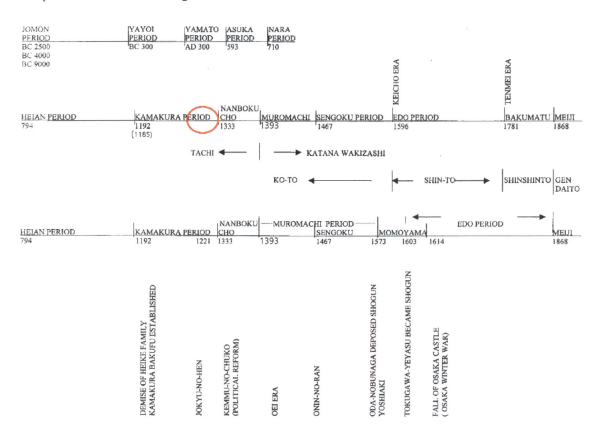

The circle above indicates the time we discuss in this section

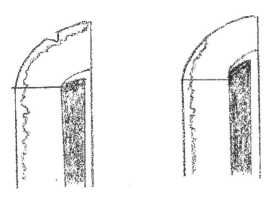

In Chapter 14, Late Kamakura Period Sword (鎌倉末太刀), the *Ikubi-kissakui sword* was explained. The above illustration shows a flaw that was caused when the damaged

area was repaired. To compensate for this flaw, swordsmiths started a new sword style in the late Kamakura period. They forged swords with a longer *Kissaki* and stopped the tip of *Hi* at a lower point than the *Yokote* line.   This way, if the *Yokote* line was lowered when it was repaired, the tip of *Hi* would stay lower than the *Yokote*-line.

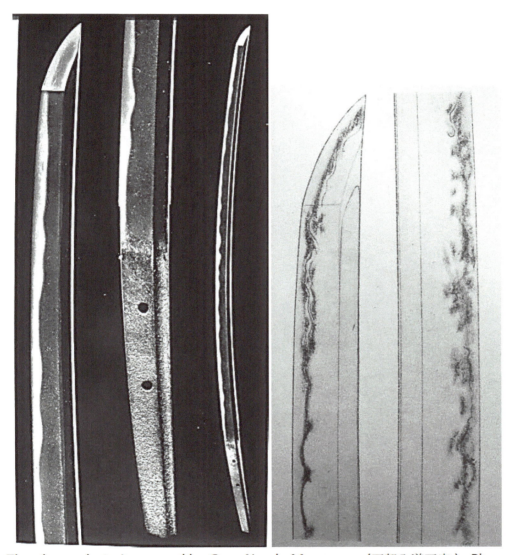

The above photo is a sword by *Goro Nyudo Masamune* (五郎入道正宗). Please look at the size and shape of the *Kissaki*. This is different from previous *Ikubi-kissaki* or *Ko-gissaki*. This is a typical late *Kamakura* period *Kissaki* style. This is O-*suriage* (largely shortened).

Under *Kamakura Bakufu,* many swordsmiths moved to Kamakura. They were *Toroku Sakon Kunituna* (藤六左近国綱) of *Yamashiro Awataguchi* group (山城粟田口), *FukuokaIchimonji Sukezane* (福岡一文字助真), and *Kunimune* (国宗) from the *Bizen* area.

They were the origin of *Soshu Den* (相州伝). Eventually, *Tosaburo Yukimitsu* (藤三郎行光) and his famous son, *Masamune* (正宗), appeared. In the drawing above, *Kinsuji* and *Inazuma* are shown inside the *Hamon*. The shining lines inside the *Hamon* are *Inazuma* and *Kinsuji*. *Inazuma* and *Kinsuji* are a collection of *Nie*. *Masamune* is famous for *Inazuma* and *Kinsuji*. *Masamune* lived in *Kamakura*; his *Hamon* looks like ocean waves when it is viewed sideways.

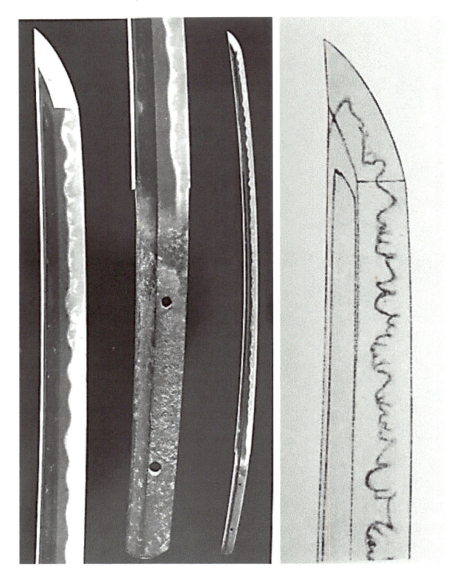

The above picture is a sword by a swordsmith, *Yoshioka Ichimonji group* (吉岡一文字). The *Kissaki* is also like the one of *Masamune's*. It is longer than the previous *Ikubi-kissaki* or *Ko-gissaki*. This is *Chu-gissaki*. The *Kissaki* like this is one of the crucial points to determine what period the sword was made. The *Hamon* has *Choji, Gunome, Togariba* (pointed-tip), and very tight *Nie*.

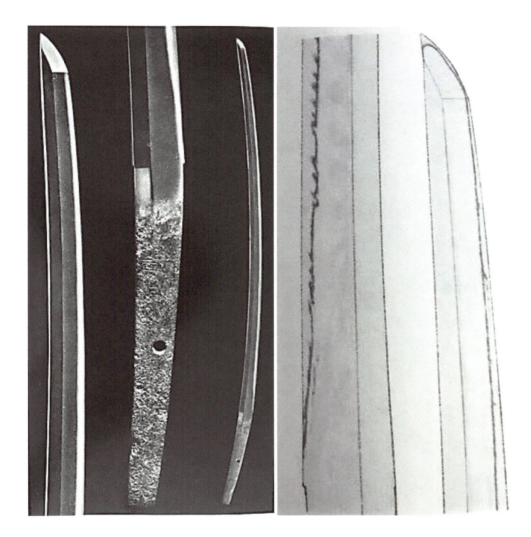

The above photo is a sword by *Ukai Unsho* (鵜飼雲生) of *Bizen Den*. This sword was also from the late *Kamakura* period. But it has *Ko-gissaki*. This sword does not have the late *Kamakura* period *Chu-gissaki* style. Narrow *Hoso-suguha* is somewhat like an earlier time than the late *Kamakura period*. This sword indicates that the sword does not always have the style of that period. To *Kantei**, first, look at the style and shape, then give yourself some idea of the period of the time it was made. But in this case, *Kissaki* does not indicate the late *Kamakura* period. The next thing is to look at the different characteristics of the sword one by one like *Hamon, Nie or Nioi, Jihada*, etc., and determine what period, which *Den,* which province and then come up with the name. This process is called *Kantei.*

*Kantei -- to determine the swordsmith's name by analyzing the sword's characteristic without seeing the *Mei* (inscribed smith name). *Mei* may be gone if it was shortened. All the photos above are from Sano Museum Catalogue. Permission to use is granted.

49 | Part 2 of -- 15 The Revival of Yamato Den (大和伝復活)

This chapter is a continued part of Chapter 15, Revival of Yamato Den. Please read Chapter 15 before reading this section.

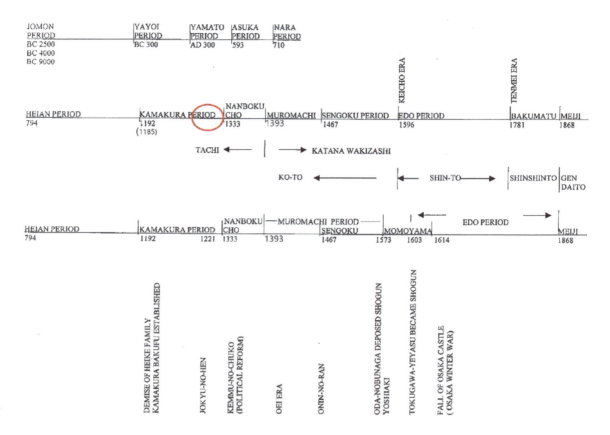

The circle above indicates the time we discuss in this section

At the end of the *Kamakura* period, in the *Yamato* area, powerful temples expanded their territories. See the map below for the location of the *Yamato* area. Several big temples, especially those with large territories, had political and military power to control the area at the end of the *Kamakura* period. Those big territories were called *Shoen* (荘園). They employed a large number of monk soldiers called *So-hei*. The demand for swords was increased by the increased number of *Sohei* (僧兵). The increased demand revived the *Yamato Den*.

Some of the prominent temples had their own swordsmiths within their territory. *Todaiji* Temple (東大寺) backed *Tegai* (手搔) sword group. The *Senjuin* (千手院) sword group lived near *Senju-do* (千手堂) where *Senju Kannon* (千手観音) was enshrined. The name of the sword group, *Taima*, came from the *Taima-ji* Temple (当麻寺). *Shikkake* group (尻懸) and *Hosho* group (保昌) were also *Yamato Den* sword groups. Those five groups are called *Yamato Goha* (*Yamato* five groups).

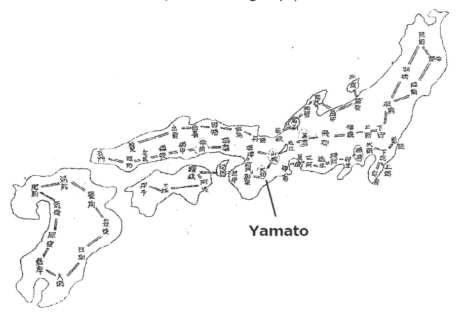

General Characteristic of Yamato Den

Yamato Den (大和伝) sword always shows *Masame* (柾目: straight grain-like pattern) somewhere on *Ji-hada*, *Jigane,* or *Hamon*. Refer to Chapter 15 Revival of Yamato Den for the general characteristic. *Masame* is sometimes mixed with *Mokume* (burl-like) or *Itame* (wood grain-like). Either way, *Yamato Den* shows *Masame* somewhere. Some swords show *Masame* on the entire body, and some show less. Because of Masame, the *Hamon* tends to show *Sunagashi* (brush stroke-like) or a double line called *Niju-ha*.

Taima (or Taema) group (当麻)

Shape --------------------------------- Middle *Kamakura* period shape and *Ikubi-kissaki* style
Hamon ------------------Mainly medium *Suguha*. Double *Hamon*. *Suguha* mixed with *Choji*. Often shows *Inazuma* and *Kinsuji*, especially *Inazuma*, appear under the *Yokote* line.
Boshi ------- Often *Yakizume*. Refer *Yakizume* on 15 Revival of Yamato Den (大和伝復活).
Ji-hada -------------------- Small wood grain pattern and well-kneaded surface. At the top part of the sword, the wood grain pattern becomes *Masame*.

Shikkake Group (尻懸)
Shape ---------------- Late Kamakura period shape. Refer 14 Late Kamakura Period Sword.
Hamon ---------------------- Mainly *Nie* (we say *Nie-hon'i*). Medium frayed *Suguha*, mixed with small irregular and *Gunome* (half-circle pattern). A double-lined, brush stroke-like pattern may appear. Small *Inazuma* and *Kinsuji* may show.

Boshi ---------- *Yakizume, Hakikake* (bloom trace like pattern) and *Ko-maru* (small round)

Ji-hada ----------------------Small burl mixed with *Masame*. The *Shikkake* group sometimes shows *Shikkake-hada*, the *Ha* side shows *Masame*, and the *mune* side shows burl.

Tegai Group (手搔)

Shape ---------- Early *Kamakura* shape and thick *Kasane* (body). High *Shinogi*. *Koshizori*.

Hamon --------------- Narrow tempered line with medium *Suguha hotsure* (frayed *Suguha* pattern). Mainly *Nie*. Double tempered line. *Inazuma* and *Kinsuji* shows.

Boshi -- *Yakizume* (no turn back), *Kaen* (flame like).

Ji-Hada -- Fine burl mixed with *Masame*.

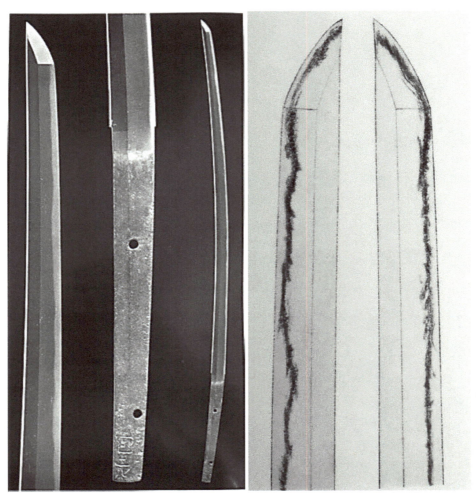

Tegai Kanenaga of Yamato. From Sano Museum Catalogue (permission granted). The illustration (called Oshigata) shows *Notare* (wave-like *hamon*) and *Suguha-hotsure* (frayed *Suguha* pattern) with *kinsuji*.

Below is my *Yamato* sword. I obtained this sword at an Annual San Francisco sword show a few years back.

Characteristics: *Munei* (shortened and no signature). *Yamato Den, Tegai-ha* (*Yamato* school *Tegai* group). Length is two *shaku* two *sun* eight &1/2 *bu* (27 1/4 inches): very small *kissaki* and *funbari.*

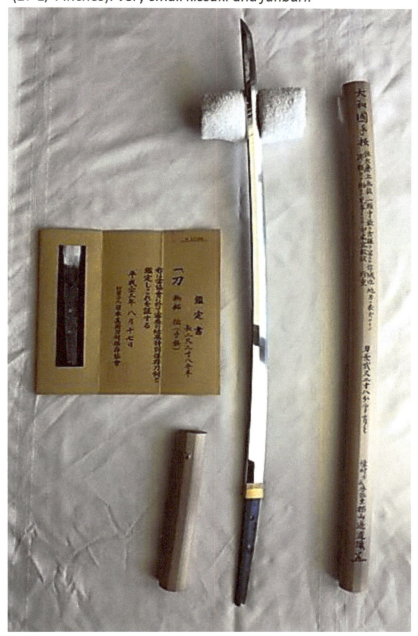

The full view of the sword and *Kantei-sho* (NBTHK Certification)
The ranking is *"Tokubetsu Hozon Token."*

In *Hamon, Sunagashi, Niju-ba* shows very faintly. My photo of *Boshi* is not good, but it looks like *Yakizume*. *Ji-hada* is *Itame* with *Masame*, almost *Nashiji-hada* (possibly because of my eyes). *Nie-hon'i*. Please ignore the cloth pattern underneath reflecting on the blade.

50 | Part 2 of --16 Late Kamakura Period Tanto: Early Soshu Den (鎌倉末短刀, 正宗墓)

Chapter 50 is a continued part of Chapter 16, Late Kamakura Period Tanto (Early Soshu-Den). Please read Chapter 16 before reading this section.

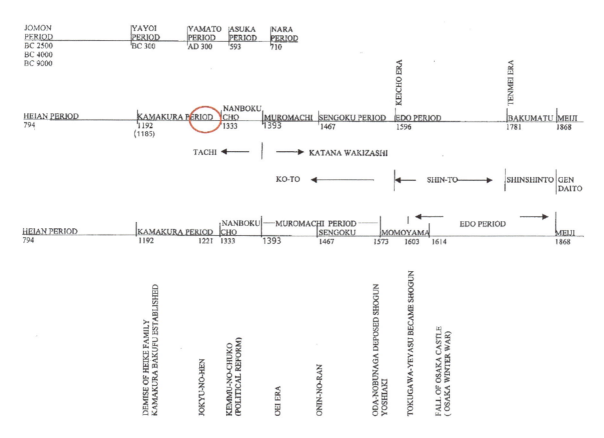

The circle above indicates the time we discuss in this section.

In Chapter 16, Late Kamakura Period Tanto (Early Soshu-Den), the general characteristics of the late *Kamakura* period *Tanto* style (early *Soshu Den*) was described. The next two photos fit in with the typical features of early Soshu *Den Tanto*.

Masamune

Goro Nyudo Masamune (五郎入道正宗) was born in *Kamakura* as a son of *Tosaburo Yukimitu* (藤三郎行光). Today, *Masamune* is a very well-known swordsmith, even among those who are not very familiar with the Japanese sword. His father, *Tosaburo*

Yukimitsu was also one of the top swordsmiths among the early *Soshu Den*. *Masamune's* tomb is in *Honkaku-JI* (本覚寺) Temple, approximately a 6 minutes' walk from Kamakura station.

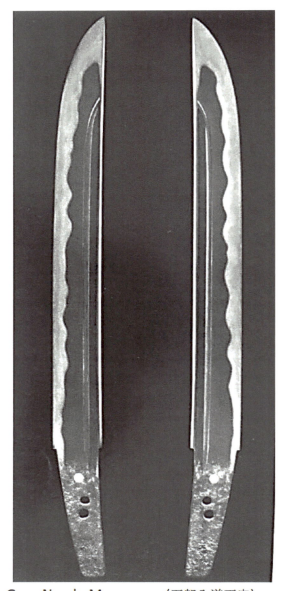
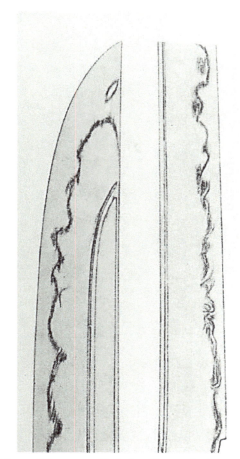

Goro Nyudo Masamune (五郎入道正宗)　　　Sano Museum Catalog (permission granted).

Masamune photo (above) ----- *Hira-zukuri* (flat). Very slightly *Sakizori* (tip area curves slightly outward). *Bo-hi* and *Tsure-hi* (parallel thin grooves). *Komaru-boshi*. *Itame-hada* (wood grain pattern). *Hamon* is *Notare* (wavy). The illustration above shows *Sunagashi* and *Niju-ba* (double *Hamon*). This type of *Nakago* is called *Tanago-bara*. *Masamune Tanto* is often *Mu-mei* (no signature). This particular *Tanto* is called *Komatsu Masamune*

(小松政宗). The Sano Museum Catalog's description stated that connoisseurs in the past had difficulty determining this is Masamune sword. Because the wide *Mihaba* with *Sori* and *Hamon* was a little different from other *Masamune's*. Judging from the clear *Nie*, *Chikei*, and *Kinsuji*, it was determined as a *Masamune Tanto*.

Enju Photo below

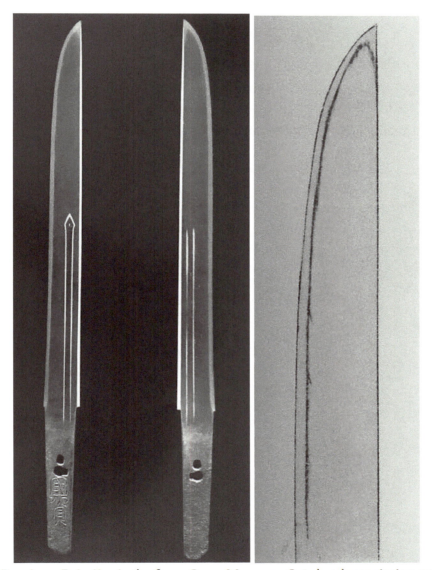

Higo Province Enju Kunisuke from Sano Museum Catalog (permission granted)

Enju (延寿) group lived in *Higo* (肥後) Province in *Kyushu*. The characteristics of the *Enju* group are very similar to that of the *Yamashiro Den's*. It is because *Enju Kunimura* was related to *Rai Kuniyuki* of *Yamashiro-Den*.

Enju (Photo above) ----*Hamon* is *Hoso-suguha* (straight temper line). *Boshi* is *Komaru*. The front engraving is *Suken* (left photo left side), and the engraving on the back is *Gomabashi* (left photo right side). *Ji-hada* is a tight *Itame*. It is confusing to *Kantei* (determining who made the sword) a sword like this because even though this sword is from the late *Kamakura* period, it does not have the typical early *Soshu Den* look.

Masamune's Tomb in Honkaku-ji Temple

Masamune's (正宗) tomb is in the *Honkakuj-Ji* Temple (本覚寺) in Kamakura. Here is a map of the *Honkaku-Ji* Temple and *Masamune Kogei* store in Kamakura. The store is owned by *Tsunahiro Yamamura,* the 24th generation of *Masamune*. *Honkaku-Ji* Temple is circled, and *Masamune Kogei* store is the circle with X. Both are approximately a 6 to 7 minutes walking distance from Kamakura station.

To get to Honkaku-Ji Temple from Tokyo

Take the *Yokosuka* line train from *Tokyo* station (approx. one hour) → Get off at *Kamakura* Station (one stop after *Kita-Kamakura*) → Exit from the East Exit (front exit) → Go straight and cross the road → Turn right and go up to the post office → Turn left at the post office (*Honkaku-ji* Temple sign is at the corner of the post office)

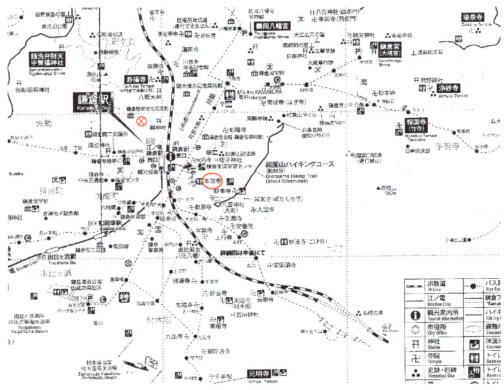

From Kamakura Tourist map

Honkakuji Temple (本覚寺) and Masamune Tomb (正宗墓)   My trip in 2019

51 | Part 2 of -- 17 Nanboku-cho Period History (南北朝歴史)

This Chapter is a detailed part of Chapter 17|Nanboku(Yoshino) Cho Period History (1333-1392). Please read Chapter 17 before reading this section.

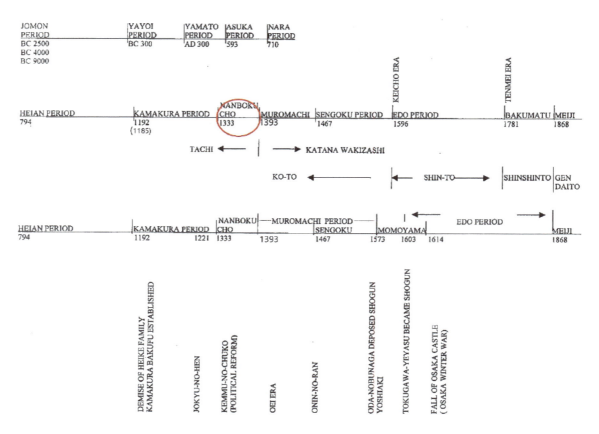

The circle above indicates the time we discuss in this section

The *Nanboku-cho* period (1333 – 1392) was between the fall of *Kamakura Bakufu* and the beginning of the *Muromachi Bakufu*. It was the time when the North Dynasty and the South Dynasty co-existed at the same time. Right around the time of the Mongolian Invasion, Emperor *Go-saga* passed away without deciding the next emperor. Because of that, his two heirs and their family lines, the *Daigakuji-to* (大覚寺統) line and the *Jimyoin-to* (持明院統) line, alternately took the emperor position after Emperor *Go-saga*'s death. This system was politically precarious. On top of that, many inconvenient problems happened; for example, while one emperor was still very young, the next-in-line emperor died young from a head injury when he was playing on a slippery stone.

203
Alpha Book Publisher

At a time like this, *Go-daigo* (後醍醐天皇) became the emperor. He was put on the throne as a temporary emperor until young emperors grew up. Around this time, the power of the emperors was declining. The *Kamakura Bakufu* (government) controlled the emperors. After the Mongolian Invasion, even though typhoons chased Mongolian troops away, *Kamakura Bakufu* was in financial trouble because of the cost of war. Many *Samurai* who fought during the Mongolian Invasion did not receive any rewards nor got paid for the expense they incurred themselves. They were also in trouble financially. All these problems piled up, and people resented the *Kamakura Bakufu*.

Emperor *Go-daigo* did not want to stay as just a filler emperor. He decided to remain as an emperor himself and decided to attack the *Kamakura Bakufu*. For some reason, the *Kamakura Bakufu* found out about the plan. Emperor *Go-daigo* somehow managed to avoid being accused as an instigator. After this happened, the *Kamakura Bakufu* appointed another heir for the next emperor. But *Go-daigo* insisted on remaining as an emperor. He planned another attack one more time. This time, he had carefully planned and allied with prominent, powerful temples in *Yamato* (*Nara* today) since the *Kamakura Bakufu* did not control them. Refer, 15 Revival of Yamato Den (大和伝復活) and 49 part 2 of-- 15 The revival of Yamato Den.

This time again, the rebellion plot came to light. *Go-daigo* sneaked out of *Kyoto* and fought against the *Kamakura* army. *Go-daigo's* army had fewer soldiers than the *Kamakura* army, but several groups opposing the *Kamakura Bakufu* rose from various places throughout Japan. Eventually, *Go-daigo* was captured and sent to *Oki Island* (the same place where Emperor *Go-toba* was sent).

Even after sending Emperor *Go-daigo* to *Oki* island, the *Kamakura Bakufu* still had to fight against other uprising groups. One of the famous rebels was *Kusunoki Masashige* (楠正成). *Go-daigo's* son was also actively fighting against the *Kamakura Bakufu* and managing to ally with more groups.

More and more people wanted to overthrow the *Kamakura Bakufu*. Even *Ashikaga Takauji* (足利尊氏), one of *the Kamakura Bakufu's* top men who fought against Emperor *Go-daigo,* betrayed the *Kamakura,* and changed sides, and became the emperor's ally. In the meantime, *Go-daigo* escaped from *Oki* Island. More and more uprisings against the *Kamakura Bakufu* emerged from everywhere. Eventually, the main political center called *Rokuhara Tandai* (六波羅探題) of the *Kamakura Bakufu* fell. *Nitta Yoshisada* (新田義貞)*, who was another uprising group attacked *Kamakura* and won. The *Kamakura Bakufu* fell in 1333.

Emperor *Go-Daigo* started a new political system called *Kenmu no Shinsei* (建武の新政). This new system was a disaster. He made a great effort to make things right and changed the old political system drastically. But this political reform created a big commotion. It was not good for anybody, and nobody would gain anything. *Ashikaga Takauji* (one of the prominent people of merit) and his men did not receive any high-ranking jobs. His new reform was very idealistic and too far advanced for the time. It was too disadvantageous for the noblemen. His new policy only invited chaos and corruption.

Now *Ashikaga Takauji* turned against *Go-daigo* and defeated him. *Go-daigo* left the Imperial Palace and opened a new government in *Yoshino*, the south of *Kyoto*. Therefore, it was called the Southern Dynasty. Meanwhile, *Ashikaga Takauji* set up a new emperor, Emperor *Komyo* (光明), in *Kyoto* and established the North Dynasty. This is how the North and South Dynasties came about.

Two dynasties co-existed for about 60 years. Little by little, many *Samurai* groups moved under the North Dynasty, and after *Go-daigo* and his several key men passed away, the South Dynasty became weakened. Eventually, the South Dynasty accepted the offer from the *Ashikaga* side, and the North and the South united in 1392. During all those fights between the emperor and *Kamakura Bakufu*, the sword style changed to broader and longer, like 3, 4, or 5 feet long. Later, most of the *Nanboku-cho* (the North and South Dynasties) style long swords were shortened.

Kibamusha (騎馬武者)   This portrait was once believed to be Ashikaga Takauji, but now some claim otherwise. "Public Domain" owned by Kyoto National Museum

*Nitta Yoshisada (新田義貞)

When *Minamoto no Yoritomo* opened the *Kamakura Bakufu*, he chose the Kamakura area as the center of the *Bakufu* because mountains surrounded Kamakura on three sides, and one side faced the ocean. That means it was hard to be attacked and easy to protect themselves. And they made seven narrow, steep roads through mountains called *Kiri Toshi* (切り通し) connecting with several major cities. Those seven roads were the only ways to go out and to come into *Kamakura*.

When *Nitta Yoshisada* tried to attack *Kamakura,* he first tried to attack through the land road but failed. So, he approached the town from the ocean side, but the cliff sticks far out to the ocean, making it impossible for them to pass. The legend says that when *Nitta Yoshisada* came to the area called *Inamura Gasaki* (稲村ヶ崎), he threw his golden sword into the ocean and prayed. Then the tide went out, and all the soldiers could go around the cliff on foot. They charged into *Kamakura*, and the *Kamakura Bakufu* fell. There are several different views on the story. Some scholars say that is not true, some say it happened, but the date was wrong, some say unusual ebb tide occurred that day, and so on.

Today, *Inamura Gasaki,* a part of the *Shonan* (湘南), is one of the favorite dating spots for young people in the evening. The evening scene of *Inamura Gasaki* is beautiful. The sunset from *Inamura Gasaki* toward *Enoshima* (江の島 ; a small island with a shrine on the hilltop) is gorgeous. My parents' house used to be above the cliff in the vicinity called *Kamakura Yama,* overlooking the ocean.

Inamura Gasaki   (Public domain)
Photo is "Creative Commons" CC 表示-継承 3.0 File: Inamuragasaki tottanbu.jpg 作成

52| Part 2 of --18 Nanboku-cho Period Sword (南北朝太刀)

This chapter is a continued part of Chapter 18, Nanboku-cho Sword. Please read Chapter 18 before reading this section.

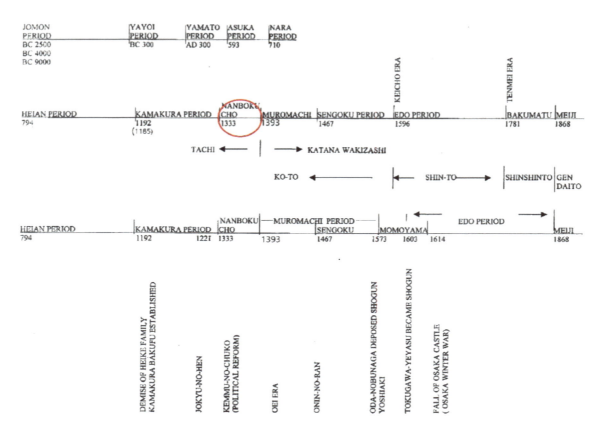

The circle above indicates the time we discuss in this section

The drawing below is the illustration from Chapter 18, Nanboku-cho Period Sword. Please compare this drawing to the photo on the right. It shows the similarity of the shape. Keep in mind this illustration is the shape of a once very long sword that was shortened at a later time. During the *Nanboku-cho* time, swordsmiths created 3, 4, or even 5 feet long blades, but later, they were shortened to approximately 2 to 2.5 feet or so.

Nanboku-Cho Period Soshu Den (shool) style
Originally much longer and it had beatiful arc line.

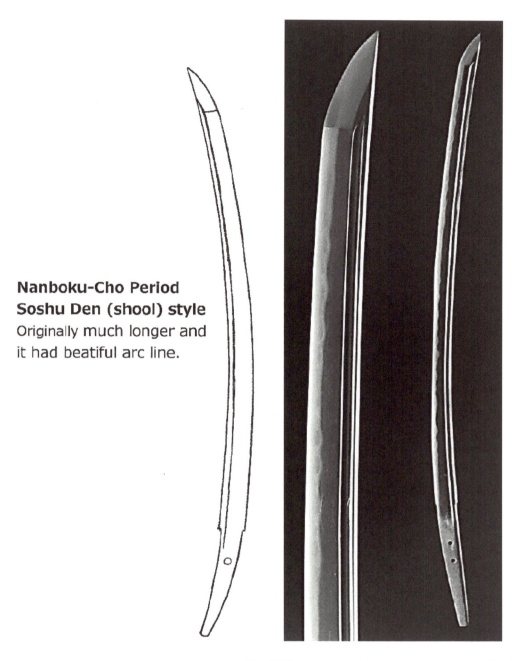

"*Sa*"* from Sano Museum Catalogue "Reborn."
(Permission granted)

* "*Sa*" is pronounced the first sound of "sabotage."

Chogi* from Sano Museum Catalogue (Permission granted)

Chogi* is pronounced: Chocho-san's "cho" and giggle "gi."

Chogi's sword style is categorized as one of the *Soden Bizen*. See, 18 Nanboku-Cho Period Sword. *Chogi* (長義) was a swordsmith from *Bizen Den* school who created swords with *Soshu Den's* characteristics. Therefore, in short, called *Soden Bizen* (*Bizen* swordsmith forged *Soshu Den*).

Chogi characteristics

Shape --------- Originally very long. It was shortened to approximately 2 to 2.5 feet.
Hamon --------Wide showy tempered line. *Nioi* and *Nie* shows.
       Sunagashi (砂流し brush stroke-like pattern) appears. *Notare* (wavy) mixed with *Gunome*. Sometimes *Chogi* created the double *Gunome*-style *Hamon* (connected one pair of half-circles). This shape resembles a pair of earlobes. Therefore, it is called *Chogi's Mimigata-midare* (irregular *Hamon* mixed with the earlobe-like pattern).

Boshi ---------- Irregular *Midare* and sharp turn back
Ji-hada -------- *Itame* (a wood grain pattern)

Aoe from Sano Museum Catalogue (Permission granted)

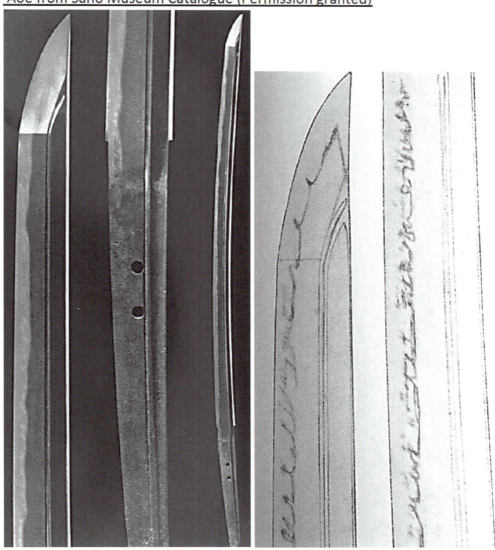

Aoe (青江) is pronounced "A" like apple, "o" like original, and "e" like egg.
Aoe was a swordsmith from *Bittchu* (備中) province, which is next to *Bizen*. Therefore, the characteristics of *Ko-aoe* (old *Aoe*) and *Ko-bizen* (old *Bizen*) are similar.

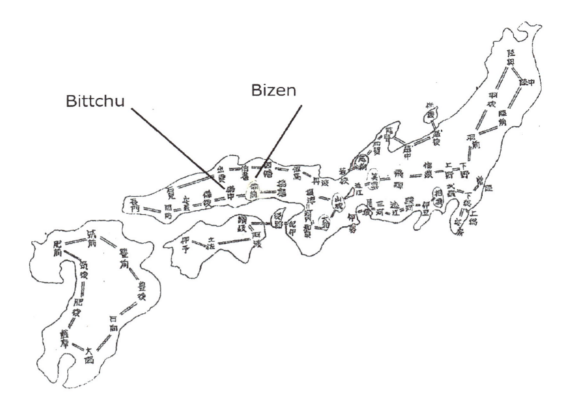

Characteristics of *Aoe* (青江)

From the middle *Kamakura* period to the *Nanboku-cho* period was the height of the **_Aoe_** group.

One of the characteristics of the *Aoe* sword is its *Aoe-zori* shape. That is to curve a lot at the lower part.
During the *Nanboku-cho* time, because the *Soshu Den* was the trendy style, even *Bizen* swordsmiths did *Nie*, though their main characteristic was *Nioi*. However, the *Bittchu* group stayed with *Nioi*.
The tempered area tends to be wide. *Sakasa-choji,* which means inverted or backward style *Choji* (see the illustration above), is the *Aoe's* most notable characteristic. Also, *Boshi* often has pointed *Hamon*. It is often said that if you see *Sakasa-choji,* the sword has a good chance of being from either the *Aoe* group or *Katayama Ichimonji* group. *Sumitetu* (澄鉄: black core metal shows through) is also *Aoe's* characteristic.

53 | Part 2 of --19 Nanboku-cho Period Tanto (南北朝短刀)

This chapter is a continued part of chapter 19. Please read Chapter 19 Nanboku-cho Period Tanto before reading this section.

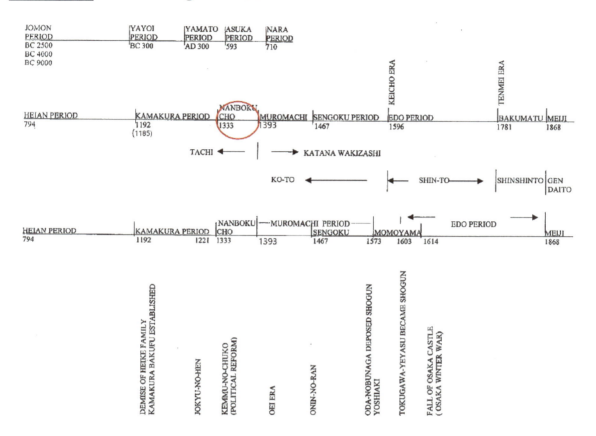

The circle above indicates the time we discuss in this section

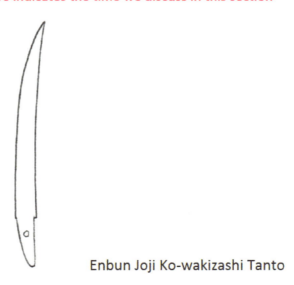

Enbun Joji Ko-wakizashi Tanto

The drawing above is a typical shape of the *Nanboku-cho* time *Tanto*. This drawing was in chapter 19. The drawing exaggerates the form of the *Enbun Joji Kowakizashi tanto*. At the end of Chapter 19, Nanboku-cho Tanto, there is a list of swordsmiths' names in the period. *Hiromitsu* (広光) and *Akihiro* (秋広) represent the Nanboku-cho features.

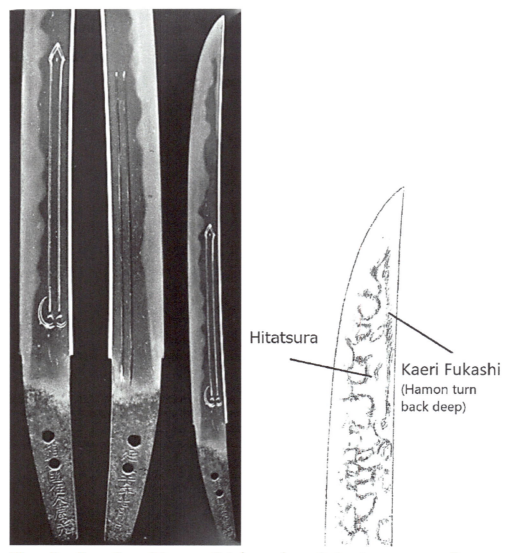

Hiromitsu From Sano Museum Catalogue (permission to use granted)

Enbun Joji Ko-wakizashi tanto is also called *Sun-nobi Tanto* (>10 inches) because the length is longer than the standard size (approx. 10 inches) *Tanto*. The top part of the *Tanto* bends outward slightly. This type of shape is called *Sakizori*.

Characteristics of Hiromitu (広光) and Akihiro (秋広)
Shape--------------- Usually, one foot and one to two inches long (*Sun-nobi*). Wide width. The blade is thin. *Sakizori*.

Hamon -------Wide *Hamon* and narrow *Hamon* are mixed. *Hamon* around *Yakidashi* (right above *Machi*) area is narrow, but it gets wider gradually as it goes up. *Hamon* around the *Fukura* area is the showiest. Mainly *Nie*. *Sunagashi*, *Kinsuji*, *Gunome*, *Umanoha-midare* (horse teeth shape *Hamon*), or *Hitatsura* appear (above drawing).
Boshi-----------Irregular, unevenly tempered. *Hamon* covers almost the entire *Boshi*. Deep turn back.

Jihada ----------------Wood-grained pattern
Nakago -------------*Tanago-bara* shape. Refer to 19 Nanboku-cho Period Tanto.

Nobukuni (Below is my sword)

Shodai Nobukuni (the first generation *Nobukuni*) was a student of *Sadamune*. He was one of the *Sadamune San Tetsu* (貞宗三哲, *Sadamune's* top three students). *Nobukuni's* characteristics were similar to those of *Hiromitsu's* and *Akihiro's* described above. *Nobukuni* also created *Sun-nobi Tanto*. The sword below has a *Hoso-suguha*, *Ko-mokume* (small burl pattern), *Ko-maru Boshi* (small round).

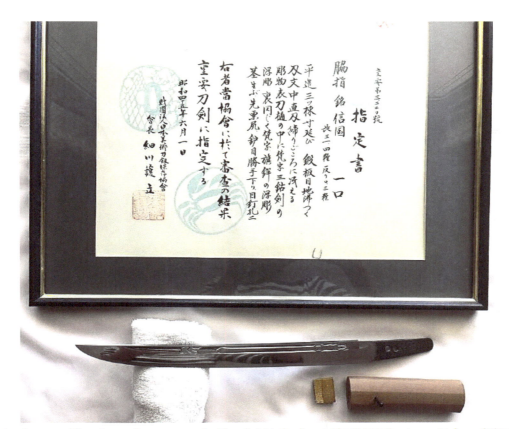

This is the certification of my sword. Shodai Nobukuni (初代信國). Juyo Token (重要刀劍)

Certification

number Juyo 3220,   Certification Juyo-Token

Wakizashi: *Nobukuni* (信国), 31.4cm length, 0.3cm curvature, *Hirazukuri*, *Mitsumune* (three-sided *Mune*), *Sun-nobi*, *Ji-hada* is wood grain and *Ji-nie* (*Nie* on the surface between *Shinogi* and *Hamon*), *Hamon* is *Chu-suguha* (medium straight), Front carving shows *Bonji* (Sanscrit), *Sanko-ken*, back engraving is *Bonji* and *Hoko* (pike*)*.   Original *Nakago*. The examination by the *Nihon Bijutu Token Hozon Kyokai*. It is certified as *Juyo Token*. The Chairman *Moritatu Hosokawa*. *Showa* 45 June 1 (1970 June 1)

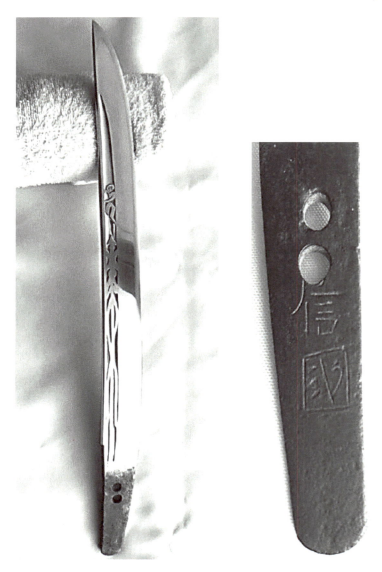

54 | Part 2 of – 20 Muromachi Period History (室町時代歴史)

This is a detailed part of Chapter 20 Muromachi Period History. Please read chapter 20 before reading this section.

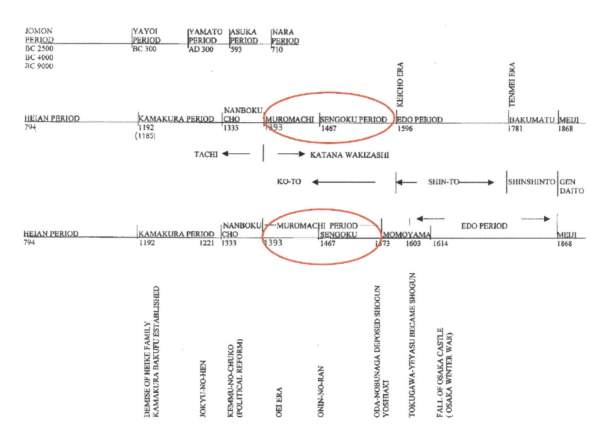

The circle above indicates the time we discuss in this chapter

Until the *Muromachi* (室町) period, the political history and the sword history are parallel in our study. The above timelines show: the middle line is for the sword history, and the bottom line is for the political history.

The styles of swords were distinctively different between those in the *Muromachi* period and the *Sengoku* period (戦国時代). Therefore, for sword study, the *Muromachi* period and *the Sengoku* period have to be separated. Japanese history textbooks define that the *Muromachi* period is from 1393 (the end of *Nanboku-cho*) until 1573 when *Oda Nobunaga* (織田信長) removed *Shogun Ashikaga Yoshiaki* (足利義昭) from

Kyoto (the fall of the *Muromachi Bakufu*). In those textbooks, the *Sengoku* period is described as a part of the *Muromachi* period. However, we need to divide the *Muromachi* period and the *Sengoku* period for the sword study's purpose.

Ashikaga Yoshimitsu (足利義満)

The best time during the *Muromachi* period was when *Shogun Ashikaga Yoshimitsu* (足利義満: Grandson of *Ashikaga Takauji*) was in power. He moved the *Bakufu* to *Muromachi* (室町) in *Kyoto*; therefore, it is called the *Muromachi* period. By the time most of the South Dynasty *Samurai* went under the North Dynasty, the South Dynasty accepted the *Shogun Yoshimitsu's* offer to end the fight against the North Dynasty. This acceptance established the power of the *Ashikaga* family in the *Muromachi Bakufu*.

Shogun Ashikaga Yoshimitsu created a tremendous amount of profit from trades with China (Ming). He built a famous beautiful resort villa in *Kyoko*, the Golden Pavillion (*Kinkaku-Ji* Temple 金閣寺*). It is said that he created the Golden Pavillion to display his power and wealth. The beautiful culture called the *Kitayama Bunka* (*Kitayama* culture 北山文化) was created around this time.

*Golden Pavilion (金閣寺: *Kinkaku-Ji* Tempe) ----- The official name is *Rokuon-Ji* Temple (鹿苑寺). *Saionji Kintsune* (西園寺公経) built it first as his resort house in the *Kamakura* period. *Shogun Yoshimitsu* acquired it in 1397, and he rebuilt it as his villa. He also used it as an official guesthouse.

After *Shogun Yoshimitsu's* death, the villa was converted to *Rokuon-ji Temple*. It is a part of *Rinzaishu Sokoku-ji Temple*, which is the head temple of a denomination of the *Zen* sect, *Rinzaishu Sokoku-ji* group(臨済宗相国寺派). *Kinkaku-ji* is a reliquary hall containing relics of Buddha. *Kinkaku-Ji* Temple represents the glorious *Kitayama Bunka* (*Kitayama* culture). In 1994, it was registered as a World Cultural Heritage Site.
https://www.shokoku-ji.jp/kinkakuji/

My photo in May 2019

Ashikaga Yoshimasa (足利義政)

After *Shogun Ashikaga Yoshimitsu* (足利義満) died, the *Muromachi Bakufu* became less financially prosperous, and the military power decreased. As a result, *Daimyo* (feudal lords) gained more control. A few generations after *Shogun Yoshimitsu*, *Ashikaga Yohimasa* became the 8th *Shogun*. His wife was the famous *Hino Tomiko* (refer to *Hino Tomiko in* Chapter 20 Muromachi Period History.

It is said that *Shogun Yoshimasa* was not interested in his job as a *Shogun*, but he was much more interested in art and culture. He created the foundation of today's Japanese art and culture, such as the Japanese garden, *Shoin-zukuri* (書院造)* interior design, tea ceremony, flower arrangements, painting, and other art forms. His cultural attribute is called *Higashiyama Bunka* (*Higashiyama* culture (東山文化).

As described in Chapter 20 Muromachi Period History (室町時代), *Shogun Yoshimasa* did not have a child. His brother *Yoshimi* (義視) was appointed to be the next *Shogun*. But his wife, *Hino Tomiko,* gave birth to a son, *Yoshihisa* (義尚). *Hino Tomiko* asked *Yamana Sozen* (山名宗全: powerful family) to back up her son. At the same time, brother, *Yoshimi*, tied up with *Hosokawa Katsumoto* (細川勝元: another powerful family). The problem was that *Shogun Yoshimasa* was paying too much attention to his cultural hobbies, and did not pay attention to the problem he created by not being clear who should be the next *Shogun*. He did not yield the Shogunate to either one.

In 1467, on top of the successor problem, because of other conflicts of interests of other powerful *Daimyo,* a civil war, "Onin-no-Run (応仁の乱)" broke out. All *Daimyo* were divided and sided either the *Hosokawa* group or the *Yamana* group. Eventually, the war spread to the rest of Japan and lasted over ten years. Finally, in 1477, after both *Hosokawa Katsumoto* and *Yamana Sozen* died, *Shogun Yoshimasa* decided to transfer the Shogunate to his son *Yoshihisa*. Because of this war, *Kyoto* was devastated. The power of the *Muromachi Bakufu* declined significantly.

While all this was happening, and people were suffering, *Yoshimasa* was still spending money to build the *Ginkaku-ji* Temple (銀閣寺: The Silver Pavillion). He died without seeing the completion of the *Ginkaku-ji* Temple. The *Onin-no-Run* would lead to the next *Sengoku* period, *the* 100-year-long Warring States Period.

*Shoin-zukuri (書院造)------------A traditional Japanese residential interior style with *Tatami* mats, a nook, and a *Shoji* screen, sliding door. This style is the base of the interior of the Japanese house today.

Shoin-zukuri style Japanese room

Public Domain   GFDL,cc-by-sa-2.5,2.0,1.0 file:Takagike CC BY-SA 3.0view terms

My Japanese Room

55| Part 2 of -- 21 Muromachi Period Sword (室町時代刀)

Chapter 55 is a detailed part of Chapter 21, Muromachi Period Sword. Please read Chapter 21 before reading this section.

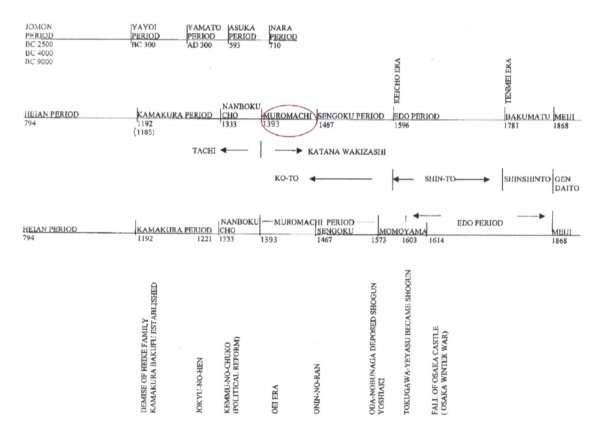

The circle above indicates the time we discuss in this section

After the *Muromachi* period, swords changed to *Katana*(刀) from *Tachi* (太刀), as described in chapter 21 Muromachi Period Sword. Refer to Chapter 21 Muromachi Period Sword. By the end of the *Nanboku-cho* period, the swords' length became shorter to approximately 2 feet ± a few inches. The 3-to-5 feet long swords seen in the *Nanboku-cho* period were no longer created. The reason was that, during the *Nanboku-cho* period, warriors fought mostly riding horses, but after the *Muromachi* time, infantry fighting became more common.

Oei Bizen (応永備前)
The pronunciation of *Oei* is "O as Oh" and "ei as A of ABC." The *Muromachi* period was the declining time in sword-making. The swords made during the early *Muromachi*

period in the *Bizen* area were called *Oei Bizen*. *Osafune Morimitsu* (長船盛光), *Osafune Yasumitsu* (長船康光), *Osafune Moromitsu* (長船師光) were the main *Oei Bizen* swordsmiths. *Soshu Hiromasa* (相州広正), *Yamashiro Nobukuni* (山城信國) were also similar to the *Oei Bizen* style. Please refer to Chapter 21 Muromachi Period Sword for *Muromachi* sword shape, *Hamon, Boshi,* and *Ji-hada*.

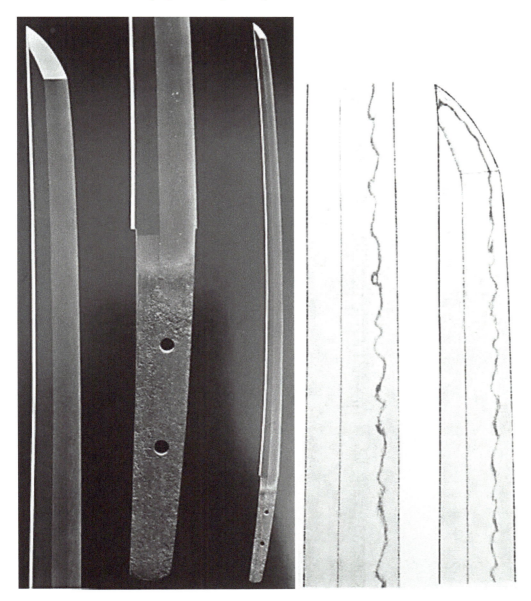

Bishu Osafune Moromitsu (備州長船師光) from *Sano* Museum Catalogue (permission granted)

The above *Osafune Moromitsu* sword is 2 feet 5 inches long with medium *Kissaki*. The *Hamon* has a small wave-like pattern with continuous *Gunome* (a lined half-circles pattern). The *Boshi* area shows irregular waviness with a slightly pointed tip. Very faint

Bo-utsuri (soft shadow shaped like a strip of wood) shows on *Ji-hada*. *Bo-utsuri* is a distinctive characteristic among all of the *Oei Bizen*.

Before the *Muromachi* period, there had been many swordsmith groups in the *Bizen* area, but Osafune (長船) was the only remaining active group by the Muromachi time.

Osafune (長船) is the name of a region, but it became the last name of the swordsmiths during the *Muromachi* time. Two other well-known swordsmiths among the *Oei Bizen* were *Osafune Morimitsu* (盛光) and *Osafune Yasumitsu* (康光). The *Hamon* by *Morimitsu* and *Yasumitsu* shows more work than that of the sword in the photo above. Chapter 21 Muromachi Period Sword shows the *Hamon* by *Morimitsu* and *Yasumitsu*, also describes typical characteristics of the swords in the *Muromachi* period.

Hirazukuri Ko-Wakizashi Tanto

Hirazukuri Ko-wakizashi Tanto Shape

Hirazukuri Ko-wakizashi Tanto was the trendy style during the early *Muromachi* time. Swordsmiths in different areas created the *Tanto* like the illustration above. But majorities of this type were made by *Oei Bizen* swordsmiths.

The characteristics of the *Hirazukuri ko-wakizashi Tanto* ------------- Usually 1 foot and 1 or 2 inches long. No *Yokote* line, no *Shinogi*, and no *Sori* (no curvature, straight back). Average thickness. Narrow width. *Gyo-no-mune* (refer <u>Chapter 12 Middle Kamakura Period Tanto</u>.

Gyo-no-Mune

(行の棟)

Hirazukuri Ko-wakizashi Tanto often shows many engravings. *Hi* with *Soe-hi* (double lines, wide and narrow side by side), *Tokko-tsuki-ken, Tsume-tsuki-ken, Bonji*, etc.

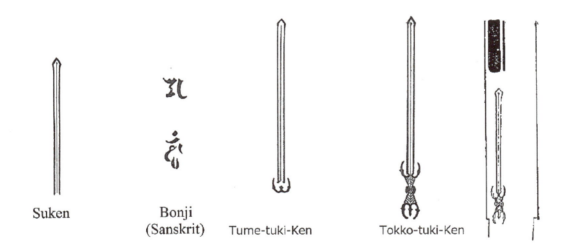

Suken   Bonji (Sanskrit)   Tume-tuki-Ken   Tokko-tuki-Ken

Drawings from "Nihonto no Okite to Tokucho" by Honami Koson

56|Part 2 of -- 22 Sengoku Period History (戦国時代歴史)

Chapter 56 is a detailed part of Chapter 22, Sengoku Period History. Please read chapter 22, Sengoku Period History, before reading this section.

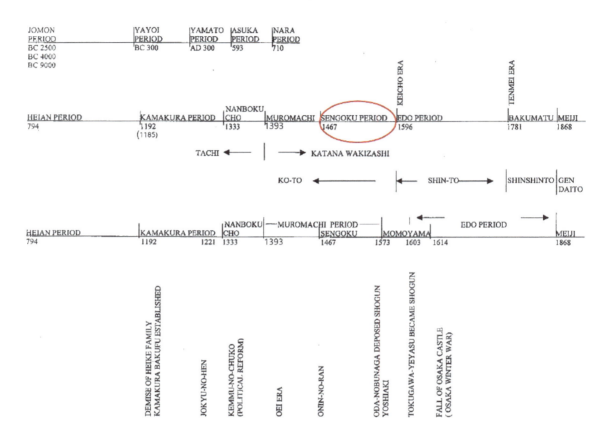

The circle above indicates the time we discuss in this section

Chapter 22 Sengoku Period History explained how we separated the timeline based on political history and sword history. The center timeline above shows the *Sengoku Period* (戦国時代) ends in 1596 for sword history.

1596 is the beginning of the *Keicho* (慶長) era. The swords made in and after the *Keicho* era are called *Shin-to* (new sword), and swords before the *Keicho* era are called *Ko-to* (old sword). Therefore, the beginning of the *Keicho* era is the dividing line. The swords made during the *Keicho* time are technically *Shin-to*, but they are specially called *Keicho Shin-to*.

Chapter 22 Sengoku Period History described the overview of the *Sengoku* Period. At the beginning of the *Sengoku* Period, 30 or so small *Sengoku Daimyo* (warlord) fought fiercely with each other. They allied with a neighboring territory on and off and sometimes betrayed each other. The stronger *Daimyo* took over weaker ones' territories. Little by little, the number of *Daimyo* became lesser. The names of known powerful *Daimyo* are *Imagawa Yoshimoto* (今川義元), *Takeda Shingen* (武田信玄), *Uesugi Kenshin* (上杉謙信), *Hojo Soun* (北条早雲), *Oda Nobunaga* (織田信長), Tokugawa *Ieyasu* (徳川家康), *Toyotomi Hideyoshi* (豊臣秀吉). Their final goal was to defeat others and advance to *Kyoto* (京都) to be the supreme political power.

Oda Nobunaga (織田信長) defeated Imagawa Yoshimoto in Okehazama (桶狭間)

Around 1560, *Imagawa Yoshimoto* (今川義元) controlled a significant part of Suruga (today's *Shizuoka* prefecture. See the map below for the location). He was a powerful *Sengoku Daimyo* who was big enough to be the top ruler of the country.

Imagawa clan decided to advance his army toward *Kyoto* to take over the government. He took 25,000 men troop with him. On his way up to *Kyoto,* they needed to pass *Owari* (尾張: *Aichi* prefecture today. See map below for the location), *Oda Nobunaga's* territory.

Oda Nobunaga (織田信長) was still a young man who had much less means than *Imagawa Yoshimoto*. It was quite apparent that there was no chance for *Oda Nobunaga* to beat *Imagawa*. He had just become the head of *Owari* after his father's death. Also, at that time, *Nobunaga* was called "The idiot of *Owari"* because of his eccentric behaviors (though he was actually a genius).

Not too many people had much confidence in *Nobunaga*. Among *Oda* vassals, some insisted on just staying inside the castle instead of going out and fighting since *Nobunaga* only managed to gather 3,000 men. But in the end, to everyone's surprise, the *Oda* side won. Here is how it happened.

While *Imagawa Yoshimoto* was advancing, *Nobunaga* scouted which route *Imagawa* would take. Imagawa*'s* side was sure to win this easy battle since the *Oda* clan was small, and the head of the clan was an idiot. *Imagawa* troops decided to stop and rest in a place called *Okehazama*. The road going through *Okehazama* was long and narrow. Knowing *Imagawa* troop would come this way, *Nobunaga* sent out his men disguised as farmers and offered food and *sake* to *Imagawa* soldiers. While they were having a good time, *Oda Nobunaga* made a surprise attack on the *Imagawa* troop. On top of that, all of a sudden, it began raining heavily. The rain was so heavy that the

Imagawa troop could not even see the *Oda* troop coming. In the end, *Imagawa Yoshimoto* was killed by the *Oda* side in the battle. After this, the *Imagawa* clan declined.

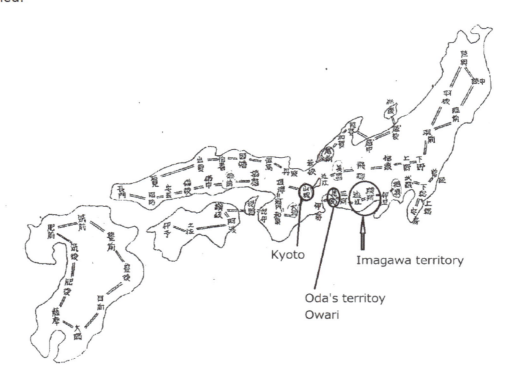

Bishu Okehazama Gassen (備州桶狭間合戦) by Utagawa Toyonobu (歌川豊信)
Public Domain   (http://morimiya.net/online/ukiyoe-big-files/U896.html)

Oda Nobunaga(織田信長) and Akechi Mitsuhide(明智光秀)

After the battle of *Okehazama,* the *Oda* clan grew bigger rapidly. *Oda Nobunaga* became the primary power. While his reign, he did several cruel things like burning *Enryaku-ji* Temple (延暦寺) and killing many people, including ordinary people, yet his economic measures encouraged commercial activities.

Things were going somewhat smoothly for *Nobunaga* late in his life. But in 1582, *Nobunaga* was killed by his own top vassal, *Akechi Mitsuhide* (明智光秀), at *Hon'nou-ji* (本能寺) Temple in *Kyoto*. *Nobunaga* was 49 years old.

A few theories about why *Akecdhi* attacked and killed *Nobunaga,* but we don't know what exactly happened. One speculation is *Akechi* had a grudge against *Nobunaga*. There were many incidents where *Nobunaga* mistreated *Akechi*. Another is that *Akechi* saw a chance to attack *Nobunaga* (*Nobunaga* was with a very few men on that day) and took the opportunity. The other is: *Shogun Ashikaga Yoshiaki* (足利義昭) and his surroundings ordered *Akechi* to kill *Nobunaga* since *Akechi* had once worked under him. *Shogun Yoshiaki* was afraid that *Nobunaga* would become too powerful. More theories go on. We don't know the real reason; we still debate over it. It is one big mystery of Japanese history.

After this happened, the news was relayed to *Toyotomi Hideyoshi,* a counterpart of *Akechi* under *Nobunaga*. At that time, *Hideyoshi* happened to be in Bicchu (備中, Okayama prefecture today), which is about 230 KM (143 miles) away from *Kyoto* (See the map below). *Hideyoshi* quickly returned to *Kyoto* with his troop to avenge his master against *Akechi* and killed him.

Here is another mystery. The time between *Nobunaga* was killed and the time *Akechi* was killed by *Hideyoshi* was only ten days. *Hideyoshi* was 230 KM (143 miles) away. There were many mountains and rivers in between. That means in 10 days, *Hideyoshi* received the information of *Nobunaga's* death, packed up and hurried back 230 KM (143 miles) to *Kyoto* with his large number of soldiers and fought against *Akechi* and killed him. Their means of transportation at the time were minimal. Even though *Hideyoshi* had a communication route established between *Nobunaga's* inner circle all the time, it is an amazing speed. There are also speculations that *Akechi* and *Hideyoshi* were behind together(?) or some other secret plot behind the incidents.

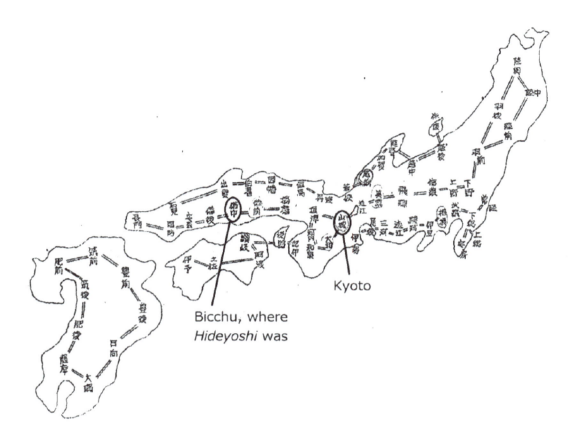

Bicchu, where Hideyoshi was

Kyoto

After *Hideyoshi* killed *Akechi, Hideyoshi* cleverly maneuvered his way up to the top of the power. While *Hideyoshi* was in charge, he mined a large amount of gold from the gold mines he possessed. There is a record stating that *Hideyoshi* buried a vast amount of gold somewhere. But we have never found it yet.

Hideyoshi was a poor farmer's son who became the most powerful man in the country. His success story fascinates the Japanese. *Nobunaga, Hideyoshi,* and *Tokugawa Ieyasu* are the three most depicted subjects on TV programs and movies. After *Hideyoshi* died of natural causes, *Tokugawa Ieyasu* became *Shogun,* and the *Edo* period started.

The reference source
*Rekijin.com/?p=31448-キャッシュ
*Bushoojapan.com/scandal/2019/06/02/51145-キャッシュ

57| Part 2 of --23 Sengoku Period Sword (戦国時代刀)

Chapter 57 is a detailed part of Chapter 23, Sengoku Period Sword. Please read Chapter 23 Sengoku period sword before reading this section.

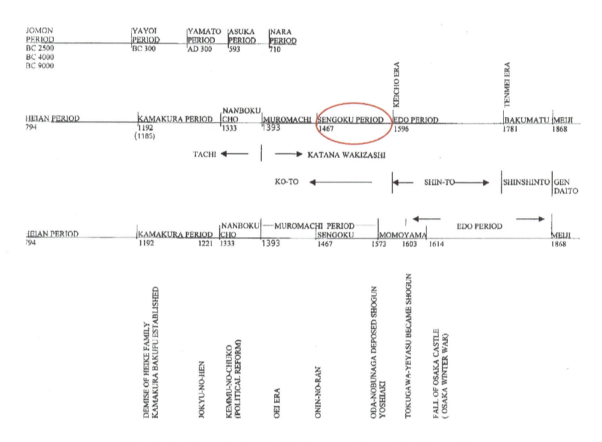

The circle above indicates the time we discuss in this section

During the *Sengoku* period (Warring States time), the *Mino Den* group and *Bizen Osafune* group were the primary sword makers. During almost 100 years of the Warring States period, all *Daimyo* needed a large number of swords. If suppliers were closer, that was even better. Many *Sengoku Daimyo* (戦国大名: Warlord) could reach the *Mino* area easily because of the central location. Since the *Heian* period, *Mino* swordsmiths were creating swords there.

One of the well-known swordsmiths of *Mino Den* at the end of the *Kamakura* period was *Shizu Kane'uji* (志津兼氏). He was one of the *Masamune Jitteru* (正宗十哲)*. But the real height for the *Mino Den* was the *Sengoku* period. During the *Sengoku* period, the

Shizu group and the *Tegai* group from the *Yamato* area and many swordsmiths from the *Yamashiro* (*Kyoto*) area moved to *Mino*. *Mino* became the busiest sword-making place. They made very practical swords for the *Sengoku* (Warring States Period) feudal lords.

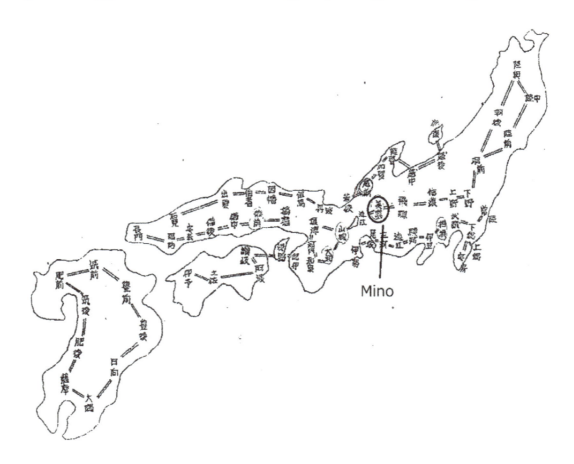

**Masamune Jittetsu* (正宗十哲) ----------The original meaning of *Masamune Jittetsu* was the top 10 *Masamune* students. However, later, this word was used more broadly. *Masamune* Jittetsu (正宗十哲)：*https://www.touken-world.jp/tips/7194/*

Three examples of Sengoku period swords

Three swords below are examples of the *Sengoku* period sword. Please note that every sword is different. Even each sword made by the same swordsmith is different. Please refer to Chapter 23 Sengoku Period Sword for the primary common characteristics of the swords made during the *Sengoku* period.

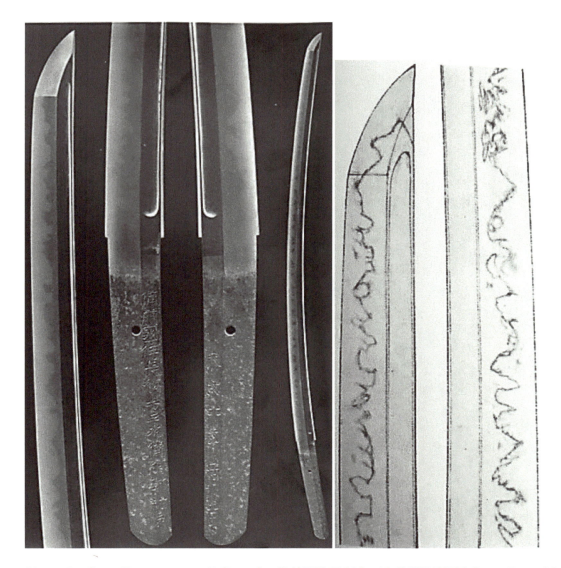

Bizen Osafune Yosozaemon Sukesada (備前国住長船与三左衛門尉祐定) from Sano Museum Catalog (permission granted).

Characteristics on the sword above.

Hamon is *Kani-no-tsume* (crab claw pattern, see above *Hamon*). *Kani-no-tsume* pattern *Hamon* never appeared in the *Heian, Kamakura,* or *Nanboku-cho* period. This type of *Hamon* is one of the decisive points to determine as a *Sengoku* Period sword. *Marudome-hi* (the end of the groove is round) often appears on the *Bizen Den* sword during the *Sengoku* period. Wide tempered area. *Midare-komi Boshi* (*Hamon* on the body and the *Boshi* is the same pattern) has a long turn-back and an abrupt stop. *Hamon* is the *Nioi* base. Most *Bizen* swords have *Nioi,* with a few exceptions.

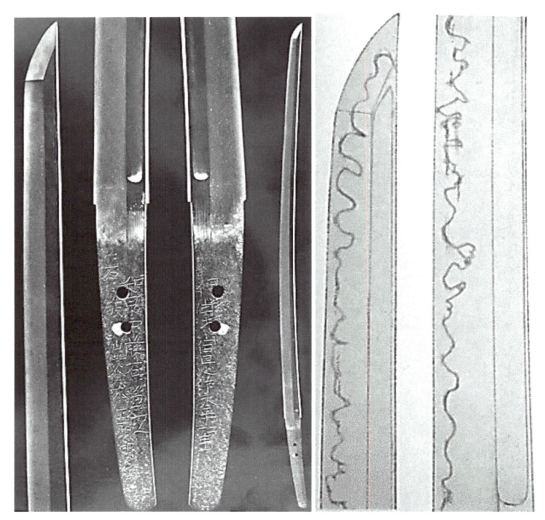

Izuminokami Fujiwara Kanesada (和泉守藤原兼㝎) From Sano Museum Catalog

Characteristic on the sword above

The last letter of the *Kanji* (Chinese characters) of the swordsmith's name above is "㝎." We use this uncommon letter in place of common "定" for him. The reason is there are two *Kanesada*. To distinguish him from the other *Kanesada* (兼定), we instead use the letter "㝎" and call him *Nosada* "のさだ."

Izuminokami Fujiwara Kanesada (AKA *Nosada*) is the top swordsmith of *Mino Den* at the time. The sword's shape is the typical *Sengoku* period style: shallow curvature, *Chu-gissaki* (medium size *Kissaki*), and pointed *Gunome Hamon*. The width of the *Hamon* is wide and narrow. Often, *Nosada* and other *Mino Den* swordsmiths have wood grain patterns with *Masame* on *Ji-hada*. *Nioi* base, mixed with coarse *Nie*.

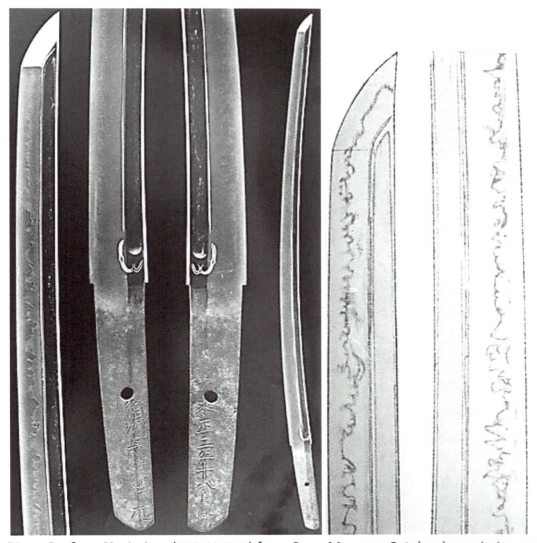

Bizen Osafune Norimitsu (備前長船法光) from Sano Museum Catalog (permission granted)

Characteristics on the sword above

Shallow curvature. Sturdy look. *Marudome-hi* (*Hi* ends round). Pointed *Hamon* called *Togari-ba* (尖り刃). *Nioi* base, mixed with *Nie*. Slight *Masame* and wood grain pattern on *Ji-hada*.

58 | Part 2 of -- 24 Sengoku Period Tanto (戦国時代短刀)

Chapter 58 is a continued part of chapter 24, Sengoku Period Tanto. Please read chapter 24, Sengoku Period Tanto, before reading this section.

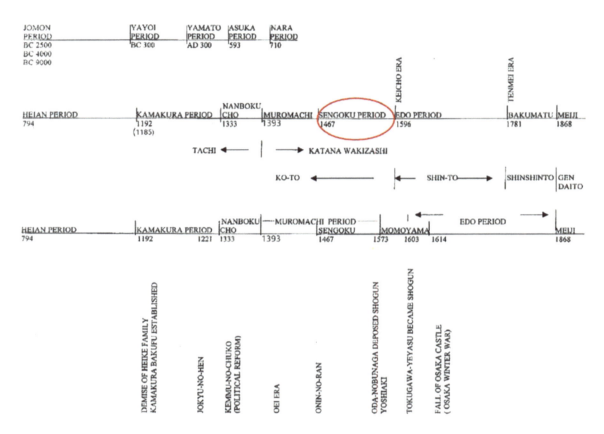

The circle above indicates the time we discuss in this section

Muramasa (村正)

The discussion of this chapter is about the famous *Muramasa* (村正). Usually, many well-known swordsmiths were from one of the *Goka Den* (五家伝：The primary five schools: *Yamashiro Den, Bizen Den, Soshu Den, Yamato Den, and Mino Den*). However, *Muramasa* was not from the *Goka Den* but *Ise* Province. The first generation *Muramasa* was known as a student of *He'ian-jo Nagayoshi* (平安城長吉) of *Yamashiro Den*. The *Muramasa* family lived through the mid-*Muromachi* period. They had three generations from the mid-*Muromachi* period to the *Sengoku* period.

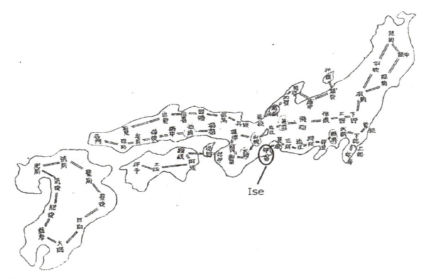

Here is one of *Muramasa's Tanto* that was made during the *Sengoku* period. Since this is the *Sengoku* period *Tanto*, the blade shows the *Sengoku* period sword style. It shows *Mino Den* characteristics, with the *Soshu Den* characteristics added.

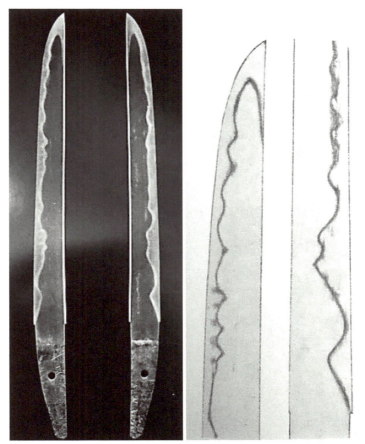

Muramasa (村正) from Sano Museum Catalogue (permission granted)

Characteristics on this Tanto

Muramasa's Tantos are often 10 inches ± half inches or so. *Hirazukuri* (平作り). Thin blade with a sharp look. *Nioi* base with small *Nie* and *Sunagashi* (brushed sand-like patterns, the illustration below) appears. *Boshi* (the top part of *Hamon*) is *Jizo* (a side view of a human's head). The tempered line has wide areas and narrow areas. Some areas are so narrow, close to the edge of the blade, while others are broad. *Hako midare* (box-like shape) and *Gunome* (lined-up beads pattern) appear. *O-notare* (large gentle waviness) is a *Muramasa's* signature characteristic. The pointed tempered line is a typical *Mino Den characteristic* (*Sanbon-sugi*). Refer to Chapter 23 Sengoku Period Sword and Chapter 24 Sengoku Period Tanto.

Sunagashi

59| Part 2 of – 25 Edo Period History (江戸時代歴史)

Chapter 59 is a detailed part of Chapter 25 Edo Period History (江戸時代歴史). Please read Chapter 25 before reading this section.

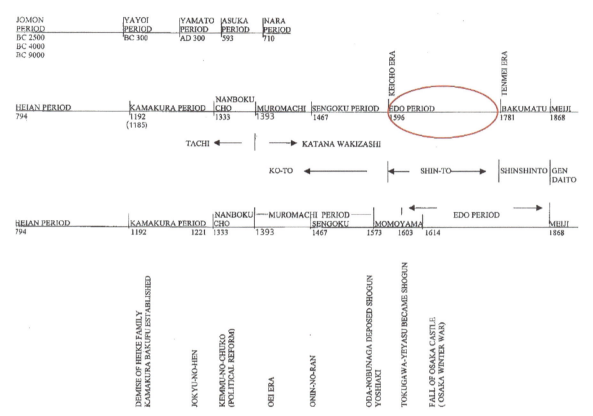

The circle above indicates the time we discuss in this section

Battle of Sekigahara (関ヶ原合戦)

Toyotomi Hideyoshi (豊臣秀吉), the most powerful man during the *Sengoku* period (and *Momoyama* period), died in 1598. At that time, his heir, *Hideyori* (秀頼), was only five years old. Before *Hideyoshi's* death, he set up a council system that consisted of the top five *Daimyo* to take care of the jobs for *Hideyori* as his regents until he grew up to be an adult.

At *Hideyoshi*'s death bed, all the five *Daimyo* agreed to be the guardians of *Hideyori*. But, little by little, *Ishida Mitsunari* (石田三成) and *Tokugawa Ieyasu* (徳川家康) began disagreeing with each other. In 1600, finally, those two main *Daimyo* clashed, and the

Battle of *Sekigahara* broke out. One side is called *Seigun* (the western army), led by *Ishida Mitsunari,* and the other, *Togun* (the Eastern army) by *Tokugawa Ieyasu*. All the *Daimyo* in the country took either *Tokugawa* or *Ishida Mitsunari's* side. It is said that the *Mitsunari's Seigun* had 100,000 men, while the *Tokugawa's Togun,* 70,000 men. *Ieyasu* had fewer soldiers, but he won in the end. *Ieyasu* became the *Toyotomi* clan's chief retainer, which means that he was virtually the top person because *Hideyori* was still a child.

In 1603 *Ieyasu* became the *Shogun*. Now *Ieyasu* seized control of Japan, and he established the *Tokugawa Bakufu* (government) in *Edo* and eliminated the council system.

Toyotomi Hideyori was still there with his mother, *Yodo-gimi* (淀君 or *Yodo-dono* 淀殿)、in *Osaka* Castle, which *Hideyoshi* built before he died. After a while, the relationship between *Hideyori-Yodo-gimi,* the *Osaka* side, and *Ieyasu,* the *Edo* side, became awkward. *Yodo-gimi* was a very proud and headstrong person with good reasons. She was a niece of *Oda Nobunaga,* the wife of *Toyotomi Hideyoshi,* and the mother of *Hideyori,* the head of the *Toyotomi* clan. Later, her pride got her into trouble and led to the destruction of the *Toyotomi* clan.

Siege of Osaka: Winter (1614) and Summer (1615) Campaigns

During the 15 years between the *Battle of Sekigahara* and the Siege of *Osaka* Castle, the tension between the *Tokugawa* Shogunate and the *Toyotomi* clan built up little by little. Before the *Battle of Sekigahara*, the *Toyotomi* clan ruled Japan. After the *Sekigahara,* the *Tokugawa Bakufu* began to rule Japan. The *Toyotomi* clan lost many top advisers and vassals in the battle. As a result, all the power of the *Toyotomi's* centered around *Yodo-gimi*.
By the time of the siege, *Hideyori* grew up to be a fine man, but *Yodo-gimi* had overprotected her son and controlled him. She even did not allow *Hideyori* to practice *Kendo* (Japanese traditional martial art of swordsmanship), saying it was too dangerous.

She persistently acted as if the *Toyotomi* clan was still in supreme power. *Tokugawa Ieyasu* tried to calm the friction by having his grand-daughter, *Sen-hime,* married to *Hideyori*. A few advisors suggested *Yodo-gimi* yield to *Tokugawa,* but she insisted that *Tokugawa* had to subordinate himself to *Toyotomi*. A rumor began to spread that the *Toyotomi* side started to hire and gather many *Ronin* (unemployed *Samurai*) inside the

Osaka Castle. Several key persons tried to mediate the *Toyotomi* clan and the *Tokugawa* clan but failed.

Finally, *Ieyasu* led his army to *Osaka,* and in November 1614, began a campaign to *siege* the *Osaka* Castle (the Winter Campaign). It is said that the *Toyotomi* side had 100,000 soldiers, but some of them were just mercenaries. However, *Osaka* Castle was built almost like a fortress itself, very hard to attack. The *Tokugawa* army attacked hard and fired cannon every day, but they realized that the castle was so solid that it was a waste of time to continue.

Eventually, both sides went to a peace negotiation. They agreed on several items of the treaty. One of them was to fill the outer moat of the *Osaka* Castle. But the *Tokugawa* side filled both the outer and the inner moats. That made the *Toyotomi* side angry, and they became suspicious that the *Tokugawa* might not keep the agreement.

Another agreement was the disarmament of the *Toyotomi* clan. Yet the *Toyotomi* side kept having their soldiers inside the castle. *Tokugawa* gave the last ultimatum to the *Toyotomi* side to dismiss all soldiers from the castle or move out from the castle. *Yodo-gimi* refused both.

After that, another siege started in the summer of 1615 (the Summer Campaign). It is said that the *Toyotomi* had 70,000 men, and the *Tokugawa* had 150,000 men. Both sides had several battles here and there, but the fights did not go well for both sides in the beginning because of the thick fog, delayed arrival of troops, miscommunications, etc. The last battlefield was in *Osaka* Castle. The *Toyotomi* decided to stay inside the castle, but soon a fire broke out from inside and burned the castle. *Yodo-gimi* and *Hideyori* hid inside the storage building, waiting for *Ieyasu's* answer to the plea for their lives. They hoped their daughter-in-law could achieve the bargain. But It was not accepted, and they both died inside the storage building.

Nene and Yodo-gimi

Nene was the lawful wife of *Toyotomi Hideyoshi*. She was a brilliant and sensible person but not a high born. Everybody respected her, including *Tokugawa Ieyasu*. Even *Hideyoshi* often followed her opinions on political matters. She helped *Hideyoshi* to climb up his ranks. However, *Nene* could not bear a child. *Toyotomi Hideyoshi* went around other women everywhere, hoping to get his heir, but nobody could have his child except *Yodo-gimi*. Naturally, a rumor went around who the true birth father was. The speculation indicated several men, and one of them was *Ishida Mitsunari*.

伝　淀殿画像 (It is said to be a portrait of *Yodo-dono* but no evidence,) Owned by Nara Museum of Art   Public Domain: Yodo-dono cropped.jpg from Wikimedia Commons, the free media repository

Nene (Kodai-in), Toyotomi Hideyoshi's lawful wife. Public domain from Wikimedia, owned by Kodai-Ji (高台寺)

60| Part 2 of -- 26 Overview of Shin-to (新刀概要)

Chapter 60 is a Continued part of Chapter 26 Overview of Shinto (新刀概要). Please read Chapter 26 before reading this section.

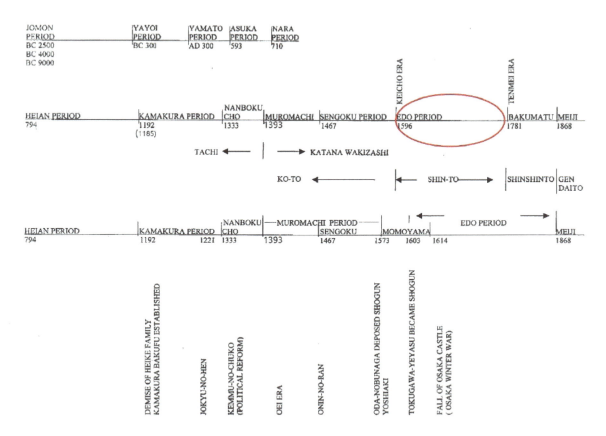

The circle above indicates the time we discuss in this section

The difficulty of Shin-to Kantei

Regarding the swords during *Ko-to* time, one can tell the approximate period when they were made by looking at the style and the shape. Several conditions indicate what period and which *Gokaden* (五ヶ伝) created the particular sword by looking at several points, like how the *Hamon* showed or how the *Ji-gane* appeared. But with the swords in the *Shin-to* time, that does not work.

Even though there are some differences among the *Shin-to* swords made in the early *Edo* period, which is around the *Keicho* (慶長: 1596 ~) era, the middle *Edo* period that is around the *Kanbun* (寛文:1661 ~) era, and the late *Edo* period that is *Genroku* era (元禄:

1688 ~), the differences are not much.

The same is true about the *Gokaden* (五ヶ伝) during the *Shin-to* time. In the *Ko-to* time, *Bizen* swordsmiths forged swords with *Bizen* characteristics. The blades *Yamato* swordsmiths made usually showed the *Yamato Den* characteristics. But in the *Shin-to* time, a swordsmith of one particular *Den* sometimes forged the style of another *Den's* features. As a result, it is hard to determine who forged a specific sword.

For *Shin-to*, we study the characteristics of seven main locations. The following chapters will go over them.

Picturesque Hamon

In and after the *Genroku* era (元禄 1688 - 1704), some picturesque *Hamon* became a trendy style. Some swordsmiths made picturesque *Hamon* on *Wakizashi* or short swords. Since it became very popular, especially among foreigners, most of them were exported outside of Japan around the *Meiji* Restoration time. Very few are left in Japan today.

The swordsmiths who made picturesque Hamon

Yamashiro (山城) area-- Iga-no-kami Kinmichi (伊賀守金道)
　　　　　　　　　　　　　　　　　　　　　　　　Omi-no-kami Hisamichi (近江守久道)
Settsu-no-Kuni (摂津) area -------------------------- Tanba-no-Kami Yoshimichi (丹波守吉道)
　　　　　　　　　　　　　　　　　　　　　　　　Yamato-no-Kami Yoshimichi (大和守吉道)

　　　　Kikusui　　　　　　　　Fuji

61 | Part 2 of -- 27 Shin-to Main 7 Regions (Part A: 主要 7 刀匠地)

This chapter is a continued part of Chapter 27 Shin-to Main 7 Regions (part A). Please read Chapter 27 before reading this section.

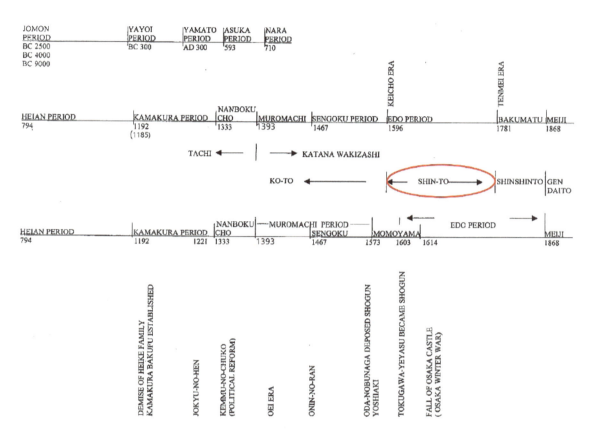

The circle above indicates the time we discuss in this section

Chapter 27, Shin-to Main 7 Regions (part A), and Chapter 28, Shin-to Main 7 Regions (part B) described an overview of the seven main regions. This chapter and the next chapter show photos of the representative swords from these regions. They are *Yamashiro* (山城 in Kyoto), *Settsu* (摂津 today's Osaka), *Musashi* (武蔵 Edo), *Satsuma* (薩摩 Kyushu). But *Echizen* (越前), *Kaga* (加賀), and *Hizen* (肥前) are skipped.

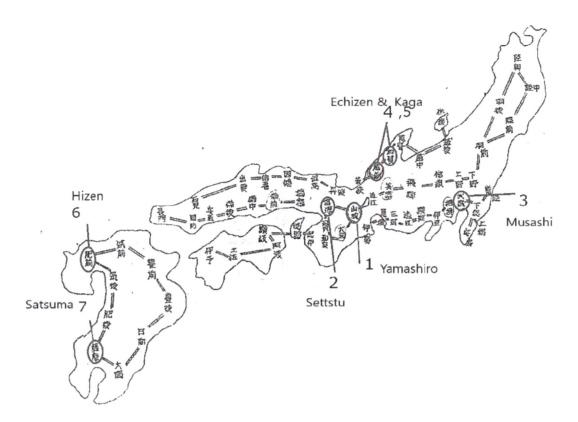

With the *Ko-to* swords, the shape, the condition of the *Hamon, Kissaki* size, the length, and the shape of the *Nakago, etc.,* indicate when the sword was forged. In *Ko-to* time, the *Bizen* swordsmiths forged the *Bizen Den* swords; the *Yamashiro* swordsmiths forged the *Yamashiro Den* swords, the *Mino* swordsmiths forged the *Mino Den* sword. But with the *Shin-to*-time, that is not the case. The *Den* and the location of a swordsmith often do not match. For *Shin-to* sword, we study the swordsmiths and their main seven regions' swords and their characteristic.

Regarding the swords made in the *Ko-to* time, if a sword has a wide *Hamon* line with *Nie*, usually, its *Ji-hada* shows large wood grain or large burl grain. Also, when you see a narrow *Hamon* line, it usually has a fine *Ji-hada*.
However, with *Shin-to* swords, if a sword has a wide *Hamon* with *Nie*, it often has small wood grain or small burl grain pattern on *Ji-hada*. And if it has a narrow *Hamon* line, it may have a large wood grain pattern *Ji-hada*. That is the *Shin-to* characteristic.

Here is an exception; some of the early *Soshu Den* swords during the late *Kamakura* period show wide *Hamon* with *Nie*, which has small burls on *Ji-hada*. Because of that, whether it is *Ko-to* or *Shin-to* is confusing. Even so, other features like *Ji-hada* or other parts should indicate the *Shin-to* or *Ko-to*.

1. Yamashiro (山城: Kyoto)

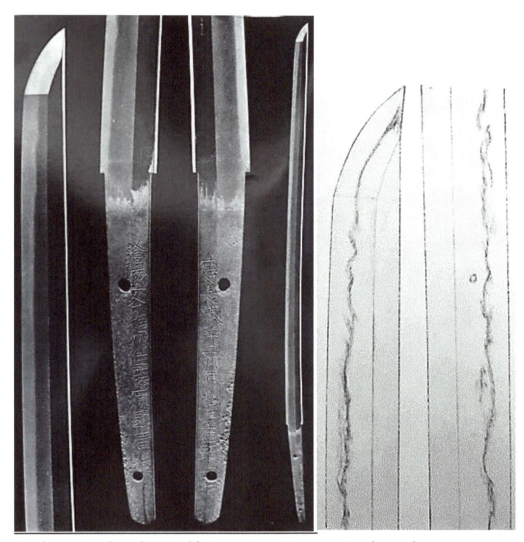

Horikawa Kunihiro (堀川国広) From Sano Museum Catalogue (permission to use granted)

Horikawa Kunihiro (堀川国広)

Horikawa Kunihiro was considered a great master swordsmith among *Shin-to* swordsmiths. He forged swords in many styles with different characteristics. *Hamon* types are *O-notare, O-gunome, Togari-ba* (pointed *hamon*), *Chu-suguha* with *Hotsure* (frayed look), *Hiro-suguha* with *Sunagashi* effect, *Inazuma*, or *Kinsuji* appears. *Kunihiro* liked to make his sword shape look like *O-suriage* (shortened *Nanboku-Cho* style long sword). *Kunihiro's* blade gives you a massive feeling. *Kunihiro's* swords often have beautiful carvings on them; designs include a dragon, Sanskrit letters, etc. Since his swords are in many different styles, there is no general characteristic on his swords other than that *Hamon* is mainly *Nie*. His *Ji-hada* is finely forged.

 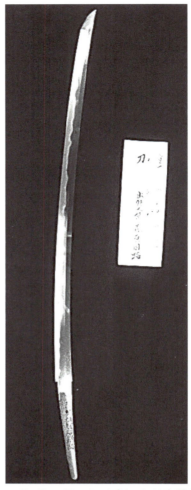

Iga-no-Kami Kin'michi (伊賀守金道)　　　　　Dewa Daijyo Kunimichi (出羽大掾国路)
Both *Juyo Token* (重要刀剣), once my family sword, photos taken by my father.

Iga-no-Kami Kinmichi (伊賀守金道)

The *Kinmichi* family is called the *Mishina* group. Refer <u>27 Shinto Main 7 Regions Part A</u>. *Iga-no-Kami Kinmichi* received the Japanese Imperial chrysanthemum crest.
<u>The characteristic of Kinmichi</u> -------- wide sword, shallow curvature, extended *Kissaki*, *Sakizori* (curvature at 1/3 top), wide tempered line, *Kyo-yakidashi* (refer <u>27 Shinto Main 7 Regions A</u>), *Hiro-suguha* (wide straight *Hamon*), *O-notare* (large wavy), *Yahazu-midare*, *Hako-midare* (refer <u>24 Sengoku Period Tanto</u>). *Boshi* is *Mishina-boshi*, refer <u>27 Shin-to Main 7 Regions A</u>. Fine wood burl, *Masame* appears on *Shinog-ji* area.

Dewa Daijo Kunimichi (出羽大掾国路)

Dewa Daijo Kunimichi was the best student of *Horikaw Kunihiro*. The right photo above. Like *Kunihiro,* shape of the sword looks like a shortened *Nanboku-cho* sword. Shallow curvature, wide-body, somewhat stretched *Kissaki,* and *Fukura-kareru* (less arch in *fukura*). Wide tempered line, large *Gunome*, *Nie* with *Sunagashi*, or *Inazuma* shows. Double *Gunome* (two *Gunome* side by side) appears. Fine *Ji-hada*.

2. Settu (摂津: Osaka 大阪)

Settu (*Osaka*) has many well-known swordsmiths. They are *Kawachi-no-Kami Kunisuke* (河内守国助), *Tsuda Echizen-no-Kami Sukehiro* (津田越前守助広), *Inoue Shinkai* (井上真改), *Ikkanshi Tadatsuna* (一竿子忠綱), etc.

The *Settsu* (*Osaka*) sword's main characteristic -------- The surface is beautiful and fine, almost like a solid look with no pattern or no design surface. The below two photos are of the *Settsu* sword.

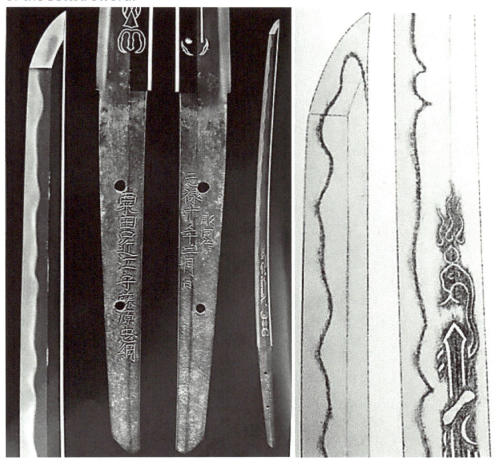

Ikkanshi Tadatsuna from Sano Museum Catalogue. (Permission to use granted)

Ikkanshi Tadatsuna (一竿子忠綱)

Ikkanshi Tadatsuna was famous for his carvings. His father was also a well-known swordsmith, *Omi-no-Kami Tadatsuna* (近江守忠綱). Therefore, he was also known as *Awataguchi Omi-no-Kami Fujiwara Tadatsuna* (粟田口近江守藤原忠綱), as you see in the *Nakago* above photo.

The characteristics of *Ikkanshi Tadatsuna* ----------- longer *kissaki*, wide tempered line with *Nie*. Osaka Yakidashi (transition between the *Suguha* above *Machi* and *Midare* is smooth. Refer to 27 Shin-to Sword - Main 7 Regions (part A) for *Osaka Yakidashi*. *O-notare* with *Gunome, Komaru-boshi* with a turn back, and very fine *Ji-hada* with almost no pattern on the surface.

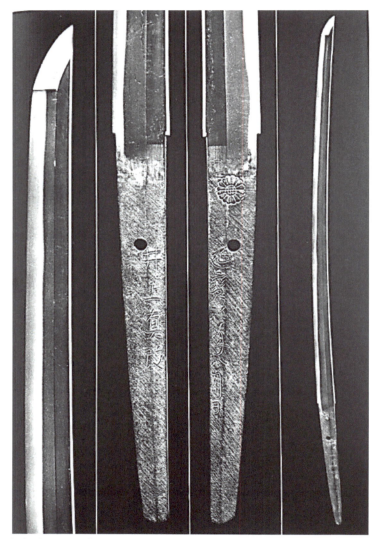

Inoue Shinkai (井上真改) from "Nippon-to Art Swords of Japan" The Walter A. Compton Collection

Inoue Shinkai (井上真改)

Inoue Shinkai was the second generation of *Izumi-no-Kami Kunisada* (和泉守国貞) who was a student of *Kunihiro*.

The characteristic of *Inoue Shinkai's* swords ------------------*Osaka Yakidashi,* the tempered line gradually becomes wider toward the top. *O-Notare* and deep *Nie*. Very fine *Ji-hada* with almost no design on the surface.

62 | Part 2 of -- 28 Shin-to Main 7 Regions (Part B: 主要7刀匠地)

This chapter is a continued part of Chapter 28 Shin-to Main 7 Regions (part B). Please read chapter 28 before reading this chapter. Below are regions 3, 7.

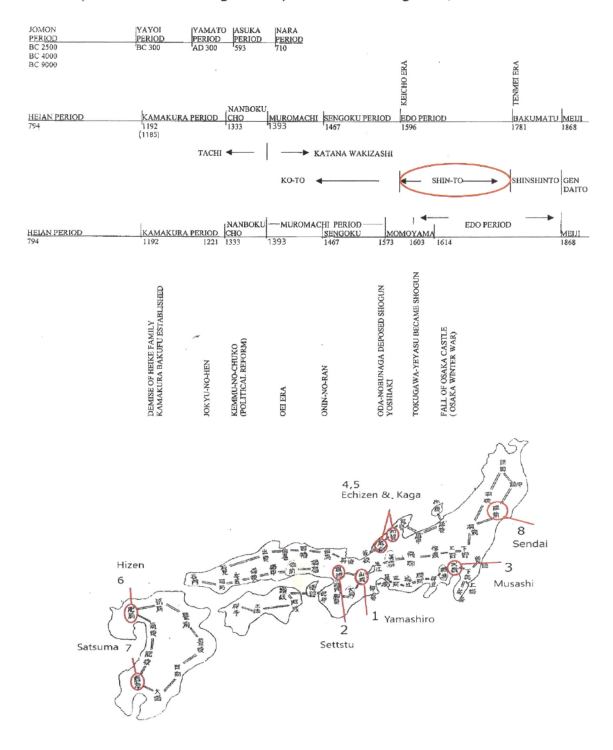

3. Musashi (Edo)

We find many famous swordsmiths in *Edo* also. They were *Yasutsugu* (康継), *Kotetsu* (虎徹), *Noda Hankei* (野田繁慶), *Hojoji Masahiro* (法成寺正弘), and their followers.

Two photos below are swordsmiths from *Musashi* (武蔵: Tokyo) area.

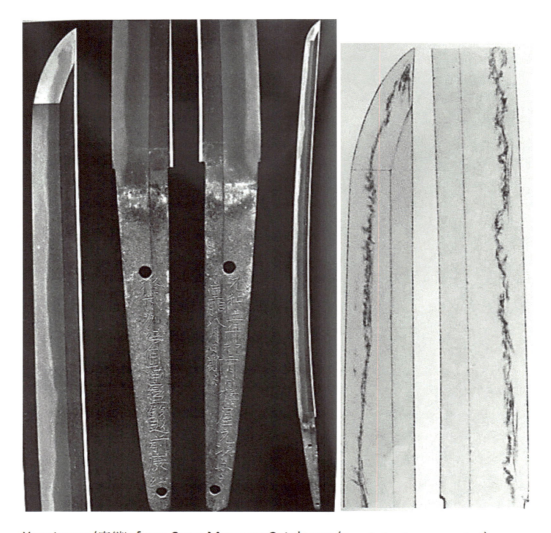

Yasutsugu (康継) from Sano Museum Catalogue (Permission to use granted).

Characteristics of *Yasutusgu* (康継) ------shallow curvature; *Chu-gissaki* (medium *Kissaki*); wide *Notare Hamon, Midare,* or *O-gunome* (sometimes double *Gunome*); a trace of *Soshu Den* and *Mino Den;* and wood-grain pattern mixed with *Masame* on *Shinogi-ji*.

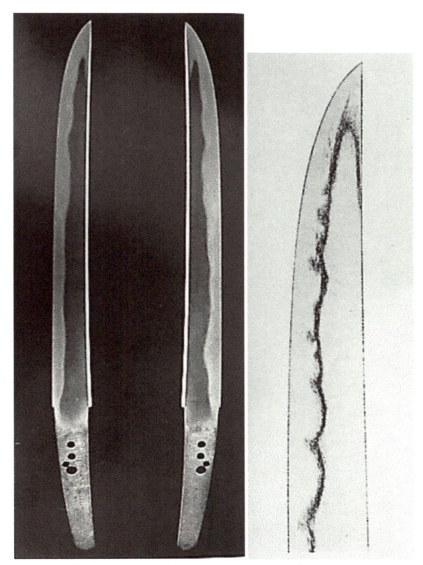

Kotetsu (虎徹) from Sano Museum Catalogue (permission to use granted)

Here is the famous *Kotetsu*. His formal name was *Nagasone Okisato Nyudo Kotetsu* (長曽祢興里入道虎徹). *Kotetsu* began to make swords after he passed 50 years old. Before that, he was an armor maker.

The characteristics of Kotetsu ------------------------------ shallow curvature and wide width, wide tempered line with *Nie*. Small irregular *Hamon* at about the *Machi* area, becoming wide *Suguha* like *Notare* at the upper area. Fine *Nie*, *Komaru-boshi* with a short turn back. *Ji-hada* is fine wood grain and burl. Sometimes, you see *O-hada* (black core iron show through) at the lower part above the *Machi* area. The illustration above shows a thick tempered line with *Nie*, which is the typical *Kotetsu's* characteristic. Once you see it, you will remember it. The next region is 7, skipping 4, 5, and 6.

7. Satsuma (Kyushu)

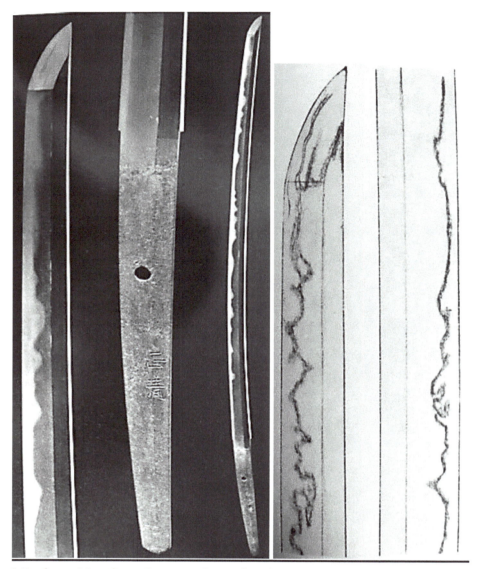

Miyahara Mondonosho Masakiyo (宮原主水正正清) from Sano Museum Catalogue, (permission to use granted).

Miyahara Mondonosho Masakiyo was highly regarded by the *Shimazu* family of *Satsuma Han* (*Satsuma* domain in *Kyushu*). Later he was chosen to go to *Edo* to forge swords for *Shogun Yoshimune*.

Mondonosho Masakiyo's characteristics-------------Well balanced sword shape, shallow curvature, and wide and narrow *Hamon* mixed with squarish *Hamon* and pointed *Hamon* as shown in the photo above. He engraved the *Aoi* crest (the hollyhock crest of the *Tokugawa* family) on *Nakago*.

63 | Part 2 of -- 29 Bakumatsu Period History (幕末歷史)

This chapter is a continued part of Chapter 29 Bakumatu Period history. Please read Chapter 29 before reading this chapter.

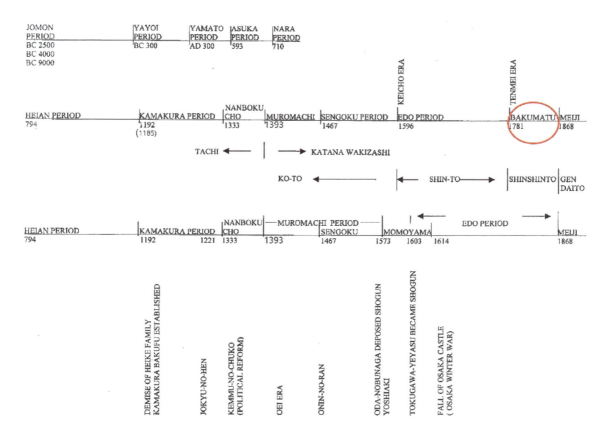

The circle above indicates the time we discuss in this section

The last part of the *Edo* period, around the *Tenmei* era (天明), from 1781 to 1868, is called *Bakumatsu*. During this time, the economy in Japan began stagnating.

The several *Tokugawa Shogun* in different generations tried to perform financial reforms, but each time, it succeeded somewhat, but it never solved the core fundamental economic problems.

Tokugawa Bakufu tried mostly to impose fiscal restraint on the government, forced people to lead a frugal life, and banned even a small luxury. You know this only shrinks the economy and gets things even worse. On top of it, they raised the prevailing interest rate, thinking that may solve the problem. It was a typical non-economist solution. The interest rate should be lowered in a situation like this. As a result, lower-level *Samurai* became more impoverished, and farmers revolted often. In addition, many natural disasters struck the farming area. The famous *Kurosawa* movie "*Seven Samurai*" was staged around this time. As we all know, "Magnificent Seven" was a Hollywood version of the "Seven *Samurai*."

Yet little by little, a small cottage industry began to grow, together with the improved farming productivity led by the local leaders. Merchants became affluent, and towns-people in the city became wealthier. However, the gap between rich and poor became wider. And the problem of *Ronin* (unemployed *Samurai*) became severe to the level where it was almost dangerous to society.

The Edo Towns-people's Culture

During this time, novels were written for ordinary people, too, instead of only for the upper-class. In the past, the paintings were related to religion and only for the upper-class. Now they became for the ordinary people too.

The Bakumatsu time was the golden time for "*Ukioe* (浮世絵)." *Kitagawa Utamaro* (喜多川歌麿 1753-1800) was well-known for portraits of ladies. *Katsushika Hokusai* (1760-1849 葛飾北斎) and *Ando Hiroshige* (1797-1858 安藤広重) were famous for scenery woodblock paintings. *Maruyama Okyo* (円山応挙) drew pictures using the European perspective method. *Katsushika Hokusai's* daughter also drew some of her paintings in perspective. Her name is "*Ooi,* 応為". Only a few of her works are left now. It is said that even her genius father was surprised at her ability to draw.

Though the number was small, some people learned the Dutch language. The Netherlands was one of the only two countries that were allowed to enter Japan then. Those people translated the European medical book into Japanese using French and Dutch dictionaries, and they wrote a book called "*Kaitai Shinsho* (解体新書)". After this book was translated, European history books, economy books, political books were translated. New ideas emerged from those books and influenced the intellects.

In society, schooling was thriving. Each feudal domain ran its schools for the sons of the *Daimyo's* retainers. Children of the towns-people went to a school called *Terakoya* (寺子屋: an unofficial neighborhood school) to learn reading, writing, and arithmetic.

Pressure from the Outside World

Even though Japan was in *Sakoku* state (鎖国: national isolation policy), people knew what was happening outside of Japan. Since the early 17th century, messengers from Russia came to Japan to demand trades (1792 and 1804). In 1808, English ships came to *Nagasaki*. In 1825, *Tokugawa Bakufu* ordered to fire guns at any ships that came close to Japan. In 1842, when England won the Opium War against the Qing dynasty, *Bakufu* decided to supply foreign ships with food and fuel. They were afraid to have the same fate as Qing. In 1846, the U.S. sent Japan a fleet commander to open diplomatic relations, but the *Bakufu* refused. The U.S. needed Japan to open the ports to supply food, water, and fuel for their whaling ships in the Pacific Ocean.

In 1853, a fleet commander, Perry*, arrived at *Uraga* (浦賀: a port of Japan) with four warships displaying American military power to open the country. *Tokugawa Bakufu* did not have any clear policy on handling such a situation and realized it is difficult to maintain the isolation policy any longer.

In 1854, "the Japan-U.S. Treaty of Amity and Friendship" was signed. After that, Japan made treaties with England, Russia, France, and the Netherlands. That ended over 200 years of *Sakoku* (national isolation policy), and Japan opened several ports for foreign ships.

However, those treaties caused many problems. The treaties were unequal. It caused Japan a shortage of daily necessities; as a result, the prices went up. Also, a large amount of gold flowed out of Japan. It was caused by the difference in the exchange rate of gold to silver between Japan and Europe. In Japan, the exchange rate was gold 1 to silver 5, but in Europe, it was gold 1 to silver 15.

On top of these problems, there was another problem; who should be the next *Shogun* after *Shogun Tokugawa Yesada* (徳川家定), since he did not have any heir. At a chaotic time like this, many feudal domains opposing each other wanted a *Shogun* whose political idea was on their side. Many other problems already had caused big battles among domains, and there were also other reasons for them to oppose the *Bakufu*.

Now the base of *Tokugawa Bakufu* began to fall apart. The *Choshu-han* (*Choshu* domain) and the *Satsuma-han* (*Satsuma* domain) were the main forces against the *Tokugawa Bakufu*. In the beginning, they opposed each other. But after many strained incidents, they decided to reconcile and went after the *Bakufu* together since they realized it was not the time to fight among themselves. England, realizing *Bakufu* did not have much power any longer, started to be closer to the Emperor's side, whereas

France sided with *Tokugawa*. England and France almost started a war in Japan.

In 1867, *Tokugawa Yoshinobu* issued "the Restoration of Imperial Rule (*Taisei Hokan,* 大政奉還)." In 1868, the *Tokugawa* clan left the *Edo* Castle, and the *Meiji* Emperor moved in. It is now called *Kokyo* (皇居: Imperial Palace). The present Emperor lives there.

Many well-known political figures were the driving forces and played an active role in toppling the *Tokugawa Bakufu*. *Ito Hirobumi* (伊藤博文), *Okubo Toshimichi* (大久保利通), *Shimazu Nariakira* (島津斉彬), and *Hitotsubashi Yoshinobu* (一橋慶喜) are among those. They established a new government system, the *Meiji Shin Seifu* (明治新政府), centering around the Emperor.

The original *Edo-jo* (Castle) was lost by a big fire, yet the original moat (you can see several swans), massive stone walls, a beautiful bridge called *Nijyu-bashi* (二重橋 below) are still there. Big garden areas are open to the public and free to walk around. This area is famous for beautiful cherry blossoms. The Imperial Palace is in front of and a walking distance from the *Marunouchi* side of Tokyo station.

Today, the Japanese like the historical dramas of the *Meiji Ishin* (*Meiji* Restoration) time, and we see them on TV and in movies quite often. Those are stories of *Saigo Takamori* (西郷隆盛), *Sakamoto Ryoma* (坂本龍馬), and *Shinnsen-Gumi* (新撰組). Though it was fiction, the Hollywood movie "Last *Samurai*" was staged around this time with a real historical character, *Saigo Takamori*.

Imperial Palace (From) Wikimedia Commons, the free media repository)

*Perry

Commodore M.C. Perry came to Japan two times with four warships. In 1853, he brought the sovereign diplomatic letter from the president of the U.S. The following year, he came back and demanded the answer to the letter. After the expedition, Perry wrote a book about his journey, "Expedition of an American Squadron to the China Seas and Japan, Under the command of Commodore M.C. Perry, United States Navy by order of the Government of the United States."   In his book, he mentioned Japan very favorably; the beautiful scenery and people's ingenuities, lively, active women, and drawings.

 Even though it was a long, tough negotiation between *Edo Bakufu* and Perry, there were several fun moments. Perry displayed and presented Japan with a 1:4-scale model steam locomotive, a sewing machine, etc. The Japanese had a *Sumo* match and presented him gifts like silk, lacquer wares, etc. The Japanese prepared elaborate banquets for the American diplomats. Perry also invited the Japanese officials for his feast. The biggest hit was when Perry served a dessert at the end of the dinner. Perry printed each guest's family crest on a small flag and put it on the desert.

Before starting his expedition, he had anticipated tough negotiations lying ahead. So, he had studied what Japanese like beforehand and discovered that the Japanese would enjoy parties a lot. He brought skilled chefs and loaded the ship with some livestock to Japan for future parties. He entertained Japanese officials with whiskey, wine, beer, etc. Initially, the U.S. wanted Japan to open five ports, whereas *Bakufu* was willing to open only one port. In the end, both sides agreed on opening three ports.

ja.wikipedia.org/wiki/黒船来航

ja.wikipedia.org/wiki/マシュー・ペリー

64| Part 2 of -- 30 Shin Shin-to: Bakumatsu Sword (新々刀)

Chapter 64 is a detailed Chapter of 30|Bakumatsu Period, Shin Shin-to. Please read Chapter 30 before reading this chapter.

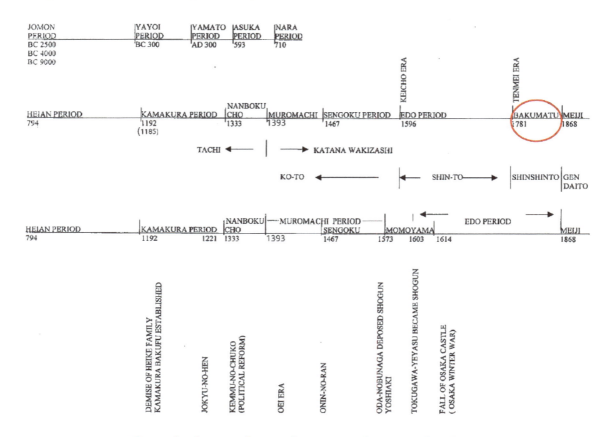

The circle above indicates the time we discuss in this chapter.

Swords made between the *Tennmei* era (天明 1781) and the end of *Keio* era (慶應) are called *Shin Shin*-to. Please see the timeline above. It was the time Japan was moving toward the *Meiji* Restoration. It was the *Bakumatsu* time. During that time, sword-making was active again. Below are the well-known swordsmiths in the main areas.

Musashi no Kuni (武蔵の国: Tokyo today)

Suishinshi Masahide (水心子正秀) ----------- When *Suishinshi Masahide* made *Yamashiro Den* style swords, the shape was similar to one of the *Ko-to* time swords; *Funbari*, elegant shape, *Chu-suguha* (medium straight), *Komaru-boshi,* fine wood grain. When he forged the *Bizen* style, he made a *Koshi-zori* shape, just like a *Ko-to* by Bizen Osafune.

Nioi with *Ko-choji,* and *Katai-ha* (Refer to 30| Bakumatsu Period Sword 新々刀). I wrote in my sword textbook that I saw *Suishinshi* in November 1970 and October 1971.

Taikei Naotane (大慶直胤) ---------------------------Although *Taikei Naotane* was within the *Suishinshi* group, he was among the top swordsmiths. He had an amazing ability to forge all kinds of different styles of swords wonderfully. When he made a *Bizen Den* style, it looked like *Nagamitsu* from the *Ko-to* time with *Nioi*. Also, he did *Sakasa-choji* as *Katayama Ichimonji* had done. *Katai-ha* appears. My note in the textbook says that I saw *Naotane* in August 1971.

Minamoto no Kiyomaro (源清麿) -------------------------- *Kiyomaro* desired to join the *Meiji* Restoration movement as a *Samurai*, still, his guardian realized *Kiyomaro's* ability as a great swordsmith and helped him become one. It is said that because *Kiyomaro* had a drinking problem, he was not so eager to forge swords. At age 42, he committed *Seppuku*. *Kiyomaro,* who lived in *Yotsuya* (a part of *Shinjuku, Tokyo,* today), was called *Yotsuya Masamune* because he was as good as *Masamune*. His swords were wide width, shallow *Sori*, stretched *Kissaki,* and *Fukura-kareru*. *Boshi* has *Komaru-boshi*. Fine wood grain *Ji-gane*.

Settsu no Kuni (摂津の国: Osaka today)

Gassan Sadakazu (月山貞一) ---------- *Gassan* was good at *Soshu Den* style and *Bizen Den* style, but he could make any kinds of style. He was as genius as *Taikei Naotane.* One needs to pay attention to notice a sword made by *Gassan* from a real *Ko-to*. He also had an amazing ability in carving. His *hirazukuri-kowakizashi* forged in *Soshu Den* style looks just like a *Masamune* or a *Yukimitsu*. He forged the *Yamashiro Den* style with *Takenoko-zori* with *Hoso-suguha* or *Chu-suguha* in *Nie*. He also forged the *Yamato Den* style with *Masame-hada*.

65 | The Sword Observation Process

This chapter shows the handling and viewing process of the sword.

1. Wear white gloves or hold a handkerchief in each hand.

 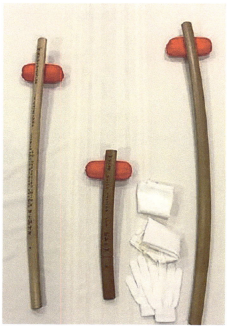

2. Bow lightly. Hold the *Tsuka* (hilt) with your right hand and the *Saya* (scabbard) with your left hand. Pull the *Saya* out. Doing this, the back of the *Saya* faces the floor, and the *Ha* faces up. The *Mune* should be resting on the inside of the *Saya*. Pull the blade carefully. Do not let the *Ha* touch the inner wall of the *Saya* to avoid getting scratches.

3. Set down the *Saya* on the left of the sword. Prepare the sword tool.

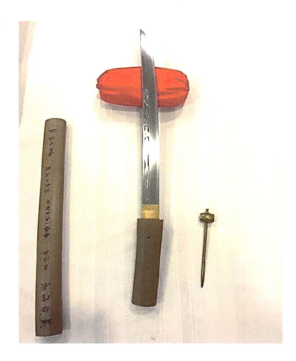

4. Using the sword tool, push the *Mekugi* (peg) out of the *Tsuka*.

5. Put *Mekugi* in the hole of the *Tsuka* so that you won't lose it.

6. Pull out the *Habaki* (metal piece above the *Tsuka,* a gold piece in the picture left) and set them down on the right.

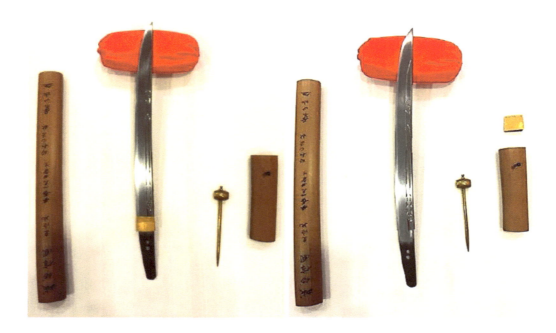

7. Hold the *Nakago* with your right hand. With *Washi* (Japanese rice paper), or handkerchief or tissue paper, support under the blade with your left hand.

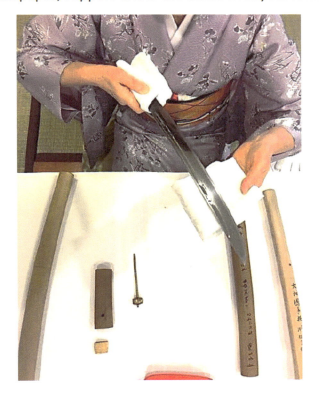

8. Using the light reflection on the blade's surface, look at *Jigane, Hamon, Boshi,* and *Mei,* etc. To see *Hamon, Jigane,* and *Boshi* well, move the sword up, down, or sideways or rotate it to reflect the light in the right position.

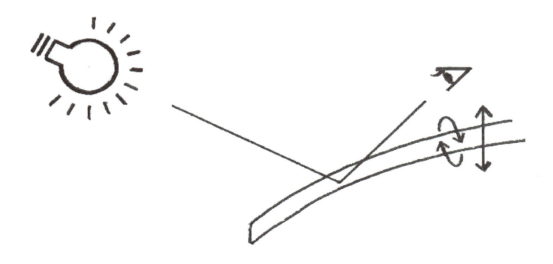

9. When you finish looking at the sword, bow lightly and reassemble it by reversing the process.

BIBLIOGRAPHY (参考資料)

Nihon Bijutsu Token Hozon Kyokai. Supervising editors: Dr. Honma, J. and Dr Sato, K.   (1966) *"Nihon-to Taikan"*   Tokyo: Otsuka Kogeisha Co.,Ltd.
日本美術刀剣保存協会　本間順次, 佐藤貫一監修　(1966) *"日本刀大鑑"*　東京: 大塚工芸社

Hon'ami, K. (1955)   "Nihonto *no Okite to Tokucho"* Tokyo: Bijutsu Club Tokenbu.
本阿弥光遜著 (1955) *" 日本刀の掟と特徴 "*　東京 : 美術倶楽部刀剣部発行

Watanabe, T. (1971)   *"Sano Bijutsu-kan Zuroku"*   Shizuoka: Sano Bijutsu-kan.
渡辺妙子著　(1971)   *" 佐野美術館図録"*   静岡 : 佐野美術館発行

Yoshihara, Y., Kapp, L., and Kapp, H. (2012) *"The art of the Japanese Sword"* Italy: Paolo Saviolo
吉原義人, リーオン & ひろ子 キャップ著　(2012) *" 日本刀美術"* イタリア:パオロ サビオロ 発行

Mochizuki, K. & Fujiki, K. (1966) *"Shousetu Nihonshi"* Tokyo: Yamakawa Shuppan-sha
High school text book by the Ministry of Education
望月圭吾, 藤木邦彦著 (1966)   *"詳説日本史"*   東京 : 山川出版発行　文部省検定済教科書

Dr. Honma, J. & Dr. Sato, K. (1972) *"Shinpan Nihon-to Koza"* Tokyo: Yuzankaku Shuppan Inc.   本間順次,佐藤貫一著 (1972) *"新版日本刀講座"*　東京: 雄山閣出版株式会社発行

Dr. Honma, J. & Dr. Sato, K. (1968) "Nihon-*to Zenshu"* Tokyo: Tokuma Shoten Co., Ltd.
本間順次、佐藤貫一著　 (1968) *"日本刀全集"* 東京: 徳間書店発行

Dr. Honma, J. & Dr. Sato, K. (1979) "Showa *Dai Meito Zufu"* Tokyo: Nihon Bijutsu Token Hozon Kyokai
本間順次、佐藤貫一著　(1979) *"昭和大名刀図譜"*　東京：日本美術刀剣保存協会

Sano Museum. (2019) *"Yomigaeru Meito (Reborn)"*   Shizuoka: Sano Museum Exhibition catalog.
佐野美術館 著 (2019) *"蘇る刀 Reborn"* 静岡 :　佐野美術館編集発行

 Hiroi, Y.   (1971) *"Token no Mikata"*   Tokyo: Dai-ichi Hoki Shuppan Co, Ltd.
　広井雄一著　(1971) *"刀剣のみかた"*　東京 : 第一法規出版株式会社発行

The Japan House Gallery. Japan Society, Inc. (1976) Nippon-To Art Sword of Japan The Walter A. Compton Collection   Tokyo: Otsuka Kogeisha Co, Ltd.

Chapter 25

*¹ ヤン ヨーステン 【Jan Joosten van Lodenstijn】 https://www.weblio.jp   6/2018

*² Names of Japan: Click the link Jipangu on Wikipedia   6/2018 (閲覧日)
Cipangu described in the 1492 Martin Beham globe From Wikimedia Commons, the free media repository (Names of Japan)

Chapter 37

Murasaki Shikibu, translated to modern Japanese by Tanizaki, J. (1967) Shin-*shinyaku Tales of Genji*.   Tokyo: Chuo Koronsha, Inc.

谷崎潤一郎訳 (1967) "*新々訳源氏物語*'   東京: 中央公論社

Chapter 43

*The three-imperial regalia   www.touken-world.jp/tips/32747   Wikipedia
　三種の神器：ウキペディア　2/2019 (閲覧日)

Chapter 45

Terukuni Jinjya website: http://terukunijinja.p-kit.com/page222400.html   2/2019
九州　照国神社　ウエブサイト：http://terukunijinja.p-kit.com/page222400.html

Chapter 47

*Number of soldiers   https://kotobank.jp/word/元寇-60419. Wikipedia
　兵力数　ウキペディア　3/2019 (閲覧日)
*Genko (元寇)　https://kotobank.jp/word/%E5%85%83%E5%AF%87-60419

Chapter 54

Golden Pavillion (金閣寺)：https://www.shokoku-ji.jp/kinkakuji/   6/2019 (閲覧日)

Chapter 56

Honouji-no-hen　(本能寺の変)
* Rekijin.com/?p=31448-キャッシュ   7/2019
* Bushoojapan.com/scandal/2019/06/02/51145-キャッシュ   7/2019 (閲覧日)

Chapter 57

Masamune Jittetsu (正宗十哲)：https://www.touken-world.jp/tips/7194/   7/2019

Chapter 59

Osaka Summer campaign (大阪夏の陣)www.thoughtco.com/toyoomi-hideyoshi-195660
Battle of Sekigahara (関ケ原の戦い)   senjp.com/Sekigahara   8/2019 (閲覧日)

Chapter 63

*Perry (ペリー)　ja.wikipedia.org/wiki/黒船来航   Wikipedia
*Perry (ペリー)　ja.wikipedia.org/wiki/マシュー・ペリー   Wikipedia   9/2019 (閲覧日)

Special Thanks

I used many sword photos from Sano Museum Catalogue in this book. The head of the Sano Museum, Ms. Taeko Watanabe, gave me special permission to use them. She had been a long-time friend of my father. I greatly appreciate her generosity. Without those photos, it was not possible to complete this book.

Sano Museum website: https://www.sanobi.or.jp

CPSIA information can be obtained
at www.ICGtesting.com
Printed in the USA
LVHW070245280422
717457LV00007B/62